PREFACE

Core Java is the backbone of modern software development, and mastering its core concepts is essential for any aspiring programmer, whether you're just starting your journey or seeking to deepen your knowledge. This book, "Core Java," is designed to be your comprehensive guide to the fundamental principles of Java programming.

In the ever-evolving landscape of technology, Java remains a constant. Its versatility and platform independence have made it the language of choice for a wide range of applications, from mobile apps to web services and enterprise systems. Whether you're a student, a professional developer, or an enthusiast eager to learn, this book is crafted to meet your needs.

Our journey through the world of Java begins with the basics. We'll guide you through setting up your development environment, writing your first lines of code, and understanding the syntax that underpins the language. From there, we'll delve into the rich world of data types, control structures, and object-oriented programming, providing a solid foundation upon which to build your Java expertise. As we progress, you'll explore advanced topics such as multithreading, I/O, and exception handling, gaining the skills necessary to develop robust and efficient Java applications. We'll demystify object-oriented design principles and guide you in applying them to your projects.

Java isn't just about syntax; it's about building real-world applications. You'll learn how to work with databases, networked systems, and graphical user interfaces, giving you the tools to create software that can truly make an impact.

Throughout this book, you'll find practical examples and hands-on exercises to reinforce your understanding and hone your programming skills. Java is a language of practice, and our aim is to equip you with the knowledge and experience needed to tackle real-world challenges confidently.

We'll also explore best practices, coding standards, and design patterns, helping you write clean, maintainable code that stands the test of time. Java isn't just about getting it to work; it's about writing code that's elegant, efficient, and easy to maintain. Java's vast ecosystem doesn't end with the language itself. We'll introduce you to popular libraries, frameworks, and tools that can streamline your development process and enhance your productivity.

As you turn the pages of this book, remember that learning Java is not just about the code you write; it's about the problem-solving mindset you cultivate. It's about thinking like a programmer, breaking down complex challenges into manageable pieces, and creating elegant solutions. Java is not just a programming language; it's a community. It's a vibrant ecosystem of developers, educators, and learners like you, all contributing to its growth and evolution. We're thrilled to have you join this community and embark on this Java journey with us.

So, without further ado, let's dive into the world of "Core Java." Whether you're here to build your career, tackle exciting projects, or simply explore the art of programming, we're excited to be your guides on this adventure.

Welcome to the world of Java.

Table of Contents

CHAPTER 1 - Introduction to Java

1.1 Introduction to Programming

Programming is the process of instructing a computer to perform specific tasks or operations by providing it with a set of instructions, often referred to as code or a program. These instructions are written in a programming language, and the computer executes them to achieve desired outcomes.

1.2 The Importance of Programming

Programming is a fundamental skill in the modern world, with applications in various fields such as software development, data analysis, web development, scientific research, and automation. It enables us to automate repetitive tasks, solve complex problems, and create innovative solutions.

1.3 Programming Languages

Programming languages are tools that allow humans to communicate with computers effectively. Some popular programming languages include Java, Python, C++, JavaScript, and Ruby. Each language has its syntax, rules, and unique features.

1.4 The Software Development Process

Software development is the process of designing, coding, testing, and maintaining software applications. It involves several stages, including requirement analysis, design, implementation, testing, deployment, and maintenance.

1.5 Programming Paradigms

There are different programming paradigms, including:

Procedural Programming: Organizes code into procedures or functions.

Object-Oriented Programming (OOP): Organizes code around objects and classes.

Functional Programming: Focuses on the use of pure functions and immutability.

Event-Driven Programming: Handles events and triggers actions in response.

1.6 Problem-Solving in Programming

Programming involves breaking down complex problems into smaller, manageable tasks and then solving them through code. Problem-solving skills are essential for programmers.

1.7 Introduction to Java

Java is a general purpose and widely used language known for its platform independence, event orientation and communi ty support. Some important features of Java are:

Platform Independence: One of the most important features of Java is platform independence. Java applications ca n run on any device or operating system with the Java Virtual Machine (JVM), making it a "write once, run anywher e" language. This is done by writing Java code to bytecode that can be run in the JVM.

Object Oriented: Java is an ObjectOriented Programming (OOP) language; i.e. it follows the principles of encapsulatio n, inheritance and polymorphism. It supports organizing code by classes and reusable objects.

Robust and Secure: Java was designed with a focus on reliability and security. It includes features such as automaic me mory management (garbage) to prevent memory leaks and powerful mode checking to catch errors while writing.

Rich Standard Library: Java comes with a rich library (Java Standard Library or Java API) that provides predefined cla sses and methods for various functions. This simplifies development and reduces the need to write low-level code.

Multithreading: Java supports multithreading, allowing developers to build complex applications. This is useful for task s like managing the UI and executing multiple tasks at once.

Community and Ecosystem: Java has a large and active developer community. It provides many opensource libraries, f rameworks and tools to extend its capabilities to various applications including web development (Java EE), mobile appl ication development (Android), and more.

Wide range of applications: Java is used in many application areas, including desktop software, web applications, mobi le applications, server-side applications, embedded systems and scientific computing.

Popular Development Environments: Developers often use integrated development environments (IDEs) such as Eclipse, IntelliJ IDEA and NetBeans to write, test and debug Java code well.

Backward Compatibility: Java is known for its commitment to backward compatibility, which ensures that lega-cy Java applications continue to work on newer versions of the language.

Strong Community Support: The Java community provides comprehensive information, tutorials, and forums to help d evelopers learn and solve problems.

Oracle Corporation: Oracle Corporation is the lead developer of the Java platform and is responsible for maint-aining the Java language, APIs and updates. They provide Java Long Term Support (LTS) versions for commercial use

OpenJDK: The Open Java Development Kit (OpenJDK) is an open source implementation of the Java Platform Standar d Edition (Java SE). It is widely used and forms the basis of many other Java distributions.

Overall Java is a versatile and reliable programming language that remains a popular choice for many applications due to its platform independence, robustness and many libraries, documentation and ecosystem tools.

Java LTS release (every three years): Oracle started a new Java cycle by releasing Long Term Support (LTS) releases every three years. These versions are updated and supported for a long time. For example, Java 11 and Java 17 are LTS r eleases.

1.7.1 History and Evolution

History of Java:

History (mid 1990s): Java was developed in the mid1990s by James Gosling and his team at Sun Microsystems (later ac quired by Oracle Corporation). It was originally developed as a language for software development for consumer electro nics, but later evolved into a general programming language.

Java 1.0 (1996): The first version of Java, Java 1.0, was released to the public in 1996. It introduced the core features of the language and the concept of "write once, run anywhere" (WORA). Platform independence from the Java Virtual Mac hine (JVM).

Java 2 Platform (1998): Java 2 introduced significant improvements, including the Swing GUI toolkit, aggregation syst em, and Java Naming and Directory Interface (JNDI). This release is a major evolution of Java.

Java Community Program (JCP) (1998): Sun Microsystems launched JCP, a collaboration that allows many partners t o collaborate to shape the future of Java through the development of Java Specification Requests (JSRs).

Enterprise Edition (Java EE) and Micro Edition (Java ME) (early 2000s): Java continues its implementation with Ja va EE for serverside applications and Java ME for mobile and embedded devices for enterprise and mobile counting.

OpenJDK (2006): Sun Microsystems is releasing Java Platform, Standard Edition (Java SE) as OpenJDK, making Java open source. This move makes Java more accessible to the open-source community.

Acquisition of Oracle (2010): Oracle acquired Sun Microsystems and became the leader of the Java platform.

Java 8 (2014): Java 8 offers lambdas, the Stream API, and the javatime package for routine date and time manipulation. These additions increase code readability and emphasize functional details.

Java 9 - 11: This release provides improvements such as process module (Project Jigsaw), variable local type inference (var), and improvements to shelf Garbage disposal algorithms.

Java Evaluation:

Platform Independence: Java's "Write Once, Run Anywhere" feature implemented by the JVM allows Java application s to run independently on platforms ranging from windows to Linux to macOS.

Robust: Java's robust type checking, custom usage, and memory management (garbage) help build robust and reliable a pplications that are less prone to crashes and memory leaks.

Community and Ecosystem: Java has a large and active developer community; This community provides a wide variet y of libraries, frameworks, and tools for a variety of applications, including web, mobile, and business development.

Security: Java's architecture includes security functions such as runtime security and sandboxing to help prevent malicio us code.

Scalability: Java is well suited for both small and large applications. The modular framework introduced in Java 9 increa ses scalability and manageability.

Performance: Although Java is not the fastest programming language, it has excellent performance and this performanc e is further enhanced by continuous improvements to the JVM and optimization in new books.

Backward Compatibility: Java's commitment to backward compatibility allows legacy applications to continue to be up dated, reducing migration difficulties.

Enterprise Adoption: Java is widely used in business and many important roles use it, including companies and large e-commerce businesses. Developed using Java technology.

Open source: With OpenJDK being open source, Java embraces open source development, encouraging community eng agement and innovation.

Looking Forward: Java continues to evolve with regular updates and LTS releases, ensuring its compatibility with mod ern software development.

Overall, Java's history and evaluation demonstrate its popularity, efficiency and functionality as a technology. Prog-ramming languages. It is also a strong choice for many constructions needs.

1.7.2 Java's Role in Modern Computing

Due to its versatility, portability and robust ecosystem, Java continues to play an important role in modern computers. Here are some key areas where Java is still influential in computing today:

Enterprise Applications: Java is the most important player in software development. It is widely used to develop mission-critical applications, including customer relationship management (CRM), enterprise resource planning (ERP) software, and accounting. The Java EE (Enterprise Edition) platform provides tools and APIs for building powerful, scalable and secure business applications.

Web Development: Java is used for web development through various technologies such as Java Server Pages (JSP), Servlets and Java Server Faces (JSF). Modern web frameworks like Spring and Java Server Faces simplify web development and make it easy to build RESTful APIs.

Mobile App Development: Java is the primary programming language for Android app development. The Android operating system is based on Java and the Android SDK provides the tools and libraries needed to build useful mobile apps.
Big Data and Analytics: Java is widely used in big data processing and analysis. Apache Hadoop is a big data system implemented in Java. In addition, tools such as Apache Spark and Apache Flink take advantage of Java for data sharing.
Cloud Computing: Java's platform independence makes it useful for cloud services and applications. Many cloud service providers offer support for Java, and containerization technologies such as Docker and Kubernetes make it easy to deploy Java applications in the cloud.
Internet of Things (IoT): Java ME (Micro Edition) and Java SE Embedded for IoT device development. Java's mobility and ability to run on non-standard devices make it particularly suitable for IoT applications in areas such as home automation and industrial IoT.
Scientific and Research Computer: Java is used for interviews because of its efficiency and ease of use. Libraries like Apache Commons Math provide math and arithmetic, making Java a good choice for scientists and researchers.
Financial Services: Java is popular in the financial industry where low-latency, high-throughput applications are required. Trading platforms, risk management, and algorithmic trading strategies often rely on Java's performance and reliability.
Game Development: Although not as important as some other languages and engines, Java is also used for game development purposes. Game engines such as libGDX and j Monkey Engine allow developers to create 2D and 3D games using Java.
Education and Learning Environment: Java is a choice for teaching programming and computer science because of its simplicity and platform independence. Most schools use Java as their primary programming language.
Open Source & Community: Java has a strong open-source community of libraries, frameworks, and tools that support innovation and collaboration among developers.
Security: Java is also a secure programming language and its architecture includes security features designed to protect against vulnerabilities and threats.
The role of Java in computing today has been strengthened by its evolution towards modern computing. Technology and its development continue with regular releases. Its long existence in many areas with constant updates and improvements ensures that Java remains relevant and effective in the world of technological change.

1.8 Java Buzzwords

Let's delve into the world of Java buzzwords in detail. These buzzwords represent key concepts, features, and technologies associated with the Java programming language. Understanding these buzzwords is essential for any Java developer. Here's an explanation of each:

1. Platform Independence:

Buzzword Explanation: Java's "Write Once, Run Anywhere" (WORA) capability allows developers to write code on one platform (e.g., Windows) and run it on another (e.g., Linux) without modification.

Key Concepts: Java achieves platform independence through the Java Virtual Machine (JVM) and bytecode compilation.

2. Java Virtual Machine (JVM):

Buzzword Explanation: The JVM is a crucial part of the Java platform. It executes Java bytecode, enabling platform independence.

Key Concepts: JVM implementations exist for various platforms, ensuring Java code can run on different systems.

3. Object-Oriented Programming (OOP):

Buzzword Explanation: Java is an object-oriented programming language, meaning it's centred around objects and classes.

Key Concepts: Classes, objects, inheritance, polymorphism, and encapsulation are core OOP principles in Java.

4. Inheritance:

Buzzword Explanation: Inheritance allows a class (subclass/child) to inherit properties and behaviours from another class (superclass/parent).

Key Concepts: Method overriding, access modifiers, and the extends keyword are essential in Java inheritance.

5. Encapsulation:

Buzzword Explanation: Encapsulation is the practice of restricting access to certain parts of an object, protecting data and ensuring it's used correctly.

Key Concepts: Access modifiers (public, private, protected), getter and setter methods, data hiding.

6. Polymorphism:

Buzzword Explanation: Polymorphism allows objects of different classes to be treated as objects of a common superclass.

Key Concepts: Method overloading, method overriding, dynamic method dispatch.

7. Exception Handling:

Buzzword Explanation: Java's robust exception handling mechanism helps manage and recover from errors or exceptional situations.

Key Concepts: try-catch blocks, checked and unchecked exceptions, custom exceptions.

8. Multithreading:

Buzzword Explanation: Multithreading enables concurrent execution of code, improving application performance.

Key Concepts: Threads, thread states (new, runnable, blocked, terminated), synchronization, race conditions.

9. Platform Security:

Buzzword Explanation: Java's security model ensures safe execution of code by restricting potentially harmful operations.

Key Concepts: Security manager, class loaders, bytecode verification.

10. Java Collections Framework:

Buzzword Explanation: A comprehensive library for data structures (e.g., lists, sets, maps) and algorithms.

Key Concepts: Collection interfaces (List, Set, Map), concrete implementations, iterators.

11. Garbage Collection:

Buzzword Explanation: Automatic memory management where Java cleans up unused objects to prevent memory leaks.

Key Concepts: java.lang.Object, finalize() method, garbage collection algorithms.

12. Java Standard Library:

Buzzword Explanation: A rich library of classes and methods that simplify common programming tasks.

Key Concepts: java.lang, java.util, java.io, java.net, and more.

13. Integrated Development Environments (IDEs):

Buzzword Explanation: IDEs like Eclipse, IntelliJ IDEA, and NetBeans provide tools to streamline Java development.

Key Concepts: Code editing, debugging, project management.

14. Version Control (e.g., Git):

Buzzword Explanation: Version control systems track changes in source code, facilitating collaboration and code management.

Key Concepts: Commits, branches, pull requests.

15. Java Ecosystem:

Buzzword Explanation: The Java ecosystem includes libraries, frameworks, and tools for various domains, from web development to data science.

Key Concepts: Spring, Hibernate, JavaFX, JUnit, Maven, and more.

16. Modern Java Features:

Buzzword Explanation: Java has evolved with features like lambda expressions, the Stream API, and modules (introduced in Java 9).

Key Concepts: Functional programming, stream processing, modularization.

17. Community and Open Source:

Buzzword Explanation: Java has a thriving community, including the Java Community Process (JCP) and numerous open-source projects.

- **Key Concepts:** Community contributions, Java User Groups (JUGs), open-source libraries.

By understanding these Java buzzwords and concepts, developers can navigate the Java programming landscape with confidence and build robust, efficient, and platform-independent applications.

1.9 Overview of Java Development Tools

Java development tools play a crucial role in the software development lifecycle. They help Java developers write, test, debug, and manage their code efficiently. Here's an overview of some essential Java development tools and their functionalities:

1. Integrated Development Environments (IDEs):

Examples: Eclipse, IntelliJ IDEA, NetBeans

Functionality: IDEs provide a comprehensive environment for Java development. They offer features like code editing, debugging, project management, version control integration, and build tools. IDEs often support plugins or extensions to enhance functionality further. Here's a breakdown of IDE features:

Code Editor: Syntax highlighting, auto-completion, code formatting, and error checking.

Debugger: Debugging tools to set breakpoints, inspect variables, and step through code.

Project Management: Project creation, organization, and dependency management.

Version Control: Integration with version control systems like Git for code versioning.

Build Tools: Integration with build tools like Maven or Gradle for project builds.

Refactoring Tools: Automated code refactoring to improve code quality.
Code Inspection: Static code analysis to identify code quality issues.
Testing Framework Integration: Seamless integration with testing frameworks like JUnit.

2. **Build Tools**
Examples: Apache Maven, Gradle, Apache Ant
Functionality: Build tools automate the process of compiling source code, running tests, and packaging applications. **They** manage project dependencies and ensure consistent and repeatable builds. Here are key functionalities of build tools:
Dependency Management: Download and manage project dependencies (libraries, frameworks) from repositories.
Build Lifecycle: Define a sequence of tasks for building, testing, and packaging.
Plugin System: Extensible through plugins to customize build processes.
Convention Over Configuration: Standardized project structures and configurations.

3. **Version Control Systems (VCS):**
Examples: Git, Subversion (SVN)
Functionality: VCS tracks changes in source code, allowing developers to collaborate, manage code versions, and roll back to previous states. Key features include:
Committing Changes: Record changes and provide descriptive commit messages.
Branching and Merging: Create branches for parallel development and merge changes.
Remote Repositories: Share code with others through remote repositories (e.g., GitHub, GitLab).
Conflict Resolution: Resolve conflicts when multiple developers modify the same code.
History Tracking: View the history of changes and who made them.

4. **Debugging Tools:**
Examples: Integrated debuggers in IDEs, Java Debug Wire Protocol (JDWP)
Functionality: Debugging tools help identify and resolve issues in Java code. They allow developers to inspect variables, set breakpoints, and step through code execution. Key capabilities include:
Breakpoints: Set breakpoints at specific code locations to pause execution.
Variable Inspection: Examine the values of variables at runtime.
Call Stack: View the call hierarchy to understand code flow.
Watch Expressions: Monitor specific variables or expressions.
Exception Handling: Catch and handle exceptions during debugging.

5. **Profiling Tools:**
Examples: VisualVM, YourKit, Java Flight Recorder (JFR)
Functionality: Profiling tools analyse application performance to identify bottlenecks and resource usage. They help optimize code for better efficiency. Key profiling capabilities include:
CPU Profiling: Identify CPU-intensive methods and threads.
Memory Profiling: Detect memory leaks, analyse heap usage, and find inefficient object creation.
Thread Analysis: Monitor thread behaviour and synchronization issues.
Code Hotspot Detection: Identify the most frequently executed code.

6. **Testing Tools:**
Examples: JUnit, TestNG, Mockito
Functionality: Testing tools help automate the testing process, ensuring code reliability and correctness. They facilitate unit, integration, and functional testing. Key functionalities include:
Test Case Management: Organize test cases into suites and groups.
Assertions: Verify expected outcomes and conditions in tests.
Mocking: Create mock objects to isolate code for testing.
Test Reporting: Generate reports and track test results.

7. **Profilers:**
Examples: VisualVM, YourKit
Functionality: Profilers are used to gather runtime information about the performance of a Java application. They help identify performance bottlenecks, memory leaks, and CPU utilization. Key profiling capabilities include:
CPU Profiling: Identify CPU-intensive methods and bottlenecks in the application.
Memory Profiling: Detect memory leaks, analyse memory usage, and optimize memory allocation.

8. **Dependency Management Tools:**
Examples: Apache Ivy
Functionality: These tools manage dependencies for a Java project by resolving and downloading required libraries and frameworks. They work in conjunction with build tools like Maven or Gradle.

9. **Continuous Integration (CI) and Continuous Deployment (CD) Tools:**
Examples: Jenkins, Travis CI, CircleCI

Functionality: CI/CD tools automate the building, testing, and deployment of Java applications. They ensure code quality and facilitate rapid and reliable deployment.

10. Code Analysis Tools:

Examples: FindBugs, PMD, SonarQube

Functionality: Code analysis tools scan codebases for potential issues, security vulnerabilities, and adherence to coding standards.

These Java development tools collectively help developers build, test, debug, and manage Java applications efficiently, ensuring code quality and robustness. The choice of tools often depends on project requirements, team preferences, and specific development workflows

1.10 Setting Up the Java Development Environment

Setting up a Java development environment is the first step in developing Java applications. It involves installing the necessary software, configuring your system, and preparing your development environment. Here's a step-by-step guide to setting up a Java development environment:

1. Install Java Development Kit (JDK):

Download JDK: Visit the official Oracle website or use OpenJDK, which is an open-source alternative to Oracle JDK.

Choose the Right Version: Select the appropriate JDK version for your project. Java 8, 11, and later versions are commonly used.

Installation: Follow the installation instructions for your operating system (Windows, macOS, Linux).

2. Set JAVA_HOME Environment Variable (Optional, but Recommended):

Setting the JAVA_HOME environment variable helps other tools and applications locate your JDK installation.

Add the JAVA_HOME variable to your system's environment variables and set its value to the path where you installed the JDK (e.g., C:\Program Files\Java\jdk1.8.0_291).

3. Install an Integrated Development Environment (IDE):

Choose an IDE that suits your needs. Popular options include Eclipse, IntelliJ IDEA, and NetBeans.

Download the IDE from the official website.

Follow the installation instructions, and you may also need to configure JDK settings within the IDE.

4. Verify Your Java Installation:

Open a command prompt (Windows) or terminal (macOS, Linux).

Run the following command to check if Java is installed and to view the installed version:

Note- You should see information about the installed JDK version.

5. Set Up a Code Editor (Optional):

If you prefer using a code editor instead of a full-fledged IDE, you can choose editors like Visual Studio Code (VSCode) or Sublime Text.

Install the code editor of your choice and consider installing Java extensions or plugins to enhance Java development support.

6. Create a Project Directory:

Create a dedicated directory on your system where you'll store your Java projects.

Organize your projects into subdirectories as needed for better project management.

7. Write and Run a Simple Java Program:

Open your chosen IDE or code editor.

Create a new Java project or file (e.g., a .java file).

Write a simple "Hello, World!" program to test your environment:

Code –

```
public class HelloWorld {
public static void main(String[] args) {
System.out.println("Hello, World!");
}
}
```

Save the file and compile and run it using your IDE or command line.

If you see "Hello, World!" printed to the console, your Java development environment is set up correctly.

8. Install Build and Dependency Management Tools (Optional):

If you plan to use build tools like Maven or Gradle, install them and configure your projects accordingly.

Dependency management tools like Apache Ivy can also be useful for managing project dependencies.

9. Explore Additional Libraries and Frameworks:

Depending on your project's requirements, you may need to install additional libraries and frameworks (e.g., Spring, Hibernate) and configure them in your development environment.

Setting up a Java development environment can vary slightly depending on your specific project needs and the tools you choose to use. However, following these general steps should help you get started with Java development. Remember to keep your JDK, IDE, and other tools updated to take advantage of the latest features and security patches.

1.11 Understand Java Syntax

Syntax:
```
public class MyCode {
        public static void main(String[] args) {
            // Your code here
    }
}
```

This Java code represents the basic structure of a Java program. Here's what each part means:

public: This keyword indicates that the `main` method is accessible from outside the class.

static: This keyword means that the `main` method belongs to the class itself, not to instances of the class. It can be called without creating an object of the class.

void: This is the return type of the `main` method, indicating that it doesn't return any value.

main: This is the name of the method.

(String [] args): These are the parameters that the `main` method accepts. In this case, it takes an array of strings named `args`, which can be used to pass command-line arguments to the program.

{}: These curly braces denote the start and end of the `main` method's block. Any code placed inside these braces is executed when the program runs.

In summary, this Java syntax defines a class named `MyCode` with a `main` method, which is where the program's execution begins. The `main` method does not return any value and can accept an array of strings as command-line arguments, but it currently doesn't contain any code (indicated by the comment "// Your code here"). Developers can add their own code within the `main` method to perform specific tasks when the program is executed.

1.12 Your First Java Program

```
public class HelloWorld {
  public static void main(String[] args) {
    System.out.println("Hello!");
  }
}
```

Here's an explanation of this program:

public class HelloWorld: This line declares a class named `HelloWorld`. In Java, everything is defined within a class.

public static void main(String[] args): This line declares the `main` method. The `main` method is the entry point of the program and is where execution begins. It takes an array of strings (`String[] args`) as a parameter, which can be used to pass command-line arguments to the program.

{}: These curly braces enclose the body of the `main` method. Any code placed inside these braces will be executed when the program runs.

System.out.println("Hello!");: This line is the actual code that gets executed. It uses `System.out.println` to print the text "Hello!" to the console. The `println` method is used to print a line of text, and it automatically adds a newline character at the end, so the next output will appear on a new line.

1.13 Java Comments

Comments in Java are words that do not affect the operation in the code, but serve as information, explanations, or warni ngs. They come in two types: single-line comments (//) for brief comments and multi-line comments (/* */) for more extensive explanations. Proper use of comments enhances code clarity and helps with maintenance and collaboration.

Example – Single-Line Comment
```
// This is a single-line comment
int age = 30; // Variable for storing age
```

Example – Multi-Line Comment
```
public class Example {
  public static void main(String[] args) {
    // This is a single-line comment

    /*
     * This is a multi-line comment
     * It can provide more detailed explanations
     * and span across multiple lines.
```

```
        */
       int a = 5; // Initialize a
       // TODO: Implement this functionality
       int b = 10;
       // FIXME: Resolve this issue
       int c = 15;
    }
}
```

1.14 Drawbacks of Procedural Languages

Procedural programming languages have been widely used for many years and have their own set of advantages, but they also come with certain drawbacks. Here are some of the drawbacks of procedural languages:

Lack of Abstraction: Procedural languages often lack the ability to create complex abstractions, which can make it harder to manage and scale large codebases. This can lead to code that is difficult to understand and maintain over time.

Limited Code Reusability: Procedural code tends to be more tightly coupled, making it less reusable than code written in more modern programming paradigms like object-oriented or functional programming. Reusing code becomes challenging because functions in procedural languages may rely heavily on global variables and side effects.

Maintenance Challenges: As procedural codebases grow, they can become difficult to maintain and extend. Changes to one part of the code can have unintended consequences in other parts, making it hard to ensure code correctness.

Poor Support for Parallelism: Procedural languages are often not well-suited for concurrent or parallel programming, which is increasingly important in modern computing environments. Handling concurrent tasks and managing shared state can be cumbersome.

Limited Encapsulation: Procedural languages often lack encapsulation mechanisms that allow data and functions to be bundled together, leading to potential data leakage and security issues.

Limited Support for Complex Data Structures: While procedural languages can work with basic data structures like arrays and structures, they may lack built-in support for more complex data structures like trees or graphs, making it less convenient to work with complex data.

Readability and Maintainability: Procedural code can become verbose and harder to read as programs grow in size. Without proper organization and naming conventions, it can be challenging for developers to understand the codebase.

Reduced Expressiveness: Procedural languages may have limited support for expressing higher-level concepts and patterns, leading to longer and more complex code for achieving certain tasks.

Code Duplication: Without the ability to create reusable abstractions, procedural code can suffer from code duplication, which increases the chances of introducing bugs and makes code harder to maintain.

Poor Error Handling: Error handling in procedural languages can be less elegant than in languages with built-in exception handling mechanisms, potentially leading to error-prone code.

It's important to note that while procedural languages have these drawbacks, they can still be a suitable choice for certain types of applications, especially when performance is a critical consideration or when dealing with legacy systems. However, many modern programming languages and paradigms, such as object-oriented and functional programming, have emerged to address some of these shortcomings and provide more powerful and expressive tools for software development

1.15 Lexical issues of Java

In Java, lexical issues refer to the rules and concerns related to the language's syntax and the way Java source code is written. These issues are important because violating Java's lexical rules can result in compilation errors or code that behaves unexpectedly. Here are some key lexical issues in Java:

Case Sensitivity: Java is case-sensitive, meaning that it distinguishes between uppercase and lowercase letters. For example, myVariable and myvariable are considered different identifiers. This rule applies to class names, method names, variable names, and keywords.

Example-

```
int myVariable = 42;
int myvariable = 23; // These are two different variables
```

Reserved Keywords: Java has a set of reserved keywords that cannot be used as identifiers (e.g., variable names, method names, class names) because they have special meanings in the language. Attempting to use a reserved keyword as an identifier will result in a compilation error.

Example-

```
int int = 10; // Error: "int" is a reserved keyword
```

Identifiers: Identifiers are used for naming variables, methods, classes, and other program elements in Java. They must follow specific rules:

Must start with a letter (uppercase or lowercase), underscore (_), or dollar sign ($).
Can contain letters, digits, underscores, and dollar signs.
Cannot be a Java keyword.
Should be descriptive and follow naming conventions for readability.

Example-

```
int myVariable = 42; // "myVariable" is a valid identifier
```

Comments: Java supports single-line comments (starting with //) and multi-line comments (enclosed between /* and */). Comments are used for documenting code and are ignored by the compiler.

Example-

```
// This is a single-line comment

/*
This is a
multi-line comment
*/
```

White Space: Java is generally lenient with white spaces, allowing spaces, tabs, and line breaks to separate tokens. However, excessive white spaces can reduce code readability.

Example-

```
int x   =  10; // Spaces can be used for readability, but too many can be distracting
```

Escape Sequences: In Java strings and character literals, you can use escape sequences to represent special characters. For example, "\n" represents a newline character, and "\t" represents a tab character.

Example-

```
String message = "Hello, \nWorld!"; // \n is an escape sequence for a newline
```

Unicode Support: Java supports Unicode characters in identifiers, strings, and comments. This allows you to use characters from various languages and symbol sets.

Example-

```
String π = "pi"; // Unicode character 'π' can be used as an identifier
```

Line Endings: Java source code files can have different line endings (e.g., CR+LF on Windows or LF on Unix-like systems). Java compilers are generally capable of handling different line ending conventions.

These lexical issues are important to understand when writing Java code, as they form the foundation of the language's syntax and determine how code is parsed and executed. Violations of these rules can lead to compilation errors, code that is difficult to read, or unexpected behaviour in your Java programs. It's essential to follow Java's lexical rules and conventions to write clean, readable, and reliable code.

1.16 JVM

JVM (Java Virtual Machine) is a critical component of the Java Runtime Environment (JRE) and the Java Development Kit (JDK). It is a software-based virtual machine that executes Java bytecode, which is the compiled form of Java source code. The primary purpose of the JVM is to provide a platform-independent runtime environment for Java applications.

Here's what the JVM does:

Execution of Java Bytecode: JVM takes compiled Java bytecode as input and executes it. Java source code is compiled into bytecode using a Java compiler, and this bytecode is platform-independent.

Platform Independence: One of the most significant advantages of Java is its platform independence. The JVM allows Java applications to run on any platform or operating system as long as there is a compatible JVM available for that platform.

Memory Management: JVM manages memory allocation and deallocation. It automatically handles memory allocation for objects, garbage collection (reclaiming memory used by objects no longer in use), and memory management for the Java heap and stack.

Just-In-Time (JIT) Compilation: Some JVM implementations include a Just-In-Time compiler that translates bytecode into native machine code at runtime. This compilation step can significantly improve the execution speed of Java applications.

Class Loading: JVM loads classes on-demand as they are needed by the application. It ensures that classes are loaded only once and provides class path management.

Execution of Threads: Java is a multi-threaded programming language, and the JVM manages the execution of threads. It allows multiple threads to run concurrently, providing support for multi-threading and concurrency.

Security: JVM includes various security features to protect against malicious code execution. It provides a secure execution environment by enforcing access control and sandboxing.
Exception Handling: JVM has built-in exception handling mechanisms to catch and handle runtime exceptions, preventing them from crashing the application.
Performance Optimization: JVMs often include various optimization techniques to improve the execution speed of Java applications. These optimizations can include inlining, loop unrolling, and more.
Dynamic Class Loading and Unloading: JVM allows for dynamic loading and unloading of classes at runtime. This feature is essential for applications like applets and dynamic class loading in certain frameworks.
Monitoring and Profiling: JVMs provide tools and APIs for monitoring the performance of Java applications, collecting profiling data, and diagnosing issues such as memory leaks or performance bottlenecks.
Compatibility: JVM ensures backward compatibility with previous versions of Java, allowing older Java applications to run on newer JVMs without modification

1.17 JVM Architecture

The JVM (Java Virtual Machine) architecture is a critical component of the Java platform, responsible for executing Java bytecode and providing a runtime environment for Java applications. The architecture of the JVM consists of several components that work together to execute Java programs. Here's an overview of the JVM architecture:

1. Class Loader Subsystem:

Class Loader: This component loads class files into memory. The Class Loader subsystem is responsible for finding and loading class files as needed by the application.

Bootstrap Class Loader: The Bootstrap Class Loader is the parent of all other class loaders and is responsible for loading core Java classes from the bootstrap class path.

2. Runtime Data Areas:

Method Area: Also known as the Permanent Generation (PermGen), this area stores class-level structures such as class metadata, static fields, and method bytecode.

Heap: The heap is the runtime data area where objects are allocated and memory for objects is reclaimed through garbage collection. It is divided into two regions: the Young Generation and the Old Generation (Tenured Space).

Java Stack: Each thread running in the JVM has its own Java stack, which stores method call frames, local variables, and operand stacks. It ensures method-level isolation.

Native Method Stack: Similar to the Java Stack, this store native method calls frames for native code executed by the JVM.

3. Execution Engine:

Interpreter: The Interpreter interprets bytecode and executes it one instruction at a time. While it is slower than compiled code, it is platform-independent and is used initially.

Just-In-Time (JIT) Compiler: Some JVM implementations include a JIT compiler that compiles bytecode into native machine code at runtime, improving execution speed. Compiled code is stored in the Code Cache.

Garbage Collector: The Garbage Collector is responsible for managing memory and reclaiming memory used by objects that are no longer reachable.

4. Native Interface:

The Native Interface allows Java applications to interact with native libraries and code written in languages like C and C++. It provides a bridge between Java and native code.

5. Java Native Interface (JNI):

JNI is a programming framework that allows Java code to call native code and vice versa. It provides a standard interface for integrating Java with other programming languages.

6. Native Method Libraries:

These libraries contain native code that can be called from Java applications using the Native Interface.

7. Java API:

The Java API includes a vast library of classes and packages that provide pre-built functionality for Java applications. Developers can use these APIs to build Java applications.

8. Native Method Interface (NMI):

NMI allows native code to invoke Java methods and manipulate Java objects directly.

9. Execution of Bytecode:

The JVM executes Java bytecode instructions, which are platform-independent and stored in class files.

10. Security Manager:

The Security Manager enforces security policies to prevent untrusted code from performing harmful actions on the system.

11. Thread Manager:

The Thread Manager manages and schedules threads, allowing for multithreading and concurrent execution of Java programs.

12. Memory Management:

Memory management is responsible for allocating and deallocating memory for objects and managing the heap.

13. Java Native Interface (JNI):

The JNI allows Java applications to interface with native code libraries, enabling interaction with non-Java code.

In summary, the JVM architecture comprises several components that work together to provide a runtime environment for Java applications. It includes class loading, memory management, bytecode execution, security, and support for native code integration, making Java platform-independent and versatile. Different JVM implementations may have variations in their architectures, but they all adhere to the Java Virtual Machine Specification.

Exercise

Exercise 1 – MCQ

Q 1. What is Java?

a) A type of coffee bean

b) A high-level programming language

c) A platform dependent language

d) A non-reliable language

Q 2. Who is the founder of Java?

a) James Gosling

b) Dennis Ritchie

c) Bjarne Stroustrup

d) Ada Lovelace

Exercise 2 – True/ False

Q 1. Java is primarily known for its use as a type of coffee bean.

Q 2. Java is a low-level programming language often used for system-level programming.

Exercise 3 – Fill in the blanks

Q 1. Java is a ____level programming language.

Q 2. Java is a platform ____language.

Exercise 4 – Match case

Q 1. Match the following Java properties with their descriptions:

i. Platform Independence

ii. Object-Oriented

iii. Automatic Memory Management (Garbage Collection)

Descriptions:

a. Allows Java code to run on different operating systems without modification

b. Emphasizes the use of objects and classes for code organization.

c. Automatically reclaims memory that is no longer in use by the program.

Exercise 5 – One word answer

Q 1. Who is the founder of Java?

Q 2. Java was created in which year?

Exercise 6 – Small answer

Q 1. What is Java?

Q 2. Write down the features of Java.

Exercise 7 – Long answer

Q 1. Explain the features of Java.

Q 2. Explain Java roles in modern computing.

Answer:

Exercise 1. Q 1: b) A high-level programming language Q 2: a) James Gosling

Exercise 2. Q 1: False Q 2: False

Exercise 3. Q 1: high Q 2: independent

Exercise 4. Q 1: i. Platform Independence – a ii. Object-Oriented – b

iii. Automatic Memory Management (Garbage Collection) - c

Exercise 5. Q 1: James Gosling Q 2: 1995

Previous Year Questions

Q 1. What are the drawbacks of procedural languages? Explain the need of object-oriented programming with suitable program. (JNTU -B.Tech.- 2018)
Q 2. Discuss the lexical issues of Java. (JNTU -B.Tech.- 2018)
Q 3. What feature of Java makes it platform independent and portable? (JNTU -B.Tech. -2017)
Q 4. Is Java a robust language? Justify your answer. (JNTU -B.Tech. -2017)
Q 5. Why is Java known as platform independent? (JNTU -B.Tech.- 2016)
Q 6. What makes compiled JAVA programs platform independent? Explain. (IGNOU MCS 2010)
Q 7. Explain the significance of each argument in the function main (string args 1) (IGNOU MCS 2010)
Q 8. Explain why is Java called platform independent language? (IGNOU MCA 2014)

Previous Year Solved Papers

Q.1. (i) What is JDK? (RU BCA 2022)
Ans. The Java Development Kit (JDK) is a cross-platformed software development environment that offers a collection of tools and libraries necessary for developing Java- based software applications and applets. It is a core package used in Java, along with the JVM (Java Virtual Machine) and the JRE (Java Runtime Environment).
if you would like to develop a Java-based software application then along with JRE you may need some additional necessary tools, which is called JDK.
The JDK has a private Java Virtual Machine (JVM) and a few other resources necessary for the development of a Java Application
JDK contains:

- Java Runtime Environment (JRE).
- An interpreter/loader (Java).
- A compiler (javac).
- An archiver (ar) and many more.

Q. 2. What the differences are between structured and object oriented programming? Explain the features of JAVA. (RU BCA 2017)
Ans- Structured programming and object-oriented programming (OOP) are two different programming paradigms with distinct approaches to organizing and building software. Here are the key differences between the two:

Structured Programming:

- **Focus:** It focuses on breaking down a program into smaller, manageable functions or procedures.
- **Data and Functions:** It separates data and functions, and the emphasis is on functions or procedures that operate on the data.
- **Procedural Approach:** It follows a procedural approach to program design, with a clear sequence of instructions.
- **Limited Reusability:** It has limited code reusability, and code tends to be more specific and less modular.
- **Data Hiding:** It lacks the concept of data hiding and does not offer ways to encapsulate data.

Object-Oriented Programming:

- **Focus:** It focuses on designing a program around objects that represent real-world entities.
- **Data and Functions:** It combines data and functions into objects, emphasizing the interaction between objects.
- **Object Interaction:** It emphasizes the interaction between objects through methods and messages.
- **Code Reusability:** It promotes code reusability and modularity through features such as inheritance and polymorphism.
- **Data Hiding:** It supports data hiding and encapsulation, allowing data to be hidden and accessed only through the methods of the object.

Features of Java:

- **Platform Independence:** Java programs can run on any system that has a Java Virtual Machine (JVM), making it platform-independent.
- **Object-Oriented:** Java is designed as an object-oriented programming language, supporting concepts such as encapsulation, inheritance, and polymorphism.
- **Robust and Secure:** Java is known for its robustness and security features, with automatic memory management, exception handling, and a robust security model.
- **Multithreading:** Java supports multithreading, allowing the execution of multiple threads simultaneously, which is essential for developing concurrent applications.
- **Rich API:** Java provides a rich set of APIs for developing various types of applications, including networking, I/O, utilities, and GUIs through libraries like AWT, Swing, and JavaFX.
- **High Performance:** With its bytecode compilation and just-in-time compilation, Java offers high performance for various applications.

Distributed Computing: Java provides extensive support for distributed computing, allowing the development of applications for networking and distributed systems.

Portability: Java code is highly portable, enabling developers to write once and run anywhere, making it suitable for a wide range of devices and platforms.

These features contribute to Java's popularity and its widespread use for developing a variety of applications, from desktop software to enterprise systems and web applications.

Q.3 Why is Java Architectural Neutral? (RU BCA 2017)

Ans- Java is considered architectural neutral due to its ability to run on any hardware or operating system that has a Java Virtual Machine (JVM) installed. This feature is a result of the design choices and principles adopted during the development of the Java language. Some key reasons why Java is considered architectural neutral include:

Bytecode and JVM: Java source code is compiled into platform-independent bytecode, which is then executed by the JVM. The JVM provides an abstraction layer between the Java program and the underlying hardware and operating system, allowing the same Java program to run on any system that has a compatible JVM, regardless of the hardware or operating system architecture.

Portability: Java's portability is a result of the platform independence achieved through the use of bytecode and the JVM. This feature enables developers to write Java programs on one platform and run them on any other platform without the need for recompilation, making Java suitable for cross-platform development.

Hardware Independence: Java's architectural neutrality allows it to be hardware independent, meaning that Java programs can run on any hardware architecture as long as there is a JVM available for that architecture. This feature simplifies the deployment of Java applications across various hardware environments without requiring modifications to the underlying code.

Operating System Independence: Java's architectural neutrality also ensures that Java applications can run on different operating systems, including Windows, macOS, and various Unix-based systems, without any modifications. This capability allows Java programs to be easily distributed and executed across a wide range of operating systems without compatibility issues.

By achieving architectural neutrality, Java has become a popular choice for developing cross-platform applications and has played a significant role in the development of various types of software, ranging from enterprise applications to mobile and web applications.

Q.4. Discuss the feature of JAVA. (RU BCA 2018)

Ans- Java, as a programming language, incorporates numerous features that contribute to its popularity and versatility. Some of the key features of Java include:

Platform Independence: Java is known for its "write once, run anywhere" capability, allowing developers to write Java code on one platform and run it on any other platform that supports Java without the need for recompilation.

Object-Oriented: Java is a pure object-oriented programming language, which means it follows the OOP principles of encapsulation, inheritance, and polymorphism, making it suitable for creating modular and maintainable code.

Simple and Familiar: Java syntax is derived from C and C++, making it familiar to many programmers. Its simple and intuitive syntax makes it easy to learn, read, and write Java programs.

Robust and Secure: Java is designed to be robust, providing automatic memory management through garbage collection, preventing memory leaks and buffer overflows. It also includes built-in security features, such as the use of a security manager and a bytecode verifier to ensure secure execution of code.

Multithreading: Java supports multithreading, allowing the concurrent execution of multiple threads within a program. This feature is essential for developing applications that require multitasking and handling multiple operations simultaneously.

High Performance: Java uses Just-In-Time (JIT) compilation and various optimization techniques to achieve high performance. JIT compiles Java bytecode into native machine code at runtime, enhancing the overall speed of execution.

Rich API: Java provides a rich set of APIs for networking, I/O, utilities, XML parsing, database connectivity, and more, enabling developers to build powerful and feature-rich applications.

Distributed Computing: Java supports distributed computing through Remote Method Invocation (RMI) and various networking APIs, making it well-suited for developing networked applications and web services.

Automatic Memory Management: Java manages memory automatically, allowing developers to focus more on the logic of the program rather than memory allocation and deallocation.

Community Support: Java has a vast and active community of developers, which contributes to the availability of numerous libraries, frameworks, and resources that can be used to simplify and expedite the development process.

Q.5. Explain Java virtual machine. (RU BCA 2018)

Ans- The Java Virtual Machine (JVM) is a crucial component of the Java Runtime Environment (JRE) that provides the runtime environment for Java applications to be executed. It is an abstract machine that enables a computer to run Java bytecode, which is the compiled form of a Java program.

Key features and functions of the Java Virtual Machine include:

Platform Independence: The JVM provides platform independence by executing Java bytecode on any platform that has an appropriate JVM implementation. This "write once, run anywhere" feature is a fundamental aspect of Java's design.

Memory Management: The JVM manages memory dynamically, allocating and deallocating memory for objects and data structures. It also includes a garbage collector that automatically reclaims memory from objects that are no longer in use, thus preventing memory leaks and improving the overall performance of Java applications.

Security: The JVM includes various security features to ensure the safe execution of Java applications. It uses a security manager to define the access control policies that restrict the actions of untrusted Java code, preventing potentially harmful operations and protecting the system from malicious activities.

Class Loading: The JVM dynamically loads and links classes as they are referenced during the execution of a Java program. It uses a class loader subsystem to locate and load classes from the file system, network, or other sources, allowing for the dynamic extension and customization of applications.

Execution Engine: The JVM includes an execution engine that interprets the Java bytecode and translates it into machine code that can be executed directly by the underlying hardware. Some JVM implementations also use Just-In-Time (JIT) compilers to improve performance by dynamically compiling bytecode into native machine code at runtime.

Exception Handling: The JVM provides a robust exception handling mechanism that allows Java programs to manage and handle various types of exceptions and errors during runtime, ensuring the stability and reliability of Java applications.

The Java Virtual Machine plays a critical role in the execution of Java applications, providing a secure, portable, and efficient runtime environment that enables developers to build a wide range of applications for different platforms without worrying about the underlying hardware and operating system.

Q.6. Java is a "platform independent language" *What does the mean? (RU BCA 2018)

Ans. The meaning of platform independent is that, the java source code can run on all operating systems. A program is written in a language which is a human readable language, It may contain words, phrases etc which the machine does not understand. For the source code to be understood by the machine, it needs to be in a language understood by machinés, typically a machine-level language, So, here comes the role Of a compiler. The compiler converts the high-level language (human language) into a format understood by the machines. Therefore, a compiler is a program that translates the source code for another program from a programming language into executable code.

Q.7. Explain some of the feature of java. (RU BCA 2019)

Ans.-1. Simple
2. Object-Oriented
3. Portable
4. Platform Independent
5. Secured
6. Robust
7. Architecture Neutral
8. Dynamic
9. High Performance
10.Multi-Threaded
11. Distributed

Q.8. Differentiate the use of JDK and JVM. (RU BCA 2020)

Ans-**JDK:-**

JDK contains tools required to write Java programs, and JRE to execute them.
It includes a compiler, Java application launcher, Appletviewer, etc.
Compiler converts code written in Java into byte code.
Java application launcher opens a JRE, loads the necessary class, and executes its main method.

JVM:

JVM provides a platform-independent way of executing Java source code.
It has numerous libraries, tools, and frameworks.

Once you run Java program, you can run on any platform and save lots of time.
JVM comes with JIT(Just-in-Time) compiler that converts Java source code into low-level machine language. Hence, it runs more faster as a regular application.

Q.9. Explain some of the important reasons for the popularity of Java language. (RU BCA 2020)
Ans. One of the biggest reasons why Java is so popular is the platform independence Programs can run on several different types of computer, as long as the computer has a Java Runtime Environment (JRE) installed, a Java program can run on it. Most types of computers will be compatible with a JRE including PCs running on Windows, Macintosh computers, Unix or Linux computers, and large mainframe computers, as well as mobile phones. Since it has been around for so long, some of the biggest organisations in the world are built using the language. Many banks, retailers, insurance companies, utilities, and manufacturers all use Java. Steve Zara, a programmer for more than 40 years, describes how there is no sign of Java declining in use. Instead, it is an evolving language which almost uniquely combines stability with innovation. Highlighting the longevity of the language, Zara states that the code you may have written 15 years ago will run on the most up- to-date JVMs and gain the speed advantage of the latest profiling, native code translating, and memory management.

Q.10 Discuss features of java in detail. (RU BCA 2021)
Ans: Java is a widely-used, powerful programming language known for its versatility, platform independence, security, and robustness. Below, I've provided a detailed discussion of some of the key features of Java:

Simple and Easy to Learn: Java was designed to be beginner-friendly, with a syntax that is easy to read and write. Its resemblance to C and C++ makes it easier for those with a background in these languages to grasp Java quickly.

Platform Independence: One of Java's most significant features is its "write once, run anywhere" capability. Java programs can run on any device that has a Java Runtime Environment (JRE) installed. This is possible because Java source code is compiled into an intermediate bytecode that can run on any Java Virtual Machine (JVM).

Object-Oriented: Java is designed around the concept of objects, which allows for the creation of modular programs and reusable code. It supports key object-oriented programming concepts such as classes, objects, encapsulation, inheritance, and polymorphism.

Security: Java is known for its robust security features. It provides a secure environment for executing untrusted code by using a combination of language features and runtime environments. The Java Runtime Environment includes a security manager that allows users to run Java applications in a secure environment.

Robust and High Performance: Java is known for its robustness and high performance. It offers strong memory management, automatic garbage collection, and exception handling. Additionally, Java's Just-In-Time (JIT) compiler enables high performance by converting bytecode into native machine code at runtime.

Distributed Computing: Java's built-in networking capability makes it well-suited for creating distributed applications. It includes a rich set of APIs for creating network applications and accessing resources over a network.

Multithreading: Java supports multithreading, allowing concurrent execution of two or more parts of a program for maximum utilization of CPU. This feature is particularly useful for creating responsive and interactive applications.

Rich API: Java provides a vast collection of APIs that simplify development. These include utilities for data structures, networking, input/output, database connectivity, XML parsing, and more. The Java API library is extensive and continually updated to meet the demands of modern development.

Open Source Libraries: Java has a vibrant open-source community that develops and maintains a wide range of libraries, frameworks, and tools. This open-source ecosystem provides developers with a rich set of resources for building complex and feature-rich applications.

Automatic Garbage Collection: Java's automatic garbage collection feature automatically reclaims memory from objects that are no longer in use. This helps developers avoid memory leaks and manage memory efficiently without manual intervention.

These features make Java a preferred choice for developing a wide range of applications, including web applications, mobile applications, enterprise software, scientific applications, and more.

Q.11. Mention any four difference between C++ and java. (BCA-III Paper IV 2021)
Ans:

Aspect	C++	Java
Memory Management	Manual memory management using pointers.	Automatic memory management via garbage collection.
Platform Dependency	Platform-dependent.	Platform-independent due to the Java Virtual Machine (JVM).
Multiple Inheritance	Supports multiple inheritance.	Doesn't support multiple inheritance but allows implementation of multiple interfaces.
Performance	Generally faster due to direct hardware access.	Slower than C++ due to the additional layer provided by the JVM and automatic memory management.

Q.12. Describe basic features of java by providing appropriate example. (RU BCA 2022)

Ans. Object Oriented "In Java, everything is an Object. Java can be easily extended since it is based on the Object model.
1. Platform Independent" Unlike many other programming languages including C and C++, when Java is compiled, it is not compiled into platform specific machine,. rather into platform independent byte code. This byte code is distributed over the web and interpreted by the Virtual Machine (JVM) on whichever platform it is being run on.
2. Simple" Java is designed to be easy to learn. If you understand the basic concept of OOP Java, it would be easy to master.
3. Secure "With Java's secure feature it enables to develop virus-free, tamper-free systems. Authentication techniques are based on public-key encryption.
4. Architecture-neutral" Java compiler generates an architecture-neutral object file format, which makes the compiled code executable on many processors, with the presence of Java runtime system.
5. Portable" Being architecture-neutral and having no implementation dependent aspects of the specification makes Java portable. Compiler in Java is written in ANSI C with a clean portability boundary, which is a POSIX subset.
6. Multithreaded" With Java's multithreaded feature it is possible to write programs that can perform many tasks
7. simultaneously. This design feature allows the developers to construct interactive applications that can run smoothly.
8. Interpreted" Java byte code is translated on the fly to native machine instructions and is not stored anywhere. The development process is more rapid and analytical since the linking is an incremental and light-weight process.
9. High Performance" With the use of Just-In-Time compilers, Java enables high performance.
10. Distributed Java is designed for the distributed environment of the internet.
11. Dynamic" Java is considered to be more dynamic than C or C++ since it is designed to adapt to an evolving environment. Java programs can carry extensive amount of run-time information that can be used to verify and resolve accesses to objects on run-time.

Q.13 Why java programs in platform independent. (RU BCA 2022)

Ans. Java is platform-independent virtual machine. The Java programming language and all APIs are compiled into bytecodes. Bytecodes platform-independent. The virtual machine takes care of the differences between the bytecodes for the different platform. The run-time requirements for Java are therefore very small. The Java virtual machine takes care of all hardware related issues, so that no code has to be compiled for different hardware

ONLINE RESOURCES

Practice Paper
Link: https://forms.gle/uX8GVoJ9XWtxSd8C7
QR Code:

Video Content
Link: https://www.youtube.com/playlist?list=PLzlh_31VWEFqq_6dtNq3PMGwN99a0zTGH
QR Code:

CHAPTER 2 - Language Fundamentals

2.1 Data Types and Variables

2.1.1 Primitive Data Types

In Java, primitive data types are the basic building blocks for defining and storing simple values. They represent fundamental data types and are used to store numeric values, characters, and boolean values. Java has eight primitive data types, categorized into four groups: integers, floating-point numbers, characters, and Booleans.

Here are the eight primitive data types in Java:

1. Integers:

byte = 8-bit signed integer. Range: -128 to 127.
short = 16-bit signed integer. Range: -32,768 to 32,767.
int = 32-bit signed integer. Range: -2^31 to (2^31 - 1).
long = 64-bit signed integer. Range: -2^63 to (2^63 - 1).

Syntax

```
byte b = 127;
short s = 32767;
int integer = 2147483647;
long l = 9223372036854775807L; // Note the 'L' suffix for long literals.
```

2. Floating-Point Numbers:

float = 32-bit IEEE 754 floating-point number. Approximate range: ±3.4 x 10^38 with limited precision.
Double = 64-bit IEEE 754 floating-point number. Approximate range: ±1.7 x 10^308 with higher precision.

Syntax

```
float f = 3.14f; // Note the 'f' suffix for float literals
double d = 3.14159265359;
```

3. Characters:

char = 6-bit Unicode character. Represents a single character in the Unicode standard.

Syntax

```
char c = 'A';
```

4. Booleans:

Boolean = Represents a true or false value.

Syntax

```
boolean isprogrammingFun = true;
boolean isProgrammingHard = false;
```

2.1.2 Non-Primitive Data Types

Non-Primitive Data Types user-defined data types created by users. These data types are used to store multiple values. When non-primitive data is defined, it refers to the memory location in the heap memory where the data is stored, i.e. the memory location where the object is located. For this reason, non-primitive data type variables are also called reference data types or object-only reference variables.There are five types of non-primitive data types in Java:

Class and Object – These are user_defined data types that you create by defining classes. When you create an instance(object)of a class, a reference variable is used to store the memory address of that object.

Syntax-

```
Class MyClass {
// Class definition
}

MyClass obj = new MyClass();
```

String- A string represents a sequence of characters for example "CoreJava", "Hello world", etc. String is the class of Java.

Syntax- String str = "Core Java Book";

Array - Arrays in Java are reference data types. They allow you to store multiple values of the same data type in a single data structure. An array variable stores the reference to the array object in memory.

Syntax –int[] num = new int[50]; // 'num' is a reference to an array of integers

Interface - Interfaces are reference data types that define a contract for classes to implement. You can use interface reference variables to store objects of any class that implements the interface.

Syntax-

```
interface MynewInterface {
    void myMethod();
```

```
}

class MyImplementation implements MynewInterface {
  public void myMethod() {
    // Implementation
  }
}

MynewInterface interfaceRef = new MyImplementation(); // 'interfaceRef' is a reference to an object of MyImplementation
```

2.1.3 "char" data type

The char data type is 16 bits, which means it uses 2 bytes of memory to represent a character. This gives the char data type a range of 65,536 different Unicode characters, allowing it to represent characters from a wide range of languages and symbol sets.

The size of the char data type in Java (2 bytes) differs from C and C++ primarily due to the historical differences in the design and goals of these programming languages:

Unicode Support: Java was designed from the beginning to be an international and platform-independent language. As a result, it uses Unicode to represent characters, which requires a larger range of values than the ASCII character set used in C and C++. Unicode is capable of representing characters from a wide variety of languages, including non-Latin scripts, symbols, and special characters, making it more suitable for global applications.

Platform Independence: Java was designed with the goal of "Write Once, Run Anywhere" (WORA). To achieve this, Java made the decision to use a fixed-width 16-bit char type, ensuring consistency in character representation across different platforms and avoiding the platform-dependent character encoding issues that C and C++ can face.

Avoiding Character Encoding Ambiguity: In C and C++, the size of the char data type can vary from one platform to another, leading to potential portability issues when dealing with character encodings. By using a fixed-width 16-bit char, Java avoids such ambiguity and simplifies character handling.

While Java's choice of a 16-bit char data type is generally suitable for its goals of platform independence and internationalization, it does mean that some characters, particularly those outside the Basic Multilingual Plane (BMP) of Unicode, require a pair of char values (a surrogate pair) to represent them fully. This is a trade-off made to ensure broader character support and portability.

2.2 Declaring and Initializing Variables-

1. Declaration: To declare a variable in Java, specify its data type followed by the variable name. For example:

```
int salary; // Declaring an integer variable named "salary"
double price; // Declaring a double variable named "price"
String name; // Declaring a String variable named "name"
```

2. Initialization: Initialization is the process of giving a variable its initial value. After declaring a variable, you can initialize it by assigning a value. For example:

```
salary = 25000; // Initializing "salary" with the value 25000
price = 19.99; // Initializing "price" with the value 19.99
name = "Jay"; // Initializing "name" with the string "Jay"
```

You have to remember some rules while giving variable names and they are as follows:

Variable names are case-sensitive so "myFunction" and "myfunction" are different.

Variable names can contain letters, digits, underscores, and dollar signs but cannot start with a digit.

Java has reserved words (keywords) that cannot be used as variable names.

2.2.1 Types of Variables

In Java, variables are categorized into different types based on their scope, lifetime, and where they are declared. Here are the main types of variables in Java:

Local Variables:

Local variables are declared within a method, constructor, or block of code.

They have limited scope, which means they are accessible only within the method, constructor, or block in which they are declared.

Local variables are created when the method is called and destroyed when the method exits.

Example-

```
public void exampleMethod() {
  int localVar = 10; // Local variable
```

```
  // ...
}
```

Instance Variables (Non-Static Fields):

Instance variables are declared within a class but outside any method, constructor, or block.
They are associated with an instance (object) of the class and have different values for each instance.
Instance variables have default values if not explicitly initialized.

Example-

```
public class MyClass {
  int instanceVar; // Instance variable
}
```

Static Variables (Class Variables):

Static variables are declared with the static keyword within a class but outside any method, constructor, or block.
They belong to the class itself rather than to any particular instance of the class.
There is only one copy of a static variable shared among all instances of the class.

Example-

```
public class MyClass {
  static int staticVar; // Static variable
}
```

Final Variables:

Final variables are declared with the final keyword.
They can be assigned a value only once and cannot be modified thereafter.
Final variables can be used for constants or to ensure that a variable's value remains constant.

Example-

```
final int myConstant = 42; // Final variable
```

Parameter Variables:

Parameter variables are declared within a method's parameter list.
They receive values when the method is called and can be used within the method.
They act like local variables within the method but are initialized with values provided as arguments.

Example-

```
public void exampleMethod(int parameterVar) {
  // parameterVar acts as a parameter variable
  // ...
}
```

Array Elements:

Elements of an array are also variables.
Each element can hold a value of the same data type as the array.
Array elements are accessed using an index.

Example-

```
int[] numbers = {1, 2, 3, 4, 5}; // Array elements
int thirdNumber = numbers[2]; // Accessing an array element
```

These are the primary types of variables in Java. Understanding their characteristics and scope is essential for writing effective and efficient Java programs.

2.3 Type Casting -

Type casting allows you to convert one data type into another. This process is essential when you want to perform operations involving different data types or store data in variables of different types. There are two types of type casting in Java:

1. Implicit Type Casting -

Implicit type casting occurs automatically when you assign a smaller data type to a larger data type. Java ensures that no data loss occurs during this conversion.

For example - byte -> short -> char -> int -> long -> float -> double (if you assign an int to a double, no explicit casting is required)

Code-

```
int intValue = 10;
double doubleValue = intValue; // Implicit casting from int to double
```

2.Explicit Type Casting – It requires manual intervention and is necessary when you want to convert a larger data type to a smaller one.This type of casting can lead to data loss and should be used with caution.To perform explicit casting, you specify the target data type in parentheses before the value you want to convert.

For Example - double -> float -> long -> int -> char -> short -> byte

Code- double doubleValue = 10.5;

int intValue = (int) doubleValue; // Explicit casting from double to int

Type Casting Rules

You can only implicitly cast between compatible data types in a certain hierarchy (e.g., from int to double).

Explicit casting is required when converting between data types that are not in a natural hierarchy (e.g., from double to int).

Be cautious with explicit casting, as it may result in data loss or unexpected behaviour.

2.4 Operators, Expressions and Keywords

Operators and expressions are fundamental concepts in Java and are used to perform various operations on data. Let's dive into the details of operators, their types, and how expressions are formed in Java:

1. Operators: Operators are symbols used to perform operations on operands. Operands can be variables, constants, or literals. Java supports a variety of operators categorized into several types:

1.1. Arithmetic Operators:

Arithmetic operators perform mathematical operations

Types: + (addition), - (subtraction), * (multiplication), / (division), % (modulus).

Example - int sum = 5 + 3; // sum is now 8

double result = 10.0 / 3.0; // result is 3.3333...

1.2. Relational Operators:

Relational operators compare two values and return a boolean result.

Types: == (equal to), != (not equal to), < (less than), > (greater than), <= (less than or equal to), >= (greater than or equal to).

Examples - boolean isGreater = 7 > 4; // isGreater is true

boolean notEqual = 5 != 5; // notEqual is false

1.3. Logical Operators:

Logical operators perform logical operations on boolean values.

Types: && (logical AND), || (logical OR), ! (logical NOT).

Examples - boolean bothTrue = true && true; // bothTrue is true

boolean eitherTrue = true || false; // eitherTrue is true

1.4. Assignment Operators:

Assignment operators assign values to variables.

Types: = (assignment), += (addition assignment), -= (subtraction assignment), *= (multiplication assignment), /= (division assignment), %= (modulus assignment), = (assignment).

Examples - int x = 10; // x is assigned the value 10

int y = 5;

y += 3; // y is now 8

1.5. Increment and Decrement Operators:

Types: Increment (++) and decrement (--) operators are used to increase or decrease the value of a variable by one.

They can be used as prefix (++i, --i) or postfix (i++, i--) operators.

Examples - int count = 2;

count++; // count is now 3

1.6. Bitwise Operators:

Bitwise operators perform operations on individual bits of integer operands.

Types: & (bitwise AND), | (bitwise OR), ^ (bitwise XOR), ~ (bitwise NOT), << (left shift), >> (right shift), >>> (unsigned right shift).

Examples - int a = 5; // binary: 0101

int b = 3; // binary: 0011

int result = a & b; // result is 1 (binary: 0001)

int m = 12; // binary: 1100

int n = 7; // binary: 0111

int result = m ^ n; // result is 11 (binary: 1011)

1.7. Conditional (Ternary) Operator:

The conditional operator (? :) is a shorthand way to write an if-else statement in a single line.

It evaluates a condition and returns one of two values based on whether the condition is true or false.

Example- int x = 5;

int y = 10;

int max = (x > y) ? x : y; // max is assigned the value of y (10)

2. Expressions: Expressions are combinations of operators and operands that produce a single value. They can be as simple as a single variable or as complex as a combination of multiple operators and variables. Here are some key points about expressions:

2.1. Arithmetic Expressions: Arithmetic expressions combine numeric values using arithmetic operators.

Example: int result = 5 + 3 * (10 / 2);

2.2. Boolean Expressions: Boolean expressions combine boolean values using logical operators.

Example: boolean isTrue = (x > 5) && (y < 10);

2.3. Assignment Expressions: Assignment expressions use assignment operators to store a value in a variable.

Example: int sum = 0; sum += 10;

2.4. Conditional Expressions: Conditional expressions use the ternary operator to conditionally assign a value based on a condition.

Example: int max = (a > b) ? a : b;

2.5. Relational Expressions: Relational expressions compare values and return a boolean result.

Example: boolean isEqual = (x == y);

2.6. Precedence and Associativity: Operators have different precedence levels, determining the order in which they are evaluated.

Parentheses can be used to override precedence.

Operators with the same precedence are evaluated from left to right (left-associative) or right to left (right-associative).

2.7. Side Effects:

Be cautious with expressions that have side effects, especially when using increment and decrement operators. The order of evaluation can affect the final result.

Understanding operators and expressions is crucial for writing effective Java code. Proper use of operators and expressions can improve code readability and efficiency while avoiding common pitfalls

3. Keywords :

In Java, keywords are reserved words that have predefined meanings and purposes in the language. They cannot be used as identifiers (e.g., variable names, method names, class names) because they are part of the language's syntax and serve specific roles. Here are the keywords in Java:

abstract: Used to declare abstract classes or methods.
assert: Used for assertion testing (typically used in debugging).
boolean: Represents a boolean data type with values true or false.
break: Used to exit a loop or switch statement prematurely.
byte: Represents an 8-bit integer data type.
case: Used in switch statements to specify different code blocks for different values.
catch: Used to catch and handle exceptions in exception handling.
char: Represents a character data type.
class: Used to declare a class.
const: Not used in modern Java; was reserved for future use but is no longer used.
continue: Used to continue to the next iteration of a loop.
default: Specifies the default case in a switch statement.
do: Used to start a do-while loop.
double: Represents a double-precision floating-point data type.
else: Used in conditional statements (if-else).
enum: Used to define enumerated types (a special data type consisting of a set of predefined constants).
extends: Indicates inheritance in class declarations.
final: Used to declare a variable, method, or class as unmodifiable or to prevent inheritance.
finally: Used in exception handling to specify a block of code that is always executed.
float: Represents a single-precision floating-point data type.
for: Used to create a for loop.
if: Used to create conditional statements.
implements: Indicates that a class implements an interface.
import: Used to include classes from other packages.
instanceof: Used to test if an object is an instance of a particular class or interface.
int: Represents a 32-bit integer data type.
interface: Used to declare an interface.
long: Represents a 64-bit integer data type.
native: Used to declare native methods (methods implemented in a language other than Java).
new: Used to create objects.

package: Used to define a package that groups related classes and interfaces.
private: Used to restrict access to members within the same class.
protected: Used to restrict access to members within the same class or its subclasses.
public: Used to make members accessible from anywhere.
return: Used to return a value from a method.
short: Represents a 16-bit integer data type.
static: Used to declare static members (belonging to the class rather than an instance).
strictfp: Ensures consistent floating-point arithmetic across different platforms.
super: Refers to the superclass in inheritance and is used to call superclass constructors and methods.
switch: Used to create a switch statement.
synchronized: Used for synchronization in multithreaded programs.
this: Refers to the current instance of a class.
throw: Used to throw an exception.
throws: Declares exceptions that a method can throw.
transient: Used to indicate that a variable should not be serialized.
try: Defines a block of code that might throw exceptions.
void: Indicates that a method does not return a value.
volatile: Specifies that a variable can be modified by multiple threads.
while: Used to create a while loop.

These keywords play a fundamental role in defining the structure, behavior, and logic of Java programs. It's essential to use them correctly and adhere to their specific meanings and usage within the language.

2.5 Control Statements (if, else, switch, loops)

Control statements in Java are essential for directing the flow of a program. They determine which blocks of code to execute based on certain conditions or for a specific number of iterations. Let's explore each of the major control statements in Java:

1. if Statement:

The if statement is used for conditional execution of code. It allows you to execute a block of code only if a specified condition is true.

Example-

```
if (condition) {
   // Code to execute when the condition is true
} else {
   // Code to execute when the condition is false (optional)
}
```

The if statement checks the condition, and if it's true, the code within the curly braces {} is executed.
You can include an optional else block to specify code to execute when the condition is false.

2. else if Statement:

The else if statement is used to test multiple conditions in a sequence. It allows you to check multiple conditions and execute code based on the first true condition encountered.

Example-

```
if (condition1) {
   // Code to execute when condition1 is true
} else if (condition2) {
   // Code to execute when condition2 is true
} else {
   // Code to execute when none of the conditions is true (optional)
}
```

The conditions are evaluated in order, and when a true condition is found, the corresponding block of code is executed.

3. switch Statement:

The switch statement is used for multi-way branching based on the value of an expression (usually an integer or character).

Example-

```
switch (expression) {
   case value1:
      // Code to execute when expression equals value1
      break;
   case value2:
      // Code to execute when expression equals value2
      break;
```

```
    // More cases...
    default:
        // Code to execute when none of the cases match (optional)
}
```

The break statement is used to exit the switch block when a match is found.
The default case is optional and is executed when none of the cases match.

4. Loops:

Loops are used to repeatedly execute a block of code as long as a specified condition is true. Java supports three main types of loops:

4.1. for Loop:

The for loop is used when you know in advance how many times the loop should run.

Example-

```
for (initialization; condition; update) {
    // Code to repeat while the condition is true
}
```

The initialization sets up loop control variables.
The condition is checked before each iteration.
The update statement changes the loop control variable(s).

4.2. while Loop:

The while loop is used when you want to repeat a block of code while a condition is true.

Example-

```
while (condition) {
    // Code to repeat while the condition is true
}
```

The loop continues to execute as long as the condition remains true.
Be careful to avoid infinite loops; ensure that the condition eventually becomes false.

4.3. do-while Loop:

The do-while loop is similar to the while loop, but it guarantees that the code block is executed at least once before checking the condition.

Example-

```
do {
    // Code to repeat at least once
} while (condition);
```

The code block is executed first, and then the condition is checked.
It's useful when you want to ensure that a certain operation is performed before checking the exit condition.

5. Java Break

"Break" is a keyword in Java used within control structures like loops and switch statements to alter the flow of the program. Here's a brief explanation of how it's used in these contexts:

1. Breaking Out of a Loop:

In a loop (e.g., for, while, do-while), the break statement is used to prematurely exit the loop, even if the loop's condition is not met.
It's commonly used when a specific condition is met, and you want to terminate the loop immediately.

Example-

```
for (int i = 0; i < 10; i++) {
    if (i == 5) {
        break; // Exit the loop when i equals 5
    }
    System.out.println(i);
}
```

2. Breaking Out of a Switch Statement:

In a switch statement, the break statement is used to exit the switch block after a case is executed.
Without break, the program would continue executing the subsequent case(s) until it encounters a break or reaches the end of the switch block.

Example-

```
int choice = 2;
switch (choice) {
    case 1:
        System.out.println("Option 1 selected");
        break;
```

```
    case 2:
        System.out.println("Option 2 selected");
        break;
    default:
        System.out.println("Invalid choice");
        break;
}
```

6. Java Continue

The continue statement in Java is used within loops (e.g., for, while, do-while) to control the flow of the loop execution. When a continue statement is encountered within a loop, it causes the current iteration of the loop to terminate prematurely, and the program proceeds with the next iteration (if applicable). In other words, it skips the remaining code within the current iteration and moves on to the next iteration.

Here's how the continue statement works:

Example-

```
for (int i = 0; i < 5; i++) {
    if (i == 2) {
        continue; // Skip the rest of the current iteration if i equals 2
    }
    System.out.println(i);
}
```

In this example, when i equals 2, the continue statement is encountered. As a result, the code within the current iteration (printing 2) is skipped, and the loop proceeds to the next iteration. Therefore, the output will be:

Output-

```
0
1
3
4
```

Key points about the continue statement:

- It only affects the current iteration of the loop in which it is placed. The loop continues with the next iteration, and subsequent iterations are not affected.
- The continue statement is typically used in combination with conditional statements (e.g., if) to control which iterations should be skipped based on certain conditions.
- Be cautious when using continue as it can lead to infinite loops if not used correctly. Ensure that the loop's exit condition is still reachable.
- You can use continue in both for loops and while loops, as well as in nested loops.

Here's an example of using continue in a while loop:

Example-

```
int i = 0;
while (i < 5) {
    i++;
    if (i % 2 == 0) {
        continue; // Skip even numbers
    }
    System.out.println(i);
}
```

This code will print only odd numbers from 1 to 5.

Control statements are a fundamental part of Java programming, allowing you to make decisions and control the flow of your programs. These statements are essential for building complex, responsive, and efficient software.

7. Java return:

The return statement is used to exit from a method and return a value to the caller of that method. It is commonly used in methods to provide a result to the calling code.

Example of using return in a method:

java

Copy code

```
public int add(int a, int b) {
    return a + b;
}
```

In this example, the add method returns the sum of a and b to the caller.

2.6 Input and Output in Java

Input and output (I/O) operations are vital in Java for interacting with users, reading data from external sources, and writing data to various destinations. Java provides a rich set of classes and methods for performing I/O operations. Let's explore input and output in Java in detail:

Input Operations:

Input operations involve reading data into a Java program. Common sources of input include the keyboard, files, and network connections.

1. Keyboard Input (Console):

Java uses the Scanner class to read input from the console (keyboard). You need to import java.util.Scanner to use it.

Code

```
import java.util.Scanner;
Scanner scanner = new Scanner(System.in);
System.out.print("Enter your name: ");
String name = scanner.nextLine();
System.out.println("Hello, " + name);
scanner.close();
```

System.in represents the standard input stream, which is connected to the keyboard.
nextLine() reads a line of text entered by the user.

2. File Input:

Java provides various classes for reading data from files, such as FileInputStream, BufferedReader, and Scanner.

Code

```
import java.io.BufferedReader;
import java.io.FileReader;
import java.io.IOException;

try (BufferedReader reader = new BufferedReader(new FileReader("input.txt"))) {
    String line;
    while ((line = reader.readLine()) != null) {
        // Process each line from the file
        System.out.println(line);
    }
} catch (IOException e) {
    e.printStackTrace();
}
```

The above code reads data from the "input.txt" file line by line using a BufferedReader.

3. Network Input (Socket Programming):

Java allows you to perform network I/O operations using classes like Socket and InputStream.
Network input typically involves connecting to a server and reading data from it.

Output Operations:

Output operations involve displaying or writing data from a Java program to various destinations, such as the console, files, or network connections.

1. Console Output:

You can display output to the console (standard output) using System.out.

Code

```
System.out.println("Hello, World!");
```

System.out represents the standard output stream, which is connected to the console.

2. File Output:

Java provides classes like FileOutputStream, BufferedWriter, and PrintWriter for writing data to files.

Code

```
import java.io.BufferedWriter;
import java.io.FileWriter;
import java.io.IOException;

try (BufferedWriter writer = new BufferedWriter(new FileWriter("output.txt"))) {
    writer.write("This is a line of text.");
    writer.newLine(); // Move to the next line
    writer.write("Another line of text.");
} catch (IOException e) {
    e.printStackTrace();
```

}

The code above writes data to the "output.txt" file.

3. Network Output (Socket Programming):

Java allows you to perform network output operations using classes like Socket and OutputStream.
Network output typically involves sending data to a remote server or client.

4. Standard Error Output:

Java provides System.err for printing error messages and diagnostic information to the console.

Code

```
System.err.println("An error occurred!");
```

System.err represents the standard error stream, which is also connected to the console by default.

5. Formatting Output:

Java offers various methods for formatting output, including String.format() and printf().

Code

```
int num = 42;
System.out.printf("The answer is %d%n", num);
```

The above code formats and prints the value of num in the specified format.

Java's I/O capabilities are versatile and allow you to interact with various data sources and destinations, making it a powerful language for handling input and output operations in different contexts, from console applications to network communication and file processing.

2.7 Exception in Java

In Java, an exception is an event that occurs during the execution of a program, disrupting the normal flow of the program's instructions. Exceptions represent abnormal or erroneous conditions that can happen at runtime. When an exceptional condition arises, Java creates an object to represent that exception, and the program can choose to handle or propagate (pass on) the exception. This mechanism provides a way to gracefully handle errors and exceptional situations in your code.

2.7.1 List of built-in exceptions in Java.

Java provides a wide range of built-in exceptions to handle different error conditions in your programs. Here are six commonly used built-in exceptions in Java:

NullPointerException: This exception is thrown when you attempt to access or invoke a method on an object that is null. It occurs when you try to perform an operation on an object reference that points to no object.

ArrayIndexOutOfBoundsException: This exception is thrown when you attempt to access an array element using an index that is outside the valid range of indices for that array. It occurs when you try to access an element that doesn't exist in the array.

ArithmeticException: This exception is thrown when an arithmetic operation results in an error, such as division by zero (/ 0). It represents mathematical errors during runtime.

FileNotFoundException: This exception is thrown when attempting to access a file that does not exist at the specified path. It occurs when you try to open or read a file that is not present in the file system.

IOException: This is a general exception for input/output (I/O) operations. It is thrown when an I/O operation (e.g., reading or writing to a file) encounters an error.

IllegalArgumentException: This exception is thrown when a method is called with an illegal or inappropriate argument. It typically occurs when a method receives an argument that is outside the expected range or doesn't meet certain conditions.

These are just a few of the built-in exceptions available in Java. Java provides a rich set of exception classes that cover a wide range of error scenarios, allowing you to handle and respond to different types of exceptions gracefully in your programs.

2.7.2 The class at the top of the exception class hierarchy is the java.lang.Throwable class. The Throwable class is the superclass for all exceptions and errors in Java. It has two main subclasses:

- **java.lang.Exception:** This class is the superclass for all checked exceptions. Checked exceptions are exceptions that your code is required to handle explicitly, either by using a try-catch block or declaring them in the method signature with the throws keyword.
- **java.lang.Error**: This class is the superclass for all errors. Errors are typically not recoverable, and they indicate severe issues in the Java runtime environment. They are not meant to be caught and handled by your application code. Examples of errors include OutOfMemoryError and StackOverflowError.

So, the hierarchy looks like this:

Example-

```
java.lang.Throwable
   |
   +-- java.lang.Exception
   |     |
```

```
|     +-- Checked Exceptions
|
+-- java.lang.Error
      |
      +-- Errors
```

All exceptions and errors in Java ultimately inherit from Throwable, making it the top-level class for exception handling in the Java language.

2.8 Exception Handling

Exception handling is a crucial aspect of Java programming that enables developers to manage errors and unexpected situations gracefully. In Java, exceptions are objects representing various types of errors that can occur during program execution. Here, we'll delve into exception handling in detail:

1. Types of Exceptions:

In Java, exceptions are categorized into two main types:

1.1. Checked Exceptions:

These exceptions must be either caught using a try-catch block or declared using the throws keyword in the method signature.

Examples: IOException, SQLException.

1.1.1 Types of Checked Exceptions:

Checked exceptions are represented by classes that inherit from the java.lang.Exception class but not from java.lang.RuntimeException. Some common checked exception classes include IOException, SQLException, ClassNotFoundException, and InterruptedException, among others.

Forced Handling or Declaration:

When a method can potentially throw a checked exception, it must either handle the exception using a try-catch block or declare (specify) the exception in its method signature using the throws keyword.

If an exception is not handled or declared in this way, the code will not compile.

Using a try-catch Block:

To handle a checked exception, you can enclose the code that might throw the exception within a try block and provide one or more catch blocks to catch and handle the exception.

For example:

```
try {
  // Code that may throw a checked exception
} catch (IOException e) {
  // Handle the exception
}
```

Using throws Declaration:

Alternatively, you can declare that a method may throw a checked exception in its method signature by using the throws keyword followed by the exception class.

For example:

```
public void readFile() throws IOException {
  // Code that may throw IOException
}
```

Propagation of Exceptions:

When a method declares that it may throw a checked exception, it is responsible for either handling the exception itself or propagating it by declaring it in its own throws clause.

If a method propagates an exception, it passes the responsibility of handling or declaring the exception to the caller method.

1.1.2 Use Cases for Checked Exceptions:

Checked exceptions are typically used for situations where it's reasonable to expect and handle errors or exceptional conditions. For example, file I/O operations may throw IOException, and handling such exceptions allows your program to recover from file-related issues gracefully.

1. Handling and Logging:

When dealing with checked exceptions, it's common to include error-handling logic that may involve logging the exception details, providing user-friendly error messages, and potentially taking corrective actions.

Here's an example of a method declaration that includes a checked exception in its throws clause:

Example-

```
import java.io.IOException;

public class FileProcessor {
   public void processFile() throws IOException {
      // Code that may throw an IOException during file processing
   }
}
```

1.2 Unchecked Exceptions (Runtime Exceptions):
These exceptions do not need to be explicitly caught or declared.
Examples: NullPointerException, ArrayIndexOutOfBoundsException.
1.2.1 List of unchecked exceptions.
Unchecked exceptions in Java, also known as runtime exceptions, are exceptions that do not need to be explicitly caught or declared in a method's throws clause. They typically represent errors or exceptional conditions that occur at runtime and are not required to be handled by the programmer. Here are four examples of unchecked exceptions in Java:
1. **NullPointerException (NPE):** This exception occurs when you attempt to access or manipulate an object that is null. It's one of the most common runtime exceptions.
Example-
```
String str = null;
int length = str.length(); // Throws NullPointerException
```
2. **ArrayIndexOutOfBoundsException:** This exception occurs when you try to access an array element with an invalid index, either by going out of bounds or using a negative index.
Example-
```
int[] arr = {1, 2, 3};
int value = arr[5]; // Throws ArrayIndexOutOfBoundsException
```
3. **ArithmeticException:** This exception occurs when an arithmetic operation results in an error, such as division by zero.
Example-
```
int result = 5 / 0; // Throws ArithmeticException
```
4. **ClassCastException:** This exception occurs when you attempt to cast an object to a class type that it is not an instance of. It typically happens when working with improper type conversions in Java.
Example-
```
Object obj = "Hello";
Integer num = (Integer) obj; // Throws ClassCastException
```
These unchecked exceptions can occur at runtime and are not required to be caught or declared in your code. However, it's still a good practice to handle them gracefully to ensure the stability and robustness of your Java applications.
2. Exception Handling Keywords:
Java provides several keywords and constructs for handling exceptions:
2.1. try-catch Blocks:
The try block encloses the code that might throw an exception.
The catch block follows try and contains code to handle exceptions.
Multiple catch blocks can be used to handle different types of exceptions.
Syntax-
```
try {
   // Code that may throw an exception
} catch (ExceptionType1 e1) {
   // Handle ExceptionType1
} catch (ExceptionType2 e2) {
   // Handle ExceptionType2
} finally {
   // Optional: Code that always executes, even if an exception occurs
}
```

You can handle multiple exceptions with multiple catch blocks in a nested try-catch structure. This allows you to catch and handle different types of exceptions at different levels of nesting. Here's an example to illustrate how this works:
Example-
```
public class NestedTryCatchExample {
   public static void main(String[] args) {
      try {
```

```
            // Outer try block
            int[] numbers = {1, 2, 3};
            int result = divideArrayElement(numbers, 0);
            System.out.println("Result: " + result);
        } catch (ArithmeticException e) {
            System.out.println("ArithmeticException caught at outer level: " + e.getMessage());
        } catch (ArrayIndexOutOfBoundsException e) {
            System.out.println("ArrayIndexOutOfBoundsException caught at outer level: " + e.getMessage());
        }
    }

    public static int divideArrayElement(int[] arr, int index) {
        try {
            // Inner try block
            int numerator = arr[index];
            int denominator = 0;
            return numerator / denominator;
        } catch (ArithmeticException e) {
            System.out.println("ArithmeticException caught at inner level: " + e.getMessage());
            return -1; // Return a special value to indicate an error
        } catch (ArrayIndexOutOfBoundsException e) {
            System.out.println("ArrayIndexOutOfBoundsException caught at inner level: " + e.getMessage());
            return -1; // Return a special value to indicate an error
        }
    }
}
```

In this example:

The main method calls the **divideArrayElement** method with an array and an index. The **divideArrayElement** method divides an element of the array by zero, potentially causing an **ArithmeticException,** and it also may access an invalid index, leading to an **ArrayIndexOutOfBoundsException.**

Inside the **divideArrayElement** method, there is an inner try-catch block. This inner block is used to catch exceptions that might occur within the method.

If an **ArithmeticException** occurs within the **divideArrayElement** method, it is caught by the inner catch block, and a message is printed. The method returns a special value (-1 in this case) to indicate an error.

If an **ArrayIndexOutOfBoundsException** occurs within the **divideArrayElement** method, it is also caught by the inner catch block, and a message is printed. Again, the method returns -1 to indicate an error.

Back in the main method, the outer try-catch block catches exceptions that might be thrown by the **divideArrayElement** method. It can catch both **ArithmeticException** and **ArrayIndexOutOfBoundsException.** Depending on the exception type, it prints a message.

This nested try-catch structure allows you to handle exceptions at different levels of the program, providing more specific error messages and handling for different scenarios.

2.2. throw Keyword:

The throw keyword is used to explicitly throw an exception within your code.

Code

```
if (someConditionIsTrue) {
    throw new CustomException("This is a custom exception message");
}
```

2.3. throws Keyword:

The throws keyword is used in a method signature to declare that the method might throw a specific exception.
It is necessary for checked exceptions.

Code

```
public void readFile() throws IOException {
    // Code that may throw IOException
}
```

2.4. finally Block:

The finally block follows the try-catch blocks (if present) and contains code that always executes, regardless of whether an exception is thrown or not.
It is often used for resource cleanup.

Code

```
try {
   // Code that may throw an exception
} catch (Exception e) {
   // Handle the exception
} finally {
   // Cleanup code (e.g., closing files or connections)
}
```

3. Custom Exceptions:

You can create your own custom exceptions by extending the Exception class or one of its subclasses. Custom exceptions are useful for handling application-specific errors.

Code

```
class CustomException extends Exception {
   public CustomException(String message) {
      super(message);
   }
}
```

4. Best Practices for Exception Handling:

Catch specific exceptions: Catch only the exceptions you expect and can handle. Avoid catching generic Exception whenever possible.

Handle exceptions appropriately: Choose the appropriate action when an exception occurs, such as logging the error, notifying the user, or performing cleanup.

Use finally for resource cleanup: If you acquire resources (e.g., files, database connections), release them in the finally block.

Keep exception messages informative: Include descriptive error messages to aid in debugging.

Minimize the scope of try-catch blocks: Place try-catch blocks around the smallest portion of code that may throw an exception.

5. The Exception Hierarchy:

Java's exception hierarchy is rooted in the Throwable class, which has two main subclasses: Error (for serious errors that should not be caught) and Exception (for exceptions that can be caught and handled). The Exception class has various subclasses for specific types of exceptions.
Understanding and effectively using exception handling in Java is crucial for writing robust and reliable applications. It enables you to gracefully handle errors, improve user experience, and ensure proper resource management.

2.9 Empty Statement

In Java, an empty statement is a statement that consists of just a semicolon (;) and nothing else. It is a valid statement in Java, and although it doesn't perform any operation or computation, it serves a specific purpose in certain situations. An empty statement is sometimes referred to as a "null statement."
The primary usefulness of an empty statement lies in its ability to act as a placeholder or a way to create a deliberate no-op (no operation) statement. Here are a few scenarios where empty statements can be useful:

Loop Control:

Empty statements can be used in loops to create loops with no executable content. This can be helpful when you want to create a loop structure that does nothing in its body but continues looping based on a condition. For example:

Example-

```
for (int i = 0; i < 10; i++) {
   // Empty statement
   ;
}
```

In this example, the loop will iterate 10 times, but the empty statement does nothing during each iteration.

Switch Statements:

In switch statements, empty cases can be used to create fall-through behavior, where the control flows from one case to another. However, when you want a case to do nothing, you can use an empty statement:

Example-

```
switch (value) {
    case 1:
        // Do something
        break;
    case 2:
        // Do nothing (empty statement)
        ;
        break;
    case 3:
        // Do something else
        break;
}
```
In this example, when value is 2, the empty statement acts as a placeholder for a case with no code.

Syntax Requirement:

In some cases, Java syntax may require a statement, but you don't want to execute any code. An empty statement can fulfil this requirement. For example, when defining an empty block in a try-catch-finally construct:

Example-

```
try {
    // Some code that may throw an exception
} catch (Exception e) {
    // Handle the exception
} finally {
    // Empty statement (required by syntax)
    ;
}
```
While empty statements can be useful in certain situations, they should be used sparingly and with care. Code with too many empty statements can become difficult to understand and maintain. It's often better to provide comments or refactor code to make it more self-explanatory, when possible, rather than relying on empty statements for clarity.

2.10 this keyword

In Java, this keyword is a reference to the current instance of the class in which it appears. It is a reference to the object on which the current method or constructor is invoked. The primary use of this keyword is to distinguish between instance variables and method parameters or to invoke one constructor from another in the same class. Here are the main uses of this keyword in Java:

Reference to Current Object:

Within an instance method or constructor, you can use this to refer to the current object. This allows you to access instance variables and invoke instance methods of the object.

Example:

```
class MyClass {
    int number;

    void setNumber(int number) {
        this.number = number; // 'this' refers to the instance variable
    }
}
```

2.11 Distinguishing between Instance Variables and Method Parameters:

When an instance variable has the same name as a method parameter, you can use this to clarify which one you are referring to.

Example:

```
class MyClass {
    int value;

    MyClass(int value) {
        this.value = value; // 'this' distinguishes the instance variable from the constructor parameter
    }
}
```
1. Invoking One Constructor from Another (Constructor Chaining):

In a constructor, you can use this to call another constructor of the same class. This is known as constructor chaining. Constructor chaining is useful when you want to reuse code or initialize common properties in multiple constructors.
Example:
```
class MyClass {
   int number;

   MyClass() {
      this(0); // Calls the parameterized constructor with a default value
   }

   MyClass(int number) {
      this.number = number;
   }
}
```
2. Returning the Current Object:
You can use this as a return value from a method to return the current object, allowing for method chaining (also known as fluent interfaces).
Example:
```
class MyClass {
   int value;

   MyClass setValue(int value) {
      this.value = value;
      return this; // Allows for method chaining
   }
}
```
3. Passing the Current Object as an Argument:
You can pass the current object (i.e., this) as an argument to another method or constructor.
Example:
```
class MyClass {
   int value;

   void process(MyClass otherInstance) {
      // Perform some operation using 'this' and 'otherInstance'
   }
}
```
This keyword is a fundamental concept in Java, allowing you to work with instance-specific data and perform various object-oriented operations. It helps clarify the context within which variables and methods are used, especially in cases where names clash between instance variables and method parameters.

Exercise

Exercise 1 – MCQ
Q 1. The expression "public static void main(String[] args)" declared in a Java program is: What means
a) Defines a method to print the output to the console.
b) Indicates the entry point where the program will start running.
c) Declares a variable that stores string arguments.
d) Represents the constructor function used to create the object.
Q 2. Which of the following statements declares a variable named "count" in Java and initializes it to the value 10?
a) count int =10;
b) int count = 10 ;
c) int count = 10
d) int count 10 ;

Exercise 2 – True/ False
Q 1. Every statement in Java must end with a semicolon (;).
Q 2. In Java, both single-line (//) and multi-line (/* */) comments are executed as part of the program.

Exercise 3 – Fill in the blanks
Q1. The main method in Java works as _________ point.
Q 2. In Java, single-line comments are denoted by ____________.

Exercise 4 – Match case
Q 1. Match the following Java syntax elements with their descriptions:
i. Variable Declaration
ii. Method Definition
iii. Class Declaration
Descriptions:
a. Defines the structure and behaviour of objects.
b. Specifies the data type and name of a value holder
c. Contains a block of code that performs a specific task.
Exercise 5 – One word answer
Q 1. How do you denote a Single-line comment in Java?
Q 2. Which keyword indicates that the `main` method is accessible from outside the class?
Exercise 6 – Small answer
Q 1. What is the purpose of a static in Java Syntax?
Q 2. How do you denote a multi-line comment in Java?
Exercise 7 – Long answer
Q 1. Explain Java Syntax.
Q 2. Write one Java program.
Answer:
Exercise 1. Q 1: b) Specifies the entry point where the program will start running.
Q 2: b) int count = 10;
Exercise 2. Q 1: True Q 2: False
Exercise 3. Q 1: entry Q 2: double slashes (//)
Exercise 4. Q 1: i. Class Declaration – A ii. Variable Declaration – B iii. Method Definition - C
Exercise 5. Q 1: // Q 2: public

Previous Year Questions

Q 1. What are the primitive data types in Java? Write about type conversions. (JNTU -B.Tech.- 2018)
Q 2. With suitable code segments illustrate various uses of 'final' keyword. (JNTU -B.Tech.- 2018)
Q 3. How to handle multiple catch blocks for a nested try block? Explain with an example. (JNTU -B.Tech.- 2018)
Q 4. What is the size of char data type? Why does it differ from C language? (JNTU -B.Tech. -2017)
Q 5. Differentiate between error and exception. (JNTU -B.Tech. -2017)
Q 6. Write a program to illustrate the use of multiple catch blocks for a try block. (JNTU -B.Tech. -2017)
Q 7. What are the uses of 'throw' and 'throws' clauses for exception handling? (JNTU -B.Tech. -2017)
Q 8. What is an exception? How are exceptions handled in Java programming? (JNTU -B.Tech.- 2016)
Q 9. What keywords are essential in handling user-defined exception? (JNTU -B.Tech.- 2016)
Q 10. Explain the use of 'final' keyword. (SPPU – BCA - 2015)
Q 11. List any six built-in exceptions in Java. (SPPU – BCA - 2015)
Q 12. Explain the purpose of checked and unchecked exception. (SPPU – BCA - 2015)
Q 13. Explain the use of 'this' keyword. (SPPU – BCA - 2015)
Q 14. Discuss Java jump statements. (SPPU – BCA - 2015)
Q 15. What is empty statement? Explain its usefulness? (Aryabhatta University BCA 2014)
Q 16. Explain how to rethrow an exception. Write a program to create a try block that is likely to generate three types of exception and then incorporate necessary catch blocks to catch and handle the appropriately. (Aryabhatta University BCA 2014)
Q 17. Name the class which is at the top of the exception class hierarchy. (SPPU – BCA - 2015)
Q 18. List memory requirement for boolean type and char type in java. (SPPU – BCA - 2015)
Q 19. Write down the methods defined by input stream. Write a java program that demonstrates random access I/O which writes six double to a file and then reads them back in non-sequential order (Aryabhatta University BCA 2014)
Q 20. What is exception handling? How is it done in java? What is the usage of throw and throws keyword in exception handling? Explain with suitable example. (Punjab Technical University MCA -2015)
Q 21. What is user - defined exceptions? (IGNOU MCS 2010)
Q 22. Differentiate checked and unchecked exception. (IGNOU MCA 2011)
Q 23. Explain static variable is used in java? (IGNOU MCA 2012)
Q 24. Explain two uses of "final" keyword with the help of example. .(IGNOU MCA 2011)
Q 25. Differentiate between throw and throws ? (IGNOU MCA 2012)

Q 26. What are shift operators ? How many types of shift operators are available in Java ? (IGNOU MCA 2012)
Q 27. What are the functions of the dot(.) operator ? Explain with suitable example. (IGNOU MCA 2012)
Q 28. When is the "this" keyword used and 4 why ? (IGNOU MCA 2013)
Q 29. Explain the uses of keywords final, finally and finalize in Java.
Q 30. List any four unchecked exceptions. (JNTU -B.Tech.- 2018)
Q 31. What is the difference between checked and unchecked exceptions (IGNOU MCS 2010)

Previous Year Solved Papers

Q.1 What are the most important features of Object Oriented Programming languages? (RU BCA 2017)
Ans- The most important features of Object-Oriented Programming (OOP) languages include:

Abstraction: The ability to represent real-world objects in a software system and focus on the essential characteristics and behaviors of those objects.

Encapsulation: The bundling of data and methods that operate on the data, restricting direct access to some of the object's components and hiding the internal state and implementation details.

Inheritance: The mechanism by which one class inherits the properties and behaviors of another class, enabling code reusability and the creation of hierarchical relationships between classes.

Polymorphism: The ability to present the same interface for different data types, allowing objects of different classes to be treated as objects of a common superclass.

Q.2. What is the difference between throw and throws? (RU BCA 2017)
Ans-

Feature	throw	throws
Purpose	Used to throw an exception explicitly.	Used in the method signature to declare exceptions.
Usage	Used within the body of a method to throw an exception.	Used in the method declaration to specify exceptions that might be thrown by the method.
Singular/Plural	Singular is used to throw a single exception.	Plural can declare multiple exceptions separated by commas.
Keyword	**throw** is a keyword.	**throws** are a keyword.
Example	**throw new IO Exception ("File not found");**	**public void readFile () throws IOException {...}**

Q.3. The Exception class has two main subclasses: IO Exception class and Runtime Exception Class. (RU BCA 2017)
Ans- The statement you provided seems to be inaccurate. In Java, the **Exception** class is a superclass for a wide range of exception classes, including both **IOException** and **RuntimeException**, which are not direct subclasses of **Exception** but rather subclasses of it indirectly. They are part of the hierarchy of exceptions in Java. Here's a more accurate representation of the relationship:

IOException Class: This class is a subclass of the **Exception** class and represents a checked exception that occurs during input-output operations, typically when dealing with files, streams, or other input-output operations. It is used to handle errors related to input-output, such as file not found, end of file, or interrupted I/O operations.

RuntimeException Class: This class is also a subclass of the **Exception** class and represents a type of exception that can be unchecked and does not need to be declared in a method's signature or handled explicitly. These exceptions typically occur due to programming errors or unexpected conditions during the execution of a Java program, such as null pointer dereference, arithmetic exceptions, or index out of bounds.

The **Exception** class serves as a superclass for a wide range of checked exceptions, while the **RuntimeException** class represents a subclass of **Exception** that includes unchecked exceptions. Both **IOException** and **RuntimeException** are important subclasses in the hierarchy of exceptions in Java, providing a way to handle and manage various types of errors and exceptional situations that may occur during the execution of Java programs.

Q.4. The switch Statement (RU BCA 2017)
Ans- The switch statement is a control flow statement that allows a variable to be tested for equality against a list of values. It provides an efficient way to execute different code blocks based on the value of a variable. The switch statement is often used as an alternative to long chains of if-else statements, making the code more readable and concise. Here is the basic syntax of the switch statement in Java:

```
switch (expression) {
   case value1:
      // code to be executed if expression matches value1
      break;
   case value2:
      // code to be executed if expression matches value2
      break;
   // more cases can be added as needed
   default:
      // code to be executed if none of the cases match
}
```

Key points to remember about the switch statement in Java:

The **expression** inside the switch should yield a value that is compatible with the data type of the cases.

Each **case** statement specifies a value to compare the **expression** against.

The **break** statement is used to exit the switch block once a match is found. If **break** is omitted, execution will continue to the next case until a **break** or the end of the switch block is reached.

The **default** case is optional and is executed if none of the other cases match the **expression**.

The **switch** expression can be of type **byte**, **short**, **int**, **char**, **String** (since Java 7), or an enumerated type.

Here's an example demonstrating the usage of the switch statement:

```
int day = 2;
String dayString;
switch (day) {
   case 1:
      dayString = "Monday";
      break;
   case 2:
      dayString = "Tuesday";
      break;
   case 3:
      dayString = "Wednesday";
      break;
   // other cases can be added here
   default:
      dayString = "Invalid day";
}
System.out.println("The day is: " + dayString);
```

In this example, the switch statement is used to match the value of the variable **day** with different cases and assign the corresponding day name to the variable **dayString**. Finally, the value of **dayString** is printed to the console.

Q.5. Explain the loop control in java? (RU BCA 2018)

Ans- In Java, loop control refers to the mechanisms that control the flow and repetition of certain code blocks. Java provides several types of loops that are used to execute a block of code repeatedly based on a specified condition. The main loop control structures in Java include the following:

for Loop: The **for** loop is used when the number of iterations is known. It consists of three parts: initialization, condition, and update. The loop continues to execute as long as the condition is true.

```
for (initialization; condition; update) {
   // code to be executed
}
```

while Loop: The **while** loop is used when the number of iterations is not known in advance. It continues to execute as long as the specified condition is true.

```
while (condition) {
   // code to be executed
}
```

do-while Loop: The **do-while** loop is similar to the **while** loop, but it checks the condition after the execution of the loop's body. This ensures that the loop's body is executed at least once.

```
do {
   // code to be executed
} while (condition);
```

break Statement: The **break** statement is used to exit a loop prematurely based on a certain condition. When the **break** statement is encountered, the loop is terminated, and the control is transferred to the next statement after the loop.

```
for (int i = 0; i < 10; i++) {
  if (i == 5) {
    break; // exit the loop when i is 5
  }
  System.out.println(i);
}
```

continue Statement: The **continue** statement is used to skip the current iteration of a loop and continue with the next iteration based on a specific condition.

```
for (int i = 0; i < 10; i++) {
  if (i == 5) {
    continue; // skip the iteration when i is 5
  }
  System.out.println(i);
}
```

These loop control structures are essential in controlling the flow of execution in Java programs, enabling developers to efficiently handle repetitive tasks and iterate through data structures. By understanding and using these loop control structures effectively, developers can write more efficient and concise code for various types of applications.

Q.6. What is java throws keyword? (RU BCA 2018)

Ans- In Java, the **throws** keyword is used in the method signature to declare that the method might throw one or more types of exceptions during its execution. It is part of Java's exception handling mechanism and is used to specify that a method can potentially throw certain types of exceptions that need to be handled by the calling method or propagated further up the call stack.

Here is an example of the **throws** keyword in Java:

```
public void readFile() throws IOException {
  // code that may throw an IOException
}
```

In this example, the method **readFile** is declared with the **throws** keyword, indicating that it may throw an **IOException** during its execution. If the method encounters an **IOException**, it will not handle the exception itself, but rather propagate it to the method that called **readFile**. It is then the responsibility of the calling method to handle the exception using a try-catch block or propagate it further up the call stack.

The **throws** keyword is particularly useful when designing methods that interact with external resources such as files, databases, or networks, where certain exceptions might occur, and the calling code needs to be aware of these potential exceptions and handle them appropriately.

It's important to note that using the **throws** keyword does not force the calling method to handle the exception immediately; it merely indicates that the method might throw the specified exceptions. However, if the calling method does not handle the exceptions, it must also declare the exceptions using the **throws** keyword or handle the exceptions using a try-catch block to prevent compilation errors.

Q.7.What is static keyword in java. (RU BCA 2018)

Ans- In Java, the keyword "static" is used to create fields, methods, and blocks that belong to the class rather than to any specific instance of the class. This means that a static member is shared among all instances of the class. It is also commonly used to create static methods, which can be called without creating an instance of the class.

Here are some key uses of the static keyword in Java:

Static Variables: A static variable is shared among all instances of a class. It is initialized only once, at the start of the execution, and its value is the same for every instance of the class. Static variables are also known as class variables.

```
public class Example {
  static int count = 0; // static variable
}
```

Static Methods: A static method belongs to the class rather than to any specific instance. It can be invoked without the need for creating an instance of the class.

```
public class Example {
  static void display() { // static method
    System.out.println("Static method.");
  }
```

}
Static Blocks: A static block is used for static initializations of a class. This block gets executed when the class is loaded into memory. It's often used to initialize static variables.

```
public class Example {
   static {
      System.out.println("Static block.");
   }
}
```

When using the static keyword, it's important to keep in mind that:

Static members can be accessed without creating an instance of the class.

Static methods cannot access instance variables and methods directly. They can only access static variables and other static methods.

Static variables and methods are associated with the class, rather than with any specific instance of the class.

Static blocks are executed only once when the class is loaded into memory.

Q. 8. Write a program to illustrate the use of socket programming with example?. (RU BCA 2019)

Ans. Java Socket programming is used for communication between the applications running on different JRE Java Socket programming can be connection-oriented or connection-less Socket and ServerSocket classes are used for connection-oriented socket programming and DatagramSocket and DatagramPacket classes are used for connection-less socket programming.

The client in socket programming must know two information:

1. IP Address of Server, and
2. Fort number

```
import java.io.*;
import java.net.*;
public class MyServer (
public static void main(String[] args){
try{
ServerSocket ss=new ServerSockct(6666)',
Socket s =ss.accept();//establishes connection
DatalnputStream dis=new DatalnputStream(s.getInputStream());
String str=(String)dis.readUTF();
System.out.println(message= "+str);
ss.close();
}catch(Exception e){System.out.println(e)}
}
}
```

PreparedStatement interface
CallableStatement interface
ResultSet interface
ResultSetMetaData interface
DatabaseMetaData interface
Row Set interface
A list of popular classes of JDBC API are given below:
DriverManager class

Q.9. Explain socket in java. (RU BCA 2019)

Ans. A server application nonnally listens to a specific port waiting for connection requests from a client. When a connection request arrives, the client and the server establish a dedicatod connection over which they can communicate During the connection process, the client is assigned a local port number, and binds a mocker to it. The client talks to the server by writing to the socket and gets information from the server by reading from it. Similarly, the server gets a new local port number (it needs a new port number so that it can continue to listen for connection requests on the original port). The server also binds a socket to its local port and communicates with the client by reading from and writing to it.

Q.10. Explain the list of operators used in Java. (RU BCA 2020)

Ans- **Arithmetic Operators:** They are used to perform simple arithmetic operations on primitive data types.

*: Multiplication

/: Division
%: Modulo
+: Addition
-: Subtraction
Unary Operators: Unary operators need only one operand. They are used to increment, decrement or negate a value.
-: Unary minus, used for negating the values.
+: Unary plus, used for giving positive values. Only used when deliberately converting a negative value to positive.
++: Increment operator, used for incrementing the value by 1. There are two varieties of increment operator.
Post-Increment: Value is first used for computing the result and then incremented.
Pre-Increment: Value is incremented first and then result is computed.
-:Decrement operator, used for decrementing the value by I. There are two varieties of decrement operator.
Post-decrement: Value is first used for computing the result and then decremented.
Pre-Decrement: Value is decremented first and then result is computed.
1: Logical not operator, used for inverting a boolean value.
Assignment Operator: Assignment operator is used to assign a value to any variable. It has a right to left associativity, ie value given on right hand side of operator is assigned to the variable on the left and therefore right hand side value must be declared before using it or should be a constant.
General format of assignment operator is.
variable = value;
In many cases assignment operator can be combined with other operators to build a shorter version of statement called Compound
Statement. For example, instead of a a+5, we can write a += 5.
+ =, for adding left operand with right operand and then assigning it to variable on the left.
-=, for subtracting left operand with right operand and then assigning it to variable on the left.
*=, for multiplying left operand with right operand and then assigning it to variable on the left.
/=, for dividing left operand with right operand and then assigning it to variable on the left.
%=,for assigning modulo of left operand with right operand and then assigning it to variable on the left.

Relational Operators: These operators are used to check for relations like equality, greater than, less than. They return boolean result after the comparison and are extensively used in looping statements as well as conditional if else statements.
General format is,
variable relation_operator value
Some of the relational operators are-
= =, Equal to: returns true if left hand side is equal to right hand side. 1,
!=,Not Equal to: returns true if left hand side is not equal to right hand side.
<, less than: returns true if left hand side is less than right hand side.
<=, less than or equal to: returns true if left hand side is less than or equal to right hand side.
>, Greater than: returns true if left hand side is greater than right hand side.
>=,Greater than or equal to: returns true if left hand side is greater than or equal to right hand side.
Logical Operators: These operators are used to perform "logical AND" and "logical OR" operation, ie the function similar to AND gate and OR gate in digital electronics. One thing to keep in mind is the second condition is not evaluated if the first one is false, ie it has a short-circuiting effect. Used extensively to test for several conditions for making a decision.
Conditional operators are-
&&, Logical AND: returns true when both conditions are true.
Logical OR: returns true if at least one condition is true.
Ternary operator: Ternary operator is a shorthand version of if-else statement.

Q.11. What is life time of a Variable? (RU BCA 2020)
Ans. A variable which is declared inside a class and outside all the methods and blocks is an instance variable. The general scope of an instance variable is throughout the class except in static methods. The lifetime of an instance variable is until the object stays in memory.

Q.12. What is checked and unchecked exception? (RU BCA 2021)
Ans: Checked Exceptions:- The exceptions that are checked during the compile-time are termed as Checked exceptions in Java. The Java compiler checks the checked exceptions during compilation to verify that a method that is throwing an exception contains the code to handle the exception with the try-catch block or not.

And, if there is no code to handle them. then the compiler checks whether the method is declared using the throws keyword. And, if the compiler finds neither of the two cases, then it gives a compilation error. A checked exception extends the exception class.

Some checked Exceptions are:

SQL Exception IO Exception

Class Not Found Exception Invocation Target Exception

File Not found Exception

Unchecked Exceptions

An exception that occurs during the execution of a program is called an unchecked or a runtime exception. The main cause of unchecked exceptions is mostly due to programming errors like attempting to access an element with an invalid index, calling the method with illegal arguments, etc. In Java, the direct parent class of Unchecked Exception Run time Exception. Unlike the checked exceptions, the compiler generally ignores the unchecked exceptions during compilation. Unchecked exceptions are checked during the runtime.

Some unchecked exceptions are

1. Arithmetic Exception
2. Null Pointer Exception
3. Array Index Out of Bounds Exception
4. Number Format Exception
5. Input Mismatch Exception
6. Illegal State Exception
7. Missing Resource Exception
8. No Such Element Exception
9. Undeclared Throwable Exception
10. Empty Stack Exception

Q.13. Define the conditional operator in java with suitable example (RU BCA 2022)

Ans- In Java, conditional operators check the condition and decides the desired result on the basis of both conditions. In this section, we will discuss the conditional operator in Java.

Types of Conditional Operator

There are three types of the conditional operator in Java:

Conditional AND &&

Conditional OR ||

Ternary Operator?

```
public class ConditionalOperatorExample
{
public static void main(String args[])
{
int x=5, y=4, z=7;
System.out.println(x>y && x>z || y<z);
System.out.println((x<z || y>z) && x<y);
}
}
```

Output

True

False

Q.14. Define stack in java. (RU BCA 2022)

Ans. The stack is a linear data structure that is used to store the collection of objects. It is based on Last-In-First- Out (LIFO). Java collection framework provides many interfaces and classes to store the collection of objects. One of them is the Stack class that provides different operations such as push, pop, search, etc. In this section, we will discuss the Java Stack class, its methods, and implement the stack data structure in a Java program. But before moving to the Java Stack class have a quick view of how the stack works. The stack data structure has the two most important operations that are push and pop. The push operation inserts an element into the stack and pop operation removes an element from the top of the stack. Let's see how they work on stack.

Practice Paper
Link: https://forms.gle/5RE8t4fUh5pLY24C8
QR Code:

Video Content
Link: https://www.youtube.com/playlist?list=PLzlh_31VWEFpzLNIlz8zQoR64L6DdxMVa
QR Code:

CHAPTER 3 - Object-Oriented Programming

3.1 Overview of Object-Oriented Programming

Object-Oriented Programming (OOP) is a fundamental programming paradigm that plays a central role in Java's design and development. In this overview, we'll explore the core principles and concepts of OOP in the context of Java:

1. Objects:

Objects are the fundamental building blocks of OOP in Java.
An object is a self-contained unit that encapsulates both data (attributes or fields) and behaviour (methods or functions).
Objects are instances of classes and represent real-world entities or concepts.
In Java, you create objects by instantiating classes using the new keyword.

2. Classes:

A class is a blueprint or template for creating objects.
It defines the structure and behaviour of objects that belong to it.
Classes in Java encapsulate data using fields (instance variables) and define methods (functions) to manipulate that data.
Java follows a class-based approach to OOP, meaning that objects are instances of classes.

3. Encapsulation:

Encapsulation is the principle of bundling data (attributes) and methods (behaviour) into a single unit (class) and controlling access to that unit.
In Java, access to the internal state of an object is controlled through access modifiers (e.g., public, private, protected) and getter and setter methods.

4. Inheritance:

Inheritance is a mechanism that allows a new class (subclass or derived class) to inherit properties and behaviours from an existing class (superclass or base class).
It promotes code reusability and the creation of a hierarchical class structure.
In Java, the extends keyword is used to establish an inheritance relationship.

5. Polymorphism:

Polymorphism allows objects of different classes to be treated as objects of a common superclass.
It enables method overriding and dynamic method dispatch.
Polymorphism simplifies code by allowing you to write code that works with objects of various types without knowing their exact types.
In Java, polymorphism is achieved through method overriding and interfaces.

6. Abstraction:

Abstraction is the process of simplifying complex reality by modelling classes based on the essential properties and behaviours.
It hides the unnecessary details and focuses on what's relevant.
Abstract classes and interfaces in Java provide a way to define abstract types with common characteristics.

7. Constructors and Destructors:

Constructors are special methods used to initialize objects when they are created.
In Java, constructors have the same name as the class and are invoked using the new keyword.
Java does not have explicit destructors like some other languages. Instead, it relies on garbage collection to automatically reclaim memory when objects are no longer in use.

8. Polymorphism and Method Overriding:

Method overriding is a technique that allows a subclass to provide a specific implementation for a method defined in its superclass.
The @Override annotation is used to indicate that a method is intended to override a method from the superclass.

9. Interfaces:

Interfaces in Java define a contract of methods that classes must implement.
Multiple inheritance is achieved in Java through interfaces, allowing a class to implement multiple interfaces.

10. Packages:

Packages provide a way to organize and group related classes and interfaces.
They help in avoiding naming conflicts and allow for modular development.
Java's strong support for OOP principles makes it a powerful and widely used programming language for building complex and maintainable software systems. By effectively applying the principles of OOP, developers can create code that is more modular, reusable, and easier to understand and maintain.

3.1.2 Appplications of Java

Here are some common applications of object-oriented programming in Java:

1. Software Development: OOP is widely used in software development to design and build complex systems. It helps in organizing code into reusable and maintainable components.
2. Graphical User Interfaces (GUIs): Java's Swing and JavaFX libraries are built using OOP principles. GUI components like buttons, windows, and menus are represented as objects with properties and behaviors.
3. Web Applications: Java Enterprise Edition (Java EE) uses OOP concepts to create scalable and maintainable web applications. Frameworks like JavaServer Faces (JSF) and Spring Framework promote OOP practices.
4. Database Interaction: Object-relational mapping (ORM) frameworks like Hibernate and JPA use OOP to map Java objects to database tables, making it easier to work with databases.
5. Game Development: Many game development frameworks in Java, such as LibGDX and jMonkeyEngine, leverage OOP for managing game objects, graphics, and interactions.
6. Mobile App Development: Android app development, using Java as one of the programming languages, relies on OOP principles to create interactive and responsive mobile applications.
7. Simulation and Modelling: OOP is used in simulations and modelling applications, such as simulating physical systems or modelling real-world scenarios.
8. Scientific Computing: Java is used in scientific computing, where OOP allows for modelling and simulating complex scientific phenomena and data analysis.
9. Financial Software: Financial applications benefit from OOP's modularity and encapsulation. Objects can represent financial instruments, transactions, and portfolios.
10. Machine Learning and AI: Java is used for machine learning and artificial intelligence applications. OOP facilitates the modelling of algorithms, neural networks, and data structures.
11. E-commerce and Online Services: Online shopping platforms and web services often use OOP for modelling products, users, transactions, and order processing.
12. Robotics and Embedded Systems: In robotics and embedded systems, OOP is used to represent sensors, actuators, and control logic in a structured way.
13. Data Structures and Algorithms: OOP is valuable for implementing data structures (e.g., lists, trees, graphs) and algorithms in a modular and reusable manner.
14. Educational Software: OOP's simplicity and modularity make it a popular choice for developing educational software and interactive learning applications.
15. Content Management Systems (CMS): CMS platforms, like Joomla and Drupal, utilize OOP for managing content, users, and plugins.
Enterprise Software: Large-scale enterprise applications often use OOP principles for creating scalable, maintainable, and extensible software solutions.

3.2 Classes and Objects

Classes: A class in Java is a blueprint or template for creating objects. It defines the structure and behaviour that objects of the class will have. Here's how you define a class in Java

Example-

```
public class Person {
   // Fields (attributes)
   private String name;
   private int age;

   // Methods (behaviours)
   public void introduce() {
      System.out.println("Hello, my name is " + name + " and I am " + age + " years old.");
   }

   // Getter and setter methods for private fields
   public String getName() {
      return name;
   }

   public void setName(String name) {
      this.name = name;
   }

   public int getAge() {
      return age;
```

```
    }

    public void setAge(int age) {
        this.age = age;
    }
}
```

Objects: Objects are instances of classes. They are created based on the blueprint defined by a class. To create an object, you use the new keyword followed by the class's constructor. Here's how you create an object of the MyClass class:

Example-

```
MyClass myObject = new MyClass(42);
```

myObject is an instance of the MyClass class.

3.3 Constructors and Methods

Constructors and methods are essential components of classes in Java. They define the behaviour and characteristics of objects created from a class. Let's explore constructors and methods in Java in detail:

3.3.1 Constructors

A constructor is a special method in a class used to initialize objects when they are created.
It has the same name as the class and does not have a return type, not even void.
Constructors are called automatically when you create an object using the new keyword.

Types of Constructors:

Default Constructor: If you don't define any constructors in your class, the compiler provides a default constructor with no arguments. It initializes fields to their default values.

Parameterized Constructor: You can define constructors with parameters to allow initialization of object attributes at the time of creation.

Example-

```
public class Person {
    private String name;
    private int age;

    // Parameterized Constructor
    public Person(String name, int age) {
        this.name = name;
        this.age = age;
    }
}
```

Multiple Constructors: You can define multiple constructors in a class, each with a different number or type of parameters (constructor overloading).

Example-

```
public class Student {
    private String name;
    private int age;

    // Parameterized Constructor
    public Student(String name, int age) {
        this.name = name;
        this.age = age;
    }

    // Default Constructor
    public Student() {
        // Initialize with default values
        this.name = "Unknown";
        this.age = 0;
    }
}
```

Constructor Chaining:

In Java, you can call one constructor from another constructor within the same class using the this() keyword. This is known as constructor chaining.

Code-

```
public class Car {
   private String make;
   private String model;

   public Car(String make, String model) {
      this.make = make;
      this.model = model;
   }

   public Car(String make) {
      // Call parameterized constructor with default model
      this(make, "Unknown");
   }
}
```

3.3.2 Methods:

A method is a block of code that performs a specific task or action.
Methods define the behaviour or operations that objects of a class can perform.
Methods can have parameters (input) and may return a value (output).

1. Method Declaration:

A method declaration consists of the method's access modifier, return type, name, parameters, and body.

Example-

```
public int add(int num1, int num2) {
   int sum = num1 + num2;
   return sum;
}
```

Access Modifiers: public, private, protected, or package-private (default).
Return Type: The data type of the value returned by the method. Use void if the method doesn't return anything.
Method Name: A unique identifier for the method within the class.
Parameters: Input values passed to the method for processing.
Method Body: Contains the code that defines the method's behavior.

2. Calling Methods:

Methods are called using an object of the class they belong to.
The syntax for calling a method is objectName.methodName(parameters).

Example-

```
Person person1 = new Person("Alice", 25);
int result = person1.calculateAgeIn5Years();
```

3. Method Overloading:

Java supports method overloading, where you can define multiple methods with the same name in a class, but with different parameter lists.
The compiler determines which method to call based on the arguments passed.

Example-

```
public int add(int num1, int num2) {
   return num1 + num2;
}

public double add(double num1, double num2) {
   return num1 + num2;
}
```

Static Methods:

Static methods belong to the class itself, not to individual objects.
They are called using the class name, not an object.

Example-

```
public class MathUtils {
   public static int add(int num1, int num2) {
      return num1 + num2;
   }
}
```

```
// Calling a static method
int sum = MathUtils.add(5, 3);
```

Constructors and methods play a crucial role in defining the **behaviour** and characteristics of objects in Java classes. Constructors initialize object attributes, while methods provide the functionality that objects can perform. Understanding how to create and use constructors and methods is fundamental to Java programming.

3.4 Inheritance and Polymorphism

Inheritance and polymorphism are two core concepts in Java's Object-Oriented Programming (OOP) paradigm. They provide the foundation for code reuse, extensibility, and abstraction. Let's explore these concepts in detail:

3.4.1. Inheritance: Inheritance is a mechanism in which one class (subclass or derived class) can inherit the properties and behaviours (fields and methods) of another class (superclass or base class). This allows you to create a hierarchy of classes with shared characteristics. Key aspects of inheritance in Java include:

a. Extending a Class: To create a subclass, you use the extends keyword followed by the name of the superclass.

Example-

```
class Subclass extends Superclass {
   // Subclass-specific members
}
```

b. Inherited Members: A subclass inherits all non-private members (fields and methods) from the superclass.
It can access these members as if they were defined in the subclass itself.

c. Method Overriding: A subclass can provide its own implementation of a method that is already defined in the superclass.

Example-

This is known as method overriding and is used to customize the **behaviour** of inherited methods.

```
class Subclass extends Superclass {
   // Override a method from the superclass
   @Override
   public void someMethod() {
      // New implementation
   }
}
```

d. Access Modifiers:

Inherited members retain their original access modifiers (e.g., public, protected, package-private) in the subclass. A subclass cannot reduce the visibility of inherited members but can increase it.

e. Constructors and Inheritance: Constructors are not inherited, but the subclass must call a constructor of the superclass using super() as the first statement in its constructor.
If the superclass has no-argument constructor, it's called by default. If not, you must explicitly call one of its constructors.

2. Benefits of Inheritance

Inheritance is a fundamental concept in object-oriented programming (OOP) that offers several benefits and advantages for software development. Here are the key benefits of inheritance:

Code Reusability: Inheritance allows you to reuse existing code from a superclass in a new subclass. This means you don't have to rewrite common functionality, reducing redundancy and promoting the reuse of well-tested and reliable code.

Modularity: Inheritance helps in organizing code into logical and manageable units. By creating subclasses that inherit from a common superclass, you can group related attributes and methods together, making the codebase more structured and easier to understand.

Extensibility: Inheritance enables you to extend the functionality of existing classes without modifying their code. You can create new subclasses to add additional features or behaviours to a class hierarchy, thus extending the capabilities of your software.

Polymorphism: Inheritance is closely related to polymorphism, which is one of the core principles of OOP. Polymorphism allows objects of different subclasses to be treated as instances of their common superclass. This promotes flexibility and the ability to work with objects in a generic way.

Consistency and Standardization: By defining common attributes and methods in a superclass, you establish a consistent interface and behaviour that all subclasses inherit. This standardization ensures that all derived classes adhere to the same conventions.

Encapsulation: Inheritance facilitates encapsulation by allowing you to control the access to and visibility of members (fields and methods) in the superclass. You can use access modifiers like protected and private to define the level of encapsulation.

Ease of Maintenance: Inheritance simplifies maintenance because changes made to the superclass automatically affect all its subclasses. This reduces the risk of introducing bugs when updating common functionality.

Code Readability: Inheritance can improve code readability by creating a hierarchical structure that represents relationships between classes. This makes it easier for developers to understand the design and purpose of the software.
Efficiency: Inheritance can lead to more efficient code because it allows you to build on existing implementations. Instead of duplicating code in multiple places, you can maintain and optimize code in a single location.
Faster Development: Reusing existing classes through inheritance can significantly speed up the development process. You can leverage pre-built components and focus on implementing only the specific features unique to your application.
Modelling Real-World Relationships: Inheritance allows you to model real-world relationships and hierarchies effectively. For example, in a vehicle simulation, you can have a superclass "Vehicle" with subclasses like "Car," "Bicycle," and "Motorcycle."
While inheritance offers many benefits, it should be used judiciously and in accordance with the principles of good object-oriented design. Overuse of inheritance can lead to complex and rigid class hierarchies, making the code harder to maintain and understand. In some cases, composition and interfaces may be more appropriate than inheritance to achieve desired behaviours and relationships in software.

3.4.2. Polymorphism:
Polymorphism is the ability to treat objects of different classes as objects of a common superclass. It simplifies code by enabling you to write code that works with objects of various types without knowing their exact types. Key aspects of polymorphism in Java include:
a. Method Overriding:
Method overriding allows a subclass to provide its own implementation of a method that is already defined in the superclass. The @Override annotation is used to indicate that a method in the subclass is intended to override a method in the superclass.
Example-
```
class Animal {
  public void makeSound() {
    System.out.println("Animal makes a sound");
  }
}

class Dog extends Animal {
  @Override
  public void makeSound() {
    System.out.println("Dog barks");
  }
}
```
b. Dynamic Method Dispatch:
In Java, method calls are resolved at runtime, which means the actual method that gets called is determined based on the object's actual type. This allows you to write code that works with objects of the superclass but executes the appropriate overridden method of the subclass.
Example-
```
Animal myPet = new Dog();
myPet.makeSound(); // Calls Dog's makeSound() method
```
c. Interfaces: Interfaces define a contract of methods that classes must implement. Polymorphism can be achieved by treating objects as instances of interfaces.
Example-
```
interface Shape {
  void draw();
}

class Circle implements Shape {
  @Override
  public void draw() {
    System.out.println("Drawing a circle");
  }
}
```
Example-
```
Shape shape = new Circle();
shape.draw(); // Calls Circle's draw() method
```

In summary, inheritance allows you to create hierarchical class structures for code reuse and organization, while polymorphism enables flexibility and code simplicity by treating objects in a more abstract manner. These concepts are foundational to Java's OOP paradigm and are essential for building modular and maintainable Java applications.

d. Method Overloading - Method overloading is a feature in Java that allows you to define multiple methods in the same class with the same name but different parameter lists. The key difference between these overloaded methods is the number or type of parameters they accept. Method overloading enhances code readability and reusability by providing multiple ways to call a method with different inputs. In this overview, we'll explore method overloading in Java, including its key concepts, syntax, usage, and best practices.

1. Key Concepts:

Method Overloading: Method overloading occurs when multiple methods in the same class have the same name but different parameter lists. Parameter lists can differ in the number, type, or order of parameters.

Signature: The method's signature includes its name and parameter list. Method overloading is based on differences in method signatures.

Return Type: Method overloading does not consider the return type when differentiating between overloaded methods.

2. Method Overloading Syntax:

To overload a method, you define multiple methods with the same name but different parameter lists. Here's an example:

Example-

```
class Calculator {
  int add(int a, int b) {
    return a + b;
  }

  double add(double a, double b) {
    return a + b;
  }
}
```

In this example, the add method is overloaded with two versions: one that takes two integers and another that takes two doubles.

3. Method Overloading Rules:

When overloading methods, you must follow these rules. The method names must be the same. The parameter lists must differ in at least one of the following ways:

- Number of parameters
- Type of parameters
- Order of parameters
- The return type is not considered when overloading methods. Two methods with the same name and parameter lists but different return types would result in a compilation error.

4. Method Overloading Usage: Method overloading is used in various scenarios, including:

- Providing convenience to users by allowing them to use methods with different data types or numbers of arguments.
- Simplifying method names, especially in utility classes or APIs, by using the same name for methods that logically perform similar operations.
- Handling default values for optional parameters.

5. Best Practices:

- Avoid overloading methods with significantly different behaviours to prevent confusion.
- Use meaningful and descriptive parameter names to differentiate overloaded methods.
- Ensure that overloaded methods have consistent behaviour for similar inputs.
- Be cautious when overloading methods with primitive and wrapper types, as it can lead to ambiguity in method resolution.

6. Example:

Here's an example of method overloading with default parameter values:

Example -

```
class Printer {
  void print(String text) {
    System.out.println(text);
  }

  void print(int number) {
    System.out.println(number);
  }
```

```
    void print(String text, int times) {
        for (int i = 0; i < times; i++) {
            System.out.println(text);
        }
    }
}
```

In this example, the print method is overloaded with different parameter lists, allowing you to print text and numbers in various ways.

e. super keyword-

The super keyword in Java is used to refer to the immediate parent class of a subclass. It is primarily used in the context of inheritance to access members (fields or methods) of the superclass. The super keyword can be used in several ways to differentiate between superclass members and subclass members and to call superclass constructors. In this overview, we'll explore the super keyword in Java, including its key usages, syntax, and examples.

1. Key Usages:

The super keyword is primarily used for the following purposes:

- **Accessing Superclass Members:** You can use super to access fields or methods of the superclass when they are hidden by the subclass. This is useful when the subclass has its own member with the same name.
- **Calling Superclass Constructors**: You can use super to call constructors of the superclass. This is useful when the subclass constructor needs to perform some additional initialization that is specific to the subclass.

2. Syntax:

To access a superclass member: super.memberName

To call a superclass constructor: super(arguments)

3. Accessing Superclass Members:

In the context of accessing superclass members, the super keyword allows you to distinguish between overridden methods or hidden fields. Consider the following example:

Example-

```
class Animal {
    String name = "Animal";

    void makeSound() {
        System.out.println("Animal makes a sound.");
    }
}

class Dog extends Animal {
    String name = "Dog";

    void makeSound() {
        super.makeSound(); // Calls the superclass method
        System.out.println("Dog barks.");
    }

    void printNames() {
        System.out.println("Name in Dog: " + name);    // Accesses the subclass field
        System.out.println("Name in Animal: " + super.name); // Accesses the superclass field
    }
}
```

In this example, super.makeSound() is used to explicitly call the makeSound method of the superclass Animal. Also, super.name is used to access the name field of the superclass Animal.

4. Calling Superclass Constructors:

The super keyword is also used to call superclass constructors. When a subclass constructor is called, it automatically calls the no-argument constructor of the superclass if no super call is specified. However, if the superclass has constructors with arguments, you can use super(arguments) to call a specific superclass constructor. For example:

Example-

```
class Animal {
    int age;

    Animal(int age) {
```

```
        this.age = age;
    }
}

class Dog extends Animal {
    String breed;

    Dog(int age, String breed) {
        super(age); // Calls the superclass constructor
        this.breed = breed;
    }
}
```

In this example, the super(age) call in the Dog constructor explicitly invokes the superclass constructor with an age argument.

5. Use Cases:

Use super to access overridden or hidden superclass members when the subclass has members with the same name.

Use super to call superclass constructors when you need to perform additional initialization in the subclass constructor.

6. Best Practices:

Use the super keyword when necessary to clarify the intent of your code, especially in cases of method overriding and field hiding.

Be cautious when using super to access superclass members, as it can make code more complex. Ensure that it is necessary for the desired behaviour.

In conclusion, the super keyword in Java is a useful tool for working with inheritance. It allows you to access superclass members and call superclass constructors, enhancing code readability and enabling proper initialization in subclass constructors.

f. Instance Initializer block –

In Java, an instance initializer block is a block of code that is defined within a class but outside of any method or constructor. It is executed when an instance of the class is created, just before the constructor of the class is called. Instance initializer blocks are useful for performing some common initialization tasks for all constructors of a class. Here's an overview of instance initializer blocks in Java:

Key Points:

Syntax: An instance initializer block is defined using a pair of curly braces {} and does not have a method or constructor name.

Usage: Instance initializer blocks are used to initialize instance variables, perform complex calculations, or execute code that needs to run for all constructors of a class.

Execution Order: Instance initializer blocks are executed in the order they appear in the class, from top to bottom, before any constructors are called.

Visibility: Instance initializer blocks can access both instance variables and static variables of the class.

Example:

```
public class MyClass {
    private int x;
    private static int y;

    // Instance initializer block
    {
        x = 10;
        System.out.println("Instance initializer block: x=" + x);
    }

    // Constructor
    public MyClass() {
        System.out.println("Constructor called");
    }

    public static void main(String[] args) {
        MyClass obj = new MyClass();
        System.out.println("Main method: x=" + obj.x);
    }
}
```

In this example, an instance initializer block is used to set the value of the instance variable x to 10. When an object of the class is created using the constructor MyClass(), the instance initializer block is executed before the constructor, ensuring that x is initialized to 10 for all instances of the class.

4. Use Cases:

Common Initialization: Instance initializer blocks are useful for performing common initialization tasks that need to be executed for all constructors of a class.

Initialization Based on Constructor Parameters: You can use instance initializer blocks to initialize instance variables based on constructor parameters.

Complex Calculations: If the initialization of instance variables involves complex calculations or logic, you can encapsulate that logic within an instance initializer block to keep constructors concise.

5. Best Practices:

Use instance initializer blocks when you need to perform common initialization tasks for all constructors of a class.

Keep the code within instance initializer blocks clean and focused on initialization tasks.

Be aware that instance initializer blocks are executed in the order they appear in the class, so ensure that the order of execution meets your requirements.

In summary, instance initializer blocks in Java provide a way to execute code that initializes instance variables or performs common initialization tasks for all constructors of a class. They are executed just before constructors and can help keep code organized and maintainable.

g final keyword –

In Java, the final keyword is used to declare entities (variables, methods, and classes) that cannot be modified or extended:

Final Variables: A final variable is a constant whose value cannot be changed once it is assigned. It must be initialized when declared or within a constructor.

Example-

```
final int constantValue = 42;
```

Final Methods: A final method in a class cannot be overridden by subclasses. It enforces that the method's behavior remains unchanged in all subclasses.

Example-

```
class Parent {
  final void doSomething() {
    // Implementation
  }
}
```

Final Classes: A final class cannot be extended or subclassed. It is typically used to prevent inheritance for security or design reasons.

Example-

```
final class FinalClass {
  // Class implementation
}
```

In summary, the final keyword is used to enforce immutability for variables, prevent method overriding, and restrict class inheritance in Java.

3.5 Interfaces and Abstract Classes

Interfaces and abstract classes are important elements of Java's Object-Oriented Programming (OOP) paradigm. They provide a way to define common behaviours and establish contracts for classes. Let's explore interfaces and abstract classes in detail:

1. Interfaces: An interface in Java defines a contract of methods that classes must implement. It's like a blueprint for methods without providing any implementation. Here are the key aspects of interfaces in Java:

a. Declaration: You declare an interface using the interface keyword.

Example-

```
interface Drawable {
  void draw();
}
```

b. Method Signatures: Interfaces contain method signatures (declaration without implementation) that participating classes must provide.

c. Implementing Interfaces: To implement an interface, a class uses the implements keyword.

Example-

```
class Circle implements Drawable {
  @Override
  public void draw() {
    System.out.println("Drawing a circle");
```

```
    }
}
```

d. Multiple Interfaces: A class can implement multiple interfaces, allowing it to adhere to multiple contracts.

Example-

```
class Square implements Drawable, Resizable {
    @Override
    public void draw() {
        System.out.println("Drawing a square");
    }

    @Override
    public void resize(int factor) {
        // Implementation for resizing
    }
}
```

e. Default Methods (Java 8+): Starting from Java 8, interfaces can have default methods with default implementations. This allows you to add new methods to existing interfaces without breaking implementing classes.

f. Static Methods (Java 8+): Java 8 introduced static methods in interfaces, which can be called without an instance of the interface.

2. Abstract Classes: An abstract class in Java is a class that cannot be instantiated on its own but can serve as a base for other classes. Abstract classes can contain both abstract (unimplemented) methods and concrete (implemented) methods. Here are the key aspects of abstract classes in Java:

a. Declaration: You declare an abstract class using the abstract keyword.

Example-

```
abstract class Shape {
    // Abstract method
    abstract double area();

    // Concrete method
    void display() {
        System.out.println("This is a shape.");
    }
}
```

b. Abstract Methods: Abstract classes can have abstract methods, which are declared but not implemented in the abstract class itself.

c. Subclassing: Concrete (non-abstract) subclasses must implement all abstract methods of the abstract class.

Example-

```
class Circle extends Shape {
    private double radius;

    Circle(double radius) {
        this.radius = radius;
    }

    @Override
    double area() {
        return Math.PI * radius * radius;
    }
}
```

d. Constructors: Abstract classes can have constructors, which are invoked when an object of a concrete subclass is created.

e. Fields and Concrete Methods: Abstract classes can have fields (attributes) and concrete methods with implementations.

f. Accessibility: Abstract methods and classes can have various access modifiers, but abstract methods in an interface are implicitly public and abstract.

In summary, interfaces define contracts for classes to implement, allowing for polymorphism and code organization. Abstract classes provide a way to create a common base for multiple classes and can include both abstract and concrete methods. Understanding when to use interfaces and abstract classes is crucial in designing flexible and maintainable Java applications.

3.6 Packages and Access Modifiers

Packages and access modifiers are fundamental concepts in Java that help organize and control access to classes, interfaces, and other elements within your code. Let's delve into packages and access modifiers in detail:

3.6.1 Packages: A package in Java is a way to organize related classes and interfaces into a single unit. It helps in avoiding naming conflicts and makes code more modular and maintainable. Here are the key aspects of packages in Java:

a. Package Declaration: You declare a package at the beginning of a Java source file using the package keyword.

Example-

```
package com.example.myapp;
```

This statement defines the package com.example.myapp for the classes in the file.

b. Directory Structure: Packages are often associated with directory structures. The package declaration maps to **the** directory structure.

Example-

```
com/
 example/
  myapp/
   MyClass.java
```

The MyClass class in the com.example.myapp package corresponds to the MyClass.java file in the directory structure.

c. Import Statements: To use classes or interfaces from other packages, you use import statements.

Example-

```
import com.example.otherpackage.OtherClass;
```

d. Default Package: If you don't specify a package, the class belongs to the default package. It's recommended to use explicit package declarations to avoid naming conflicts.

e. Access Control: Classes and members with package-private access are accessible only within the same package.

f. Java Standard Packages: Java provides a set of standard packages (e.g., java.util, java.io) for common functionalities. These packages are automatically available to all Java programs.

2. Accessing a Package:

To access classes or interfaces in a package, you need to import them into your Java code using the import statement. Here's how you can access a class from a package:

a. Single Class Import:

If you want to use a single class from a package, you can import it by specifying its fully qualified name (including the package name) at the beginning of your Java file.

Example-

```
import com.example.myproject.MyClass;

public class Main {
  public static void main(String[] args) {
    MyClass myObject = new MyClass();
    // Use myObject here
  }
}
```

b. Import the Entire Package:

You can also import all classes and interfaces from a package by using a wildcard * after the package name. This way, you don't need to import each class individually.

Example-

```
import com.example.myproject.*;

public class Main {
  public static void main(String[] args) {
    MyClass myObject = new MyClass();
    // Use myObject here
  }
}
```

c. Using Fully Qualified Names: Alternatively, you can use the fully qualified name (including the package name) every time you refer to a class or interface from the package without importing it explicitly.

Example-

```
public class Main {
  public static void main(String[] args) {
    com.example.myproject.MyClass myObject = new com.example.myproject.MyClass();
    // Use myObject here
  }
```

}

Remember to compile and run your Java code correctly based on your project's directory structure and package organization. Properly structuring your code into packages helps maintain code organization and avoids naming conflicts in larger projects.

3.6.2 Interfaces of the Java IO package.

Java's java.io package provides a set of interfaces and classes for input and output operations, including file I/O, character and byte streams, and more. Here are explanations of five important interfaces from the java.io package:

1. Serializable Interface:

The Serializable interface is a marker interface that does not declare any methods.

It is used to indicate that a class can be serialized, meaning its objects can be converted into a stream of bytes and then deserialized to recreate the object.

Serialization is commonly used for data persistence, network communication, and storing object states.

2. Closeable and AutoCloseable Interfaces:

The Closeable and AutoCloseable interfaces are used for classes that represent resources that need to be closed after they are no longer needed.

Closeable declares a single method, void close() throws IOException, which is used to close the resource, such as a file or network connection. It is commonly used with I/O streams and readers/writers.

AutoCloseable is a more general interface introduced in Java 7. It also declares a single method, void close() throws Exception. Classes that implement AutoCloseable can be used in a try-with-resources statement to ensure automatic resource management and proper cleanup.

3. Flushable Interface:

The Flushable interface declares a single method, void flush() throws IOException, which is used to flush any buffered data to the underlying destination.

It is often implemented by classes that have a buffering mechanism, such as output streams and writers, to ensure that data is written to the destination immediately or when needed.

4. DataInput and DataOutput Interfaces:

The DataInput interface provides methods for reading primitive data types (e.g., int, double, boolean) and strings from a binary input stream.

The DataOutput interface provides methods for writing primitive data types and strings to a binary output stream.

These interfaces are typically implemented by classes like DataInputStream and DataOutputStream to facilitate reading and writing structured binary data.

5. FileFilter and FilenameFilter Interfaces:

The FileFilter interface defines a single method, boolean accept(File pathname), which is used to filter files in a directory based on a certain criterion. Implementations of this interface decide whether a file should be included in a list or not.

The FilenameFilter interface defines a single method, boolean accept(File dir, String name), which is similar to FileFilter but allows filtering based on both the directory and the file name.

These interfaces are commonly used when working with file and directory listings.

3.6.3 Access Modifiers: Access modifiers control the visibility and accessibility of classes, fields, methods, and other members within a class. Java offers four main access modifiers:

a. public: Members declared as public are accessible from any class or package. For example, a public class can be used from anywhere.

b. private: Members declared as private are accessible only within the same class. This is the most restrictive access modifier.

c. protected: Members declared as protected are accessible within the same package and by subclasses (even if they are in different packages).

d. Default (No Modifier): Members with no access modifier (package-private) are accessible only within the same package. This is the default access level when no modifier is specified.

e. Access Modifiers and Inheritance: Access modifiers also apply to inherited members. A subclass cannot reduce the visibility of inherited members but can increase it.

f. Access Modifiers and Top-Level Classes: For top-level classes (classes not nested within other classes), only public and package-private access modifiers **are allowed.**

g. Using Access Modifiers for Encapsulation: Access modifiers are often used for encapsulation, which hides the internal implementation details of a class and exposes a controlled interface.

By using packages and access modifiers effectively, you can create well-organized, modular, and secure Java code. Packages help structure your codebase, and access modifiers control the visibility and accessibility of your classes and members, ensuring proper encapsulation and code maintainability.

3.7 Anonymous inner classes

In Java, an anonymous inner class is a class that's defined without a name and is typically used for creating instances of a class with a specific implementation of methods or interfaces on the fly. Anonymous inner classes are a convenient way to implement one-off classes or interfaces without the need to explicitly define a separate class with a name.
Here are some key points to understand about anonymous inner classes:

No Explicit Class Name: Anonymous inner classes do not have a name. They are defined and instantiated in a single expression, often at the point of use.

Syntax: Anonymous inner classes are typically created by extending an existing class or implementing an interface. They are defined as part of an expression, within a method, constructor, or block. The syntax looks like this:

Example-

```
ClassName variableName = new ClassName() {
   // Anonymous inner class body
   // You can override methods or add new ones here
};
```

Usage: Anonymous inner classes are often used in scenarios where you need to provide a specific implementation for a single-use case, such as event handling, callbacks, or custom comparators for sorting.

Example: Here's an example of an anonymous inner class implementing a Runnable interface:

Example-

```
Runnable myRunnable = new Runnable() {
   @Override
   public void run() {
      System.out.println("This is a runnable task.");
   }
};

// Execute the runnable task
Thread thread = new Thread(myRunnable);
thread.start();
```

In this example, we create an anonymous inner class that implements the run() method of the Runnable interface.

Access to Local Variables: Anonymous inner classes have access to local variables and parameters of the enclosing method (this is known as "capturing" variables). However, these variables must be effectively final (i.e., not modified after being captured).

Use Cases: Common use cases for anonymous inner classes include event listeners in GUI programming, custom comparators for sorting, and one-time implementations of interfaces.

Limitations: Anonymous inner classes cannot have explicit constructors, and they cannot be used for interfaces with more than one method (functional interfaces are an exception starting from Java 8, where you can use lambda expressions instead).

It's important to note that while anonymous inner classes provide a concise way to define and use classes with specific behaviour, they can make code less readable when used extensively. For more complex cases or for classes that need to be reused, it's often better to define a named class or use lambda expressions (Java 8 onwards) for functional interfaces.

3.1 Static keyword

In Java, the static keyword is used to define members (fields or methods) that belong to the class itself rather than to individual instances (objects) of the class. When a member is declared as static, it means there is only one instance of that member shared by all instances of the class. Here's an explanation of how the static keyword is used in Java:

a. Static Fields (Class Variables):

When a field (also called a variable) is declared as static, it becomes a class variable, also known as a static variable. Class variables are shared by all instances of the class. They are stored in a common memory location associated with the class itself, rather than each instance having its own copy.

You can access a static field using the class name, without creating an instance of the class.

Example:

```
class MyClass {
   static int count = 0; // Static field
}
// Accessing the static field without an instance
int myCount = MyClass.count;
```

b. Static Methods:

When a method is declared as static, it becomes a class method.

Class methods can be called on the class itself, without the need to create an instance of the class. They cannot access instance-specific data.

Common use cases for static methods include utility methods or factory methods.

Example:

```
class MathUtils {
  static int add(int a, int b) { // Static method
    return a + b;
  }
}
// Calling the static method without an instance
int sum = MathUtils.add(5, 3);
```

c. Static Blocks:

A static block is a block of code enclosed within {} and marked with the static keyword. It is executed when the class is loaded into memory.

Static blocks are used for one-time initialization of class-level resources or for performing tasks that need to be done when the class is first loaded.

Example:

```
class MyClass {
  static {
    System.out.println("Static block executed.");
  }
}
```

d. Static Nested Classes:

A static nested class is a class defined within another class and declared as static. It is associated with the outer class, not with instances of the outer class.

Static nested classes are typically used when a nested class does not require access to instance-specific data of the outer class.

Example:

```
class Outer {
  static class InnerStatic {
    // Static nested class
  }
}
// Creating an instance of the static nested class
Outer.InnerStatic inner = new Outer.InnerStatic();
```

It's important to note that static members are shared across all instances of a class and can be accessed through the class name itself. They are often used for utility functions, constants, and other elements that should be associated with the class as a whole rather than with individual objects.

Exercise

Exercise 1 – MCQ

Q 1. In Java, which of the following data types is used to store whole numbers without decimal points?

a) double

b) float

c) int

d) char

Q 2. What keyword in Java is used to define a constant variable, which cannot be modified once assigned a value?

a) final

b) static

c) const

d) immutable

Exercise 2 – True/ False

Q 1. In Java, a variable declared with the "final" keyword can be reassigned a new value after its initial assignment.

Q 2. The "char" data type in Java is used to store Unicode characters and is represented using single quotation marks (").

Exercise 3 – Fill in the blanks

Q 1. In Java, the _______ keyword is used to declare a constant variable that cannot be modified after initialization.

Q 2. To store whole numbers without decimal points in Java, you typically use the _______ data type.

Exercise 4 – Match case

Q 1. Match the Java Data Types with Their Descriptions:

i. int

ii. double

iii. char

iv. boolean
Descriptions:
a. Used to store single characters
b. Stores true or false values.
c. Stores whole numbers.
d. Stores numbers with decimal points.

Exercise 5 – One word answer

Q 1. Which Java data type is used to represent numbers with decimal points?
Q 2. What is the term for a variable that cannot be changed after it is initially assigned a value in Java?

Exercise 6 – Small answer

Q 1. What are the types of Type Casting?
Q 2. How to declare a variable in Java?

Exercise 7 – Long answer

Q 1. Compare and contrast the int and double data types in Java. Provide examples of when to use each of these data types in variable declarations.
Q 2. What is Type Casting? Explain in detail.

Answer:

Exercise 1. Q 1: c) int	Q 2: a) final		
Exercise 2. Q 1: False	Q 2: True		
Exercise 3. Q 1: final	Q 2: int		
Exercise 4. Q 1: i. int – c	ii. double – d	iii. char - a	iv. boolean - b
Exercise 5. Q 1: double	Q 2: final		

Previous Year Questions

Q 1. What is constructor? What are its special properties? (Aryabhatta University BCA 2014)
Q 2. List the applications of object-oriented programming. (JNTU -B.Tech.- 2018)
Q 3. Differentiate class, abstract class and interface. (JNTU -B.Tech.- 2018)
Q 4. What is a constructor? What is its requirement in programming? Explain with program. (JNTU -B.Tech.- 2018)
Q 5. Discuss about anonymous inner classes. (JNTU -B.Tech.- 2018)
Q 6. What are the benefits of inheritance? Explain the various forms of inheritance with suitable code segments. (JNTU -B.Tech.- 2018)
Q 7. Define data abstraction. (JNTU -B.Tech. -2017)
Q 8. What is the use of anonymous inner class? (JNTU -B.Tech. -2017)
Q 9. What is a package? How to define it and access it? (JNTU -B.Tech. -2017)
Q 10. Differentiate between interface and abstract class. (JNTU -B.Tech. -2017)
Q 11. between a class and object. (JNTU -B.Tech. -2017)
Q 12. Demonstrate constructor overloading concept. (JNTU -B.Tech. -2017)
Q 13. What is inheritance? Explain different forms of inheritance with suitable program segments and real world example classes. (JNTU -B.Tech. -2017)
Q 14. Explain multilevel inheritance with the help of abstract class in your program. (JNTU -B.Tech.- 2016)
Q 15. Can inheritance be applied between interfaces? Justify your answer. (JNTU -B.Tech.- 2016)
Q 16. What are the drawbacks of procedural languages? Explain the need of object-oriented programming with suitable program. (JNTU -B.Tech.- 2016)
Q 17. Define polymorphism. (JNTU -B.Tech.- 2016)
Q 18. Differentiate between abstract class and interface. (JNTU -B.Tech.- 2016)
Q 19. How to create and access a package? (JNTU -B.Tech.- 2016)
Q 20. What is Package? Explain steps to create Package. (SPPU – BCA - 2015)
Q 21. Explain wrapper classes. (SPPU – BCA - 2015)
Q 22. Comment "Class is logical and object is physical representation of an Entity" (SPPU – BCA - 2015)
Q 23. Create a Package Vehicle, which will have two classes- two-wheeler and four-wheeler. Two-wheeler with method disp (cc, price), four-wheeler with method show (regno, reg. year). (SPPU – BCA - 2015)
Q 24. Describe various forms of Implementing Interface. Give example of each case. (SPPU – BCA - 2015)
Q 25. What is data abstraction? (JNTU – B.Tech.- 2015)
Q 26. Differentiate between interface and abstract class. (SPPU – BCA - 2015)
Q 27. What is a nested class? Differentiate between static nested classes and non-static nested classes. (SPPU – BCA - 2015)

Q 28. How to define a package? How to access, import a package? Explain with examples. (SPPU – BCA - 2015)
Q 29. What is the significance of' super' keyword in an inheritance? Explain with an example how Subclass class can superclass constructor and how super keyword can access superclass member. (Aryabhatta University BCA 2014)
Q 30. Explain method overriding with a suitable example program. (SPPU – BCA - 2015)
Q 31. Explain the basic concepts of object-oriented programming. (SPPU – BCA - 2015)
Q 32. Can we override a constructor"? Comment. (SPPU – BCA - 2015)
Q 33. When sub class cannot access the super class properties? (SPPU – BCA - 2015)
Q 34. What is an interface? How does it differ from an abstract class? (SPPU – BCA - 2015)
Q 35. Discuss the methods of Stack class. (SPPU – BCA - 2015)
Q 36. Distinguish between abstract class and concrete class. (JNTU -B.Tech.- 2016)
Q 37. How multiple inheritance is achieved in Java ? Explain with an example. (IGNOU MCS 2010)
Q 38. Differentiate between method overloading and method overriding with an example.(IGNOU MCA 2011)
Q 39. What is the use of class path ? How it helps in the execution of a java program? (IGNOU MCA 2011)
Q 40. What is the use of Interface ? .(IGNOU MCA 2011)
Q 41. What is object oriented programming ? Explain basic concepts of object oriented programming, briefly. (IGNOU MCA 2012)
Q 42. What is object oriented programming? How is it different from structured programming? Explain advantages of using object oriented programming. (IGNOU MCA 2014)
Q 43. What is abstraction? Explain why classes in OOP, known as abstract data types. (IGNOU MCA 2014)
Q 44. Explain the significance of PATH and CLASS PATH (IGNOU MCS 2010)
Q 45. The members of which classes can access members of a class in a particular package? (IGNOU MCS 2010)
Q 46. Why cannot the "abstract" method modifier be used together with the "native" modifier (IGNOU MCS 2010)
Q 47. Differentiate the following and support (IGNOU MCS 2010)
Final and static member
Inheritance and Aggregation
Abstract class and Interface
Q 48. State different uses of Super Keywords? Explain with suitable examples. (SPPU – BCA - 2015)
Q 49. Explain any five interfaces of the Java IO package. (IGNOU MCA 2014)
Q 50. How to create and use a package in Java program? (JNTU -B.Tech.- 2018)
Q 51. What is static import? How is it useful? Using package access and importing packages Technique, write a program to find the largest among three numbers. (Aryabhatta University BCA 2014)
Q 52. How do we tell Java that we want to use a particular package in a file (Aryabhatta University BCA 2014)
Q 53. With suitable program segments describe the usage of 'super' keyword. (SPPU – BCA - 2015)

Previous Year Solved Papers

Q.1. What is Inheritance? Explain its different types. Write a java program to implement multiple inhe ritances. (RU BCA 2017)

Ans- Inheritance is a fundamental concept in object-oriented programming (OOP) that allows a new class (derived class) to inherit properties and behaviors from an existing class (base class or superclass). It promotes code reusability and establishes a hierarchical relationship between classes. In Java, inheritance is implemented using the **extends** keyword. The derived class inherits the fields and methods of the superclass, and it can also define its own unique fields and methods.
There are different types of inheritance in Java, including:
Single Inheritance: In single inheritance, a class inherits from only one superclass. It represents a simple parent-child relationship between two classes.
Multilevel Inheritance: In multilevel inheritance, a derived class serves as the base class for another class, forming a chain of inheritance. It establishes a hierarchical structure with multiple levels of parent and child classes.
Hierarchical Inheritance: In hierarchical inheritance, multiple classes are derived from a single base class. It allows for the creation of multiple subclasses that share the same superclass.
Multiple Inheritance (not supported in Java): Multiple inheritance refers to the concept of a class inheriting properties and behaviors from multiple classes. Java does not support multiple inheritance for classes to avoid the diamond problem, where ambiguities may arise if two superclasses have a method with the same name.
Here's a simple Java program demonstrating multiple inheritance using interfaces, as Java does not support multiple inheritance for classes:

```
interface Interface1 {
   void display1();
}

interface Interface2 {
```

```
    void display2();
}

class MultipleInheritance implements Interface1, Interface2 {
    public void display1() {
        System.out.println("Displaying from Interface1");
    }

    public void display2() {
        System.out.println("Displaying from Interface2");
    }

    public static void main(String[] args) {
        MultipleInheritance obj = new MultipleInheritance();
        obj.display1();
        obj.display2();
    }
}
```

In this example, the **MultipleInheritance** class implements two interfaces, **Interface1** and **Interface2**, and provides implementations for their respective methods. Through interfaces, Java supports a form of multiple inheritance, allowing a class to inherit behaviors from multiple interfaces.

Q.2. (a) Is java a pure object-oriented language? If not why? (RU BCA 2017)

Ans- Java is not considered a pure object-oriented language due to the presence of certain non-object-oriented features and concepts in the language. While Java is primarily designed to be object-oriented and follows many object-oriented principles, there are a few aspects that deviate from the pure object-oriented paradigm. Here are some reasons why Java is not considered a pure object-oriented language:

Primitive Data Types: Java includes primitive data types such as **int**, **double**, **char**, and **boolean**, which are not objects and do not inherit from a common class. Operations on these types do not involve the use of methods or objects.

Static Methods and Variables: Java allows the use of static methods and variables that belong to a class rather than to instances of the class. Static members are associated with the class itself and are not tied to specific objects, deviating from the instance-based nature of pure object-oriented languages.

Procedural Programming Elements: Java supports procedural programming constructs such as control statements (**if**, **else**, **for**, **while**) that are not specific to objects. These constructs enable developers to write code in a procedural style, mixing object-oriented and procedural programming paradigms.

Primitive Type Wrappers: Although Java provides wrapper classes for primitive types, the existence of these wrapper classes alongside primitive types introduces a concept that does not adhere strictly to the pure object-oriented model.

Despite these non-object-oriented aspects, Java remains a predominantly object-oriented language, as it supports key object-oriented principles such as encapsulation, inheritance, and polymorphism. The use of objects and classes as the fundamental building blocks for software development in Java makes it a powerful and widely used language for creating object-oriented applications.

Q.3. Why Packages are used? (RU BCA 2017)

Ans- Packages in Java are used for various reasons, offering several benefits that contribute to the organization, modularity, and reusability of code in large-scale software development. Some key reasons why packages are used in Java include:

- **Namespace Management:** Packages provide a way to manage namespaces by organizing classes into different packages. This prevents naming conflicts and allows developers to create classes with similar names that can coexist within different packages.
- **Encapsulation:** Packages facilitate encapsulation by grouping related classes and providing a clear boundary for the visibility and accessibility of classes and their members. This helps in controlling the access to classes and prevents unauthorized access from outside the package.
- **Modularity:** Packages enable modularity in Java applications by allowing developers to create a modular and maintainable codebase. By organizing classes into packages based on their functionalities, it becomes easier to manage and maintain the code, leading to a more organized and scalable application.
- **Access Control:** Packages provide access control mechanisms that allow classes to be visible only within the same package or to specific classes within other packages. This helps in hiding the implementation details of certain classes and ensuring that only relevant classes can access and interact with them.

Code Reusability: Packages promote code reusability by providing a way to organize and manage classes and resources. By grouping related classes into packages, developers can reuse code across multiple projects and applications, leading to a more efficient and streamlined development process.

Distribution and Deployment: Packages facilitate the distribution and deployment of Java applications by allowing developers to package classes, resources, and libraries into a single unit. This simplifies the deployment process and makes it easier to distribute applications and libraries to other developers or end-users.

By utilizing packages effectively, developers can create well-organized, secure, and reusable codebases, leading to the development of robust and scalable Java applications.

Q.4. Explain the Package in Java with example and also write advantage of Package.(RU BCA 2018)

Ans- In Java, a package is a namespace that organizes a set of related classes and interfaces, providing a way to encapsulate and group Java classes. It helps in avoiding naming conflicts, controlling access, and providing a way to categorize classes and interfaces based on functionality. Packages are used to create a hierarchical structure for the Java classes, similar to directories in a file system.

For example, consider the following Java code:

```
package mypackage;

public class MyClass {
  public void display() {
    System.out.println("This is a simple package example.");
  }
}
```

In this example, the class **MyClass** is defined within the package **mypackage**. To use this class in another Java file within the same package or in a different package, you would use the following import statement:

```
import mypackage.MyClass;

public class Main {
  public static void main(String[] args) {
    MyClass obj = new MyClass();
    obj.display();
  }
}
```

Here, the **import** statement is used to import the **MyClass** from the **mypackage** package, allowing the **Main** class to access and use the functionalities provided by **MyClass**.

Advantages of using packages in Java include:

Namespace Management: Packages help in organizing classes into different namespaces, preventing naming conflicts and ensuring that classes with similar names can coexist within different packages.

Access Control: Packages allow for the access control of classes and their members. Using access modifiers like public, private, protected, and default, you can control the accessibility of classes and their members within and outside the package.

Encapsulation: Packages provide a way to achieve encapsulation by grouping related classes and providing a clear and well-defined boundary for the visibility and access of classes and their members.

Modularity: Packages facilitate modularity in Java applications, allowing developers to create modular and maintainable code by grouping related classes together and separating them from unrelated classes.

Code Reusability: Packages promote code reusability by providing a way to organize and manage classes and resources, making it easier to reuse code across multiple projects and applications.

Q.5. What is object oriented programming? Explain the basic concepts of object oriented programming in detail? (RU BCA 2018)

Ans- Object-oriented programming (OOP) is a programming paradigm that organizes software design around objects rather than functions or logic. It is based on the concept of "objects," which can contain data in the form of fields (attributes or properties) and code in the form of procedures (methods or functions). OOP promotes the reusability, flexibility, and modularity of code by allowing developers to create objects that can be used and manipulated within their programs.

Key concepts of object-oriented programming include:

Class: A class is a blueprint or template that defines the attributes and behaviors of an object. It serves as a model for creating objects, specifying their initial state and behavior.

Object: An object is an instance of a class that encapsulates data and behavior. It represents a real-world entity and can interact with other objects through methods and messages.

Abstraction: Abstraction is the process of hiding the complex implementation details and showing only the essential features of an object. It allows developers to focus on the relevant information and ignore unnecessary details.

Encapsulation: Encapsulation is the mechanism of bundling the data (attributes) and the methods (behavior) that operate on the data into a single unit, i.e., the object. It prevents the direct access of the internal state of an object from the outside, ensuring data integrity and security.

Inheritance: Inheritance is a mechanism that allows a class (subclass or derived class) to inherit properties and behaviors from another class (superclass or base class). It promotes code reuse and the creation of a hierarchy of classes with shared attributes and methods.

Polymorphism: Polymorphism allows objects of different classes to be treated as objects of a common superclass. It enables a single interface to represent multiple types, allowing for flexibility and extensibility in the design of software.

OOP helps in managing complex software projects by organizing code into self-contained objects with their own properties and behaviors. It promotes the development of modular, maintainable, and scalable software that is easier to understand and modify. By leveraging the concepts of OOP, developers can create more robust and flexible applications that can effectively model real-world entities and interactions.

Q.6 What is java inner class? What are the advantages of java inner classes. (RU BCA 2018)

Ans- In Java, an inner class is a class that is defined within another class. It is a way to logically group classes that are only used in one place, allowing for more readable and maintainable code. Java supports several types of inner classes, including static nested classes, non-static nested classes (inner classes), local classes, and anonymous classes.

Advantages of using inner classes in Java include:

Encapsulation: Inner classes can access private members of the outer class, enabling a tighter and more cohesive encapsulation of related functionalities.

Readability and Maintainability: By logically grouping classes within the same file, inner classes improve the readability and maintainability of the code, especially when the classes have a strong logical connection and are not useful outside the context of the outer class.

Improved Code Organization: Inner classes allow you to keep related classes together, making it easier to understand and navigate the codebase.

Easy Access to Outer Class Members: Inner classes have access to the members of the outer class, including its private members, enabling them to manipulate the state of the outer class.

Implementation of Callbacks: Inner classes are often used to implement callback functions, event handling, and listeners in Java, as they can directly access the methods and fields of the outer class.

Increased Security and Control: Inner classes can help in securing the implementation details of a class by restricting the visibility of the inner class to the outer class only, preventing external classes from accessing it.

Q.7. What's the difference between constructors and Other methods? (RU BCA 2018)

Ans-

Feature	Constructors	Other Methods
Name	Constructor names are always the same as the class name.	Method names can be chosen freely, following the rules of identifier naming.
Return Type	Constructors do not have a return type, not even void.	Other methods have a specified return type: a primitive data type, a reference type, or a void.
Invocation	Constructors are invoked implicitly when an object is created using the **new** keyword.	Other methods are invoked explicitly by calling the method on an object or class.
Purpose	Constructors are used to initialise the newly created object.	Other methods are used to perform various operations or provide functionality to the objects.
Overloading	Constructors can be overloaded, which means a class can have multiple constructors with different parameters.	Other methods can be overloaded, allowing the same method name with different parameters and return types.
Inheritance	Constructors are not inherited, but the superclass's constructor can be invoked using the **super** keyword.	Other methods are inherited if they are not private and can be overridden in the subclasses.

Q.8. What is interface in java? (RU BCA 2018)

Ans- In Java, an interface is a reference type that is similar to a class but is a collection of abstract methods. It can also contain constants, default methods, static methods, and nested types. It is a way to achieve full abstraction in Java, as it specifies what a class must do, but not how it should do it.

Key features of interfaces in Java include:

Declaration: Interfaces are declared using the **interface** keyword.

```
interface MyInterface {
  // method signatures
  void doSomething();
}
```

Implementation: A class that implements an interface must provide an implementation for all of the interface's methods.

```
class MyClass implements MyInterface {
  public void doSomething() {
    // provide implementation
  }
}
```

Multiple Inheritance: Java allows multiple inheritance through interfaces, which means a class can implement multiple interfaces.

```
interface Interface1 {
  void method1();
}

interface Interface2 {
  void method2();
}

class MyClass implements Interface1, Interface2 {
  // implementation of both methods
  public void method1() {
    // implementation
  }

  public void method2() {
    // implementation
  }
}
```

Default and Static Methods: Java 8 introduced default methods and static methods in interfaces, allowing developers to add new methods to an interface without affecting the classes that implement the interface.

```
interface MyInterface {
  void doSomething();

  default void doSomethingElse() {
    // provide default implementation
  }

  static void doStaticThing() {
    // provide static method implementation
  }
}
```

Interfaces are widely used to achieve abstraction, allow multiple inheritance, and support the development of loosely coupled systems in Java. They play a crucial role in achieving the goal of the Java programming language, which is "write once, run anywhere" (WORA). They are also used to define the contract for the subclasses and promote code maintainability and flexibility.

Q.9. What is difference between an inheritance and an abstract class? (RU BCA 2018)

Ans-

Feature	Inheritance	Abstract Class
Basic Function	A way to establish a relationship between two or more classes, allowing one class to inherit properties and behaviour from another.	A class that cannot be instantiated on its own and is meant to be subclassed by other classes. It can contain both regular and abstract methods.
Keyword Usage	Inheritance is achieved using the **extends** keyword.	Abstract classes are declared using the **abstract** keyword.
Multiple Inheritance	Java does not support multiple inheritances. A class can only inherit from one superclass.	A class can implement multiple interfaces and also inherit from an abstract class.
Implementation	It allows the reuse of code through the concept of parent and child classes.	It provides a way to partially implement a class and leave the implementation details to its subclasses.
Constructors	Subclasses can call the constructor of the superclass using the **super** keyword.	Abstract classes can have constructors that are called when a subclass is instantiated.
Method Definition	Subclasses can override the superclass's methods to provide their implementation.	Abstract classes can contain both regular and abstract methods. Subclasses must implement the abstract methods.
Object Instantiation	Objects of subclasses are independent of the superclass and can be instantiated separately.	Abstract classes cannot be instantiated directly, but they can be used as reference types for polymorphism.

Q.10. Explain the inheritance in java. (RU BCA 2018)

Ans- Inheritance is a fundamental feature in object-oriented programming (OOP) languages like Java. It allows a class (subclass or derived class) to inherit properties and behavior from another class (superclass or base class). This helps in creating a hierarchy of classes that share common attributes and methods, reducing code redundancy, and promoting reusability.

In Java, the concept of inheritance is implemented through the "extends" keyword. When a class inherits from another class, it acquires all the non-private fields and methods of the superclass. The subclass can then add its own unique fields and methods or override the inherited methods.

Here's an example to illustrate inheritance in Java:

```
// Base class or superclass
class Animal {
   private String name;

   public Animal(String name) {
      this.name = name;
   }

   public void makeSound() {
      System.out.println("Some sound");
   }
}

// Subclass inheriting from the Animal class
class Dog extends Animal {
   public Dog(String name) {
      super(name);
   }

   // Overriding the makeSound method
   @Override
   public void makeSound() {
      System.out.println("Bark!");
   }

   public void fetch() {
```

```
        System.out.println("Fetch the ball!");
    }
}

// Subclass inheriting from the Animal class
class Cat extends Animal {
    public Cat(String name) {
        super(name);
    }

    // Overriding the makeSound method
    @Override
    public void makeSound() {
        System.out.println("Meow!");
    }

    public void play() {
        System.out.println("Play with a ball of yarn.");
    }
}

// Main class
public class Main {
    public static void main(String[] args) {
        Dog dog = new Dog("Buddy");
        Cat cat = new Cat("Kitty");

        dog.makeSound(); // Outputs "Bark!"
        dog.fetch(); // Outputs "Fetch the ball!"

        cat.makeSound(); // Outputs "Meow!"
        cat.play(); // Outputs "Play with a ball of yarn."
    }
}
```

In this example, the classes **Dog** and **Cat** inherit from the **Animal** class. They both override the **makeSound** method and provide their own implementation. Additionally, they have their own unique methods **fetch** and **play** respectively.

Inheritance facilitates code reusability, promotes the use of a hierarchical structure, and allows for polymorphism, where objects of the subclass can be treated as objects of the superclass.

Q. 11. Design a program in java to implement the different type of inheritance and also write a code for handling exception in that? (RU BCA 2019)

Ans-
```
class Teacher {
String designation= "Teacher",

String collegeName="Beginnersbook";
void does(){
    System.out.println("Teaching");
    }
}
public class Physics Teacher extends Teacher(
    String mainSubject = "Physics";
    public static void main(String args[]){
    Physics Teacher obj = new Physics Teacher();
    System.out.println(obj.collegeName);
    System.out.println(obj.designation);
```

```
    System.out.println(obj.mainSubject);
    obj.docs();
```
Output:
Beginnersbook
Teacher
Physics
Teaching
Exception headling
```
public class JavaExceptionExample{
   public static void main(String args[]){
    try{
       //code that may raise exception
       int data 100/0;
       }catch(ArithmeticException e)(System.out.println(e);)
       //rest code of the program
       System.out.println("rest of the code...");
       }
    }
```

Q.12. Why do you say that java is a pure object oriented programming language? Explain by defining most of the supporting features of OPPs by java?
Ans. Pure Object Oriented Language or Complete Object Oriented Language are Fully Object Oriented Language which supports or have features which treats everything inside program as objects. It doesn't support primitive datatype(like int, char, float, bool, etc.). There are seven qualities to be satisfied for a programming language to be pure Object Oriented. They are:
1. Encapsulation/Data Hiding
2. Inheritance
3. Polymorphism
4. Abstraction
5. All predefined types are objects
6. All user defined types are objects
7. All operations performed on objects must be only through methods exposed at the objects.

Object-Oriented Features Of Java:
Since it is an object-oriented language, it will support the following features:
Class
Object
Encapsulation
Abstraction.
Inheritance
Polymorphism

An object is a real-world entity that has three basic characteristics Identity, State, and Behaviour, A class is a collection of objects. The process of grouping these attributes and behaviours into a single unit is known as encapsulation
This process of sustaining only essential and relevant information and discarding the rest is known as abstraction When one class acquires properties of another class, it is known as inheritance. The class that gives the properties is called superclass and the class that acquires the properties is called subclass. The major benefit of inheritance is reusability of code The last major concept of object-oriented programming is the polymorphism. Poly' means many and "morph means forms. This means it has statements that have many forms or the same statements can have different meanings in different contexts.

Q.13. Differentiate inner class and sub class. (RU BCA 2019)
Ans- An Inner class is a class which is nested within another class. An Inner class has access rights for the class which is nesting it and it can access all variables and methods defined in the outer class.
A sub-class is a class which inherits from another class called super class. Sub-class can access all public and protected methods and fields of its super class. inner classes are in the same file, whereas subclasses can be in another file, may be in another package.

You cannot get an instance of an inner class without an instance of the class that contains it. inner classes have the methods they want, whereas subclasses have the methods of their parent class Subclasses can of course define additional methods, but they'll always have those of their parent.

Q.14. What is the use of inheritance? And its types. (RU BCA 2019)
Ans. Inheritance is a mechanism of acquiring the features and behaviors of a class by another class. The class whose members are inherited is called the base class, and the class that inherits those members is called the derived class. Inheritance implements IS-A relationship. For example, mammal IS-A animal, dog IS-A mammal; Hence dog IS-A animal as well.
Different Types of Inheritance
OOPS support the six different types of inheritance as given below.
1. Single inheritance
2. Multi-level inheritance
3. Multiple inheritance
4. Multipath inheritance
5. Hierarchical Inheritance
6. Hybrid Inheritance

Q.15. Explain class and object?
Ans.-Object Objects have states and behaviour's. Example: A dog has states-color, name, breed as well as behaviours-wagging the tail, barking, eating. An object is an instance of a class • Class" A class can be defined as a template/blueprint that describes the behaviour/state that the object of its type support.

Q.16. Explain object oriented programming? (RU BCA 2019)
Ans- Object-oriented programming (OOP) refers to a type of computer programming (software design) in which programmers define not only the data type of a data structure, but also the types of operations (functions) that can be applied to the data structure. In this way, the data structure becomes an object that includes both data and functions. In addition, programmers can create relationships between one object and another. For example, objects can inherit characteristics from other objects.

Q.17. Why do we say that java is a platform independent language? Ans. The meaning of platform independent is that, the java source code can run on all operating systems. (RU BCA 2019)
Ans- A program is written in a language which is a human readable language. It may contain words, phrases etc which the machine does not understand. For the source code to be understood by the machine, it needs to be in a language understood by machines, typically a machine-level language. So, here comes the role of a compiler. The compiler converts the high-level language (human language) into a format understood by the machines. Therefore, a compiler is a program that translates the source code for another program from a programming language into executable code.
This executable code may be a sequence of machine instructions that can be executed by the CPU directly, or it may be an intermediate representation that is interpreted by a virtual machine. This intermediate representation in Java is the Java Byte Code.

Q.18. Design a program in Java to illustrate the usages of Single and Multiple Inheritance (if possible) by taking any suitable example. (RU BCA 2020)
Ans.

```
interface Backend {
//abstract class
 public void connectServer();
}
```

exception is raised in method C. then the search for appropriate handler will move from CBOA If appropriate exception handler is found, exception object is passed to the handler to process it. The handler is said to be "catching the exception". If there are no appropriate exception handler found then program terminates printing information about the exception.

Q.19. Design a code in Java to find out the factorial of a given number.
Ans.

```
class Factorial Example{
public static void main(String args[])
int i,fact-1:
int number-5/It is the number to calculate factorial
```

fact-fact*i;
System.out.println("Factorial of"+number+ is "+fact).
output:-
Factorial of 5 is: 120

Q.20. Discuss the importance of object oriented programming over structure cultural programming. Also explain some of the important features, which makes Java differ from other languages. (RU BCA 2020)
Ans- Structured Programming is designed which focuses on process/ logical structure and then data required for that process. Structured programming follows top-down approach.
Structured Programming is also known as Modular Programming and a subset of procedural programming language. small self contained functions.
In Structured Programming, Programs are divided into Structured Programming is less secure as there is no way of data hiding
Structured Programming can solve moderately complex programs.
Structured Programming provides less reusability, more function dependency.
Less abstraction and less flexibility.
The primary objective of Java programming language creation was to make it portable, simple and secure programming language. Apart from this, there are also some excellent features which play an important role in the popularity of this language. The features of Java are also known as java buzzwords.

A list of most important features of Java language is given below. Java Features
Simple
Object-Oriented
Portable
Platform independent
Secured
Robust
Architecture neutral
Interpreted
High Performance
Multithreaded
Distributed
Dynamic

Q.21. Design a class using Java to illustrate the use of class and object.
Ans. Objects in Java

Let us now look deep into what are objects. If we consider the real-world, we can find many objects around us, cars, dogs, humans, etc. All these objects have a state and a behaviour.
If we consider a dog, then its state is - name, breed, color, and the behaviour is-barking, wagging the tail, running.
If you compare the software object with a real-world object, they have very similar characteristics.
Software objects also have a state and a behavior. A software object's state is stored in fields and behavior is shown via methods.

So in software development, methods operate on the internal state of an object and the object-to-object communication is done via methods
Classes in Java
A class is a blueprint from which individual objects are created. A class can contain any of the following variable types. Local variables" Variables defined inside methods, constructors or blocks are called local variables. The variable will be declared and initialized within the method and the variable will be destroyed when the method has completed. Instance variables" Instance variables are variables within a class but outside any method. These variables are initialized when the class is instantiated. Instance variables can be accessed from inside any method, constructor or blocks of that particular class.
Class variables "Class variables are variables declared within a class, outside any method, with the static keyword.

Q.22. Explain Abstraction using a simple example. (RU BCA 2020)
Ans. "Abstraction is the process of selecting data to show only the relevant information to the user "abstraction "displays" only the relevant attributes of objects and "hides" the unnecessary details.

Q.23. Discuss any of the 2 disadvantages of array in Java. (RU BCA 2020)

Ans. 1. Arrays does not have add or remove methods
2. We need to mention the size of the array. Fixed length.

Q.24. What is instance of a Class? (RU BCA 2020)
Ans. In object-oriented programming (OOP), an instance is a concrete occurrence of any object, existing usually during the runtime of a computer program. Each realized variation of that object is an instance of its class. That is, it is a member of a given class that has specified values rather than variables.

Q.25. What is inheritance and how it beneficial for building components? How does java support inheritance? Show using an example. (RU BCA 2021)
Ans: In Java, it is possible to inherit attributes and methods from one class to another. We group the "inheritance concept" into two categories:
subclass (child)- the class that inherits from another class
superclass (parent) - the class being inherited fromTo inherit from a class, use the extends keyword.
Benefits of Inheritance:-
Inheritance helps in code reuse. The child class may use the code defined in the parent class without rewriting it. Inheritance can save time and effort as the main code need not be written again. Inheritance provides a clear model structure which is easy to understand. An inheritance leads to less development and maintenance costs.
With inheritance, we will be able to override the methods of the base class so that the meaningful implementation of the base class method can be designed in the derived class. An inheritance leads to less development and maintenance costs.
In inheritance base class can decide to keep some data private so that it cannot be altered by the derived class Types of inheritance
Here are five types of inheritances in Object-Oriented programming as described below:
(1) Single Inheritance: When a derived class or subclass inherits from only one base or superclass then it is single inheritance.
(2) Multilevel Inheritance: In Multilevel Inheritance.we have more than one level wherein a class inherits from a base class and the derived class in turn is inherited by another class.
(3) Hierarchical Inheritance: An inheritance hierarchy is formed in this type of inheritance when a superclass is inherited by more than one class.
(4) Multiple Inheritance: Multiple inheritance is the one in which a class can inherit properties and behaviour from more than one parent.
(5) Hybrid Inheritance: When one or more types of inheritance are combined, then it becomes a hybrid inheritance.
Note that Java supports only single, multilevel, and hierarchical type of inheritance using classes. Java does not support multiple and hybrid inheritance with classes. Java Doesn't Support Multiple Inheritance. Java aims at simplicity in programs. This applies even to OOP features. So when it comes to multiple inheritance. some ambiguous situations may arise when we derive a class from more than one class. Let's implement a simple example in Java to demonstrate inheritance.

```
#example class demonstrating Inheritance in Java class BaseClass{
        public void display()) {
          System.out.println("BaseClass: Display").}
        }
    }
    //create a new class from BaseClass
    class Derived Class extends BaseClass {
        public void print() {
            System.out.println("DerivedClass print");
        }
    }

class Main{
   public static void main(String[] args) {
        //create an object of DerivedClass
        Derived Class di= new DerivedClass():
        dl.display(); //call BaseClass method
        dl.print(); //call DerivedClass method
        }
    }
```
Output:

Base Class::Display

DerivedClass: : print

Q.26 Discuss about various decision making statement in java with example. (RU BCA 2021)
Ans: Decision making in Java executes a particular segment of code based on the result of a boolean condition. It is important because conditions define the flow of programs and the output of a particular program. There are the 6 ways of exercising decision making in Java:
1. if
2. if-else
3. nested-if
4. if-elsc-if
5. switch-case
6. jump-break,continue,return
1. If Statement in Java
Java if statement is the simplest decision making statement. It encompasses a boolean condition followed by a scope of code, which is executed only when the condition evaluates to true. However if there are no curly braces to limit the scope of sentences to be executed if the condition evaluates to true, then only the first line is executed.
```
if(condition)
{
//code to be executed
}
```
if else statement in Java
This pair of keywords is used to divide a program to be executed into two parts, one being the code to be executed if the condition evaluates to true an be other one to be executed if the value is false.
syntax
```
if(condition)
{
//code to be executed if the condition is true
}
else
{
//code to be executed if the condition is false
}
```
Nested if Statements in Java
If the condition of the outer if statement evaluates to then the inner if statement is evaluated. true Nested if's are important if we have to declare extended conditions to a previous condition
Syntax:
```
if(condition)
{
//code to be executed if(condition)
{
code to be executed
}
}
```
if-else-if Statements in Java
These statements are similar to the if else statements.The only difference lies in the fact that each of the else statements can be paired with a different if condition statement. This renders the ladder as a multiple choice option for the user.
Syntax
```
If
{
#code to be executed
}

else if(condition)
{
//code to be executed
}
else if(condition)
```

```
{
//code to be executed
}
else
{
//code to be executed
}
```

Switch Statement in Java

Java switch statement is a different form of the if else if ladder statements. This saves the hassle of writing else if for every different option. It branches the flow of the program to multiple points as and when required or specified by the conditions. It bases the flow of the program based on the output of the expression. As soon as the expression is evaluated, the result is matched with each and every case listed in the scope. If the output matches with any of the cases mentioned, then the particular block is executed. A break statement is written after every end of the case block so that the remaining statements are not executed.

The default case is written which is executed if none of the cases are the result of the expression. This is generally the block where error statements are written.

Syntax:

```
switch(expression)
{
case <value>:
//code to be executed
break;
case <value2>:
//code to be executed
break;
default:
//code to be defaultly executed
}
```

Java break statement

The break statement, as the name signifies, is useful to break out of the normal workflow of a program. We can use it to terminate loops, end cases of switch statements, and as a goto statement. Break statements, if used in a nested loop. terminates the innermost loop. The outermost loop still functions.

Continue Statement in Java

The continue statement is useful for early iteration of a particular loop. Sometimes rather than breaking out of a loop and halting it for good we want to skip some iterations based on our requirements of a program. This results in the usage of continue statements.

Return Statement in Java

This keyword, when executed by the compiler, returns the control back to the method it was called from. This is generally used in methods which are not of the void type and return some values. When the statement is executed, the return function returns to the caller method along with whatever variable is mentioned in the definition.

Q.27. Discuss in detail the features of object oriented programming. (BCA-III Paper IV 2021)

Ans: Object-oriented programming (OOP) is a programming paradigm that uses objects and classes to design and create applications. Here's a detailed discussion of the key features of object-oriented programming:

- **Classes and Objects:** OOP allows the creation of classes, which serve as blueprints for creating objects. A class defines the data and behavior that objects can have. Objects are instances of classes and represent real-world entities.
- **Encapsulation:** Encapsulation is the process of binding data (attributes) and methods (functions) that operate on the data within a single unit, called an object. It helps in data hiding, preventing access to the inner workings of an object and allowing access only through a defined interface. This promotes security and modularity in the code.
- **Inheritance:** Inheritance allows a class (subclass or derived class) to inherit properties and behavior from another class (superclass or base class). It facilitates code reusability, enabling the creation of a new class from an existing class. The subclass can extend or override the functionality of the superclass.
- **Polymorphism:** Polymorphism means the ability of objects to respond in different ways to the same message or method invocation. It allows objects of different classes to be treated as objects of a common superclass, and it enables methods to be implemented differently in different classes. Polymorphism is achieved through method overriding and method overloading.

Abstraction: Abstraction involves the concept of hiding the complex implementation details and showing only the necessary features of an object. It allows the creation of simple models for representing real-world objects and their interactions. Abstract classes and interfaces are used to achieve abstraction in Java.
Association: Association represents the relationship between multiple objects. It can be one-to-one, one-to-many, or many-to-many. Objects can interact with each other through methods, and this relationship can be represented as an association in the code.
Aggregation and Composition: Aggregation and composition are types of association that represent the relationship between objects. Aggregation implies a "has-a" relationship, where one object contains or is composed of other objects, while composition implies a stronger relationship where the child object cannot exist without the parent object.
Message Passing: Objects communicate with one another by sending and receiving information through method calls. Message passing allows objects to request actions from other objects and to trigger methods to perform specific tasks.

These features make OOP a powerful and flexible programming paradigm that is widely used in the development of complex and scalable software applications. By promoting code reusability, encapsulation, and modular design, OOP facilitates the creation of efficient and maintainable codebases.

Q.28. What are inner classes and how is it beneficial. (RU BCA 2021)
Ans: Inner classes are used to develop a more readable and maintainable code because they logically group classes and interfaces in one place. Easy access, as the inner object, is implicitly available inside an outer Code optimization requires less code to write. It can avoid having a separate class. Inner classes are the concept where we want to add more encapsulation to the given code. When we declare a class within a class, the inner class can access all the private members, in addition to the inner class, it can hide from the outside world.
An advantage of inner classes
In Java, there are three advantages of inner classes. They are as follows:
The inner class could be used only by outer class. Inner classes represent a special type of relationship that allows access to all members (data members and methods) of the outer class, including the private class.
Inner classes are used to develop a more readable and maintainable code because they logically group classes and interfaces in one place.
Easy access, as the inner object, is implicitly available inside an outer Code optimization requires less code to write. It can avoid having a separate class.

Q.29. What are differences between regular loop and for-each loop? (RU BCA 2021)
Ans:

Aspect	Regular Loop (for loop)	For-Each Loop (Enhanced for loop)
Syntax	More complex syntax requiring initialization, condition, and increment/decrement statements.	Simple syntax that directly iterates over elements of an array or a collection.
Use	Used when the index of each element is required or when looping with a specific increment or condition.	Used when the complete iteration of elements is needed without concern for the index.
Applicability	Applicable to arrays, collections, and other data structures.	Specifically designed for arrays and collections.
Accessibility	Allows both read and write operations within the loop block.	Allows only read operations; modifying elements requires using the original collection or array.
Performance	Offers slightly better performance in terms of faster execution.	Might incur slightly more overhead due to additional method calls and hidden iterators.
Index manipulation	Enables manual control over the index, allowing flexibility in array manipulation.	Hides the index, providing a simplified approach but limiting control over the index itself.

Q.30. What are interface and how are they different from abstract class. (RU BCA 2021)
Ans: An interface in Java is a blueprint of a class. It has static constants and abstract methods. The interface in Java is a mechanism to achieve abstraction. There can be only abstract methods in the Java interface, not method body. It is used to achieve abstraction and multiple inheritance in Java. In other words, you can say that interfaces can have abstract methods and variables. It cannot have a method body. Java Interface also represents the IS-A relationship.

Aspect	Abstract Class	Interface
Declaration and Definition Part	Contains both declaration and definition parts.	Contains only the declaration part.
Multiple Inheritance	Does not support multiple inheritance but allows implementation of multiple interfaces.	Supports multiple inheritance through multiple interface implementation.
Implementation	Can provide a complete. default implementation of methods.	Cannot provide any method implementations.
Constructor	Can have a constructor.	Cannot have a constructor

Q.31. What is meant by package scope of members. (RU BCA 2021)
Ans: Java provides the following levels of visibility (in general order of encapsulation).
Package: The container used to hold a number of classes. When working with a simple directory structure, as the examples in this book do. the package is a directory that holds a number of class files.

Q.32.How can you prevent inheritance in java. (RU BCA 2021)
Ans: While one of Java's strengths is the concept of inheritance, in which one class can derive from another, sometimes it's desirable to prevent inheritance by another class. To prevent inheritance, use the keyword "final" when creating the class.
For example, if a class is likely to be used by other programmers, you may wish to prevent inheritance if any subclasses created could cause problems.

Q.33. Discuss loops in java with example. (RU BCA 2022)
Ans. Looping in programming languages is a feature that facilitates the execution of a set of instructions/functions repeatedly while some condition evaluates to true.
Types of looping statements in Java:
There are three types of looping statements in Java. They are as follows:
1. For loop
2. While loop
3. Do while loop
For Loop in Java:
The Java for loop repeats the execution of a set of Java statements. A for loop executes a block of code as long as some condition is true. The syntax to use for the loop is given below.

```
for(initialization; condition; increment/decrement)
{
Statement(s);
}
```

The initialization expression initializes the loop and is executed only once at the beginning when the loop begins. The termination condition is evaluated in every loop and if it evaluates to false, the loop is terminated. And lastly, increment/decrement expression is executed after cach iteration through the loop.

```
class ForLoopDemo
{
public static void main(String args[])
{
for(int num 1; num < 5: num++)
{
System.out.print(mm):
}
}
}
```

Output:12345

Q.34.Enhanced for loop in Java. (RU BCA 2022)
Ans- Enhanced for loop provides a simpler way to iterate through the elements of a collection or array. It is inflexible and should be used only when there is a need to iterate through the elements in a sequential manner without knowing the index of the currently processed element.

Also, note that the object/variable is immutable when enhanced for loop is used. i.e it ensures that the values in the array cannot be modified, so it can be said as a read-only loop where you can't update the values as opposed to other loops where values can be modified. The syntax to use the enhanced for loop in java is given below.

```
for(Telement:Collectionobject/array)
{
Statement(s):
}
```

Example to Understand Enhanced for loop in Java:

```
public class EnhancedforloopDemo
{
public static void main(String args[])
{
String array[]=("Ray", "Harsh", "Himani"):
//enhanced for loop
for (String x:array)
{
System.out.println(x),
}
/*for loop for same function
for (int i=0;i< array length; i++) (
{
System.out.println(array[i]).
}
*/
}
}
```

Output:

Ray
Harsh
Himani

While Loop in Java:

The while statement or loop continually executes a block of statements while a particular condition is true. The while statement continues testing the expression and executing its block until the expression evaluates to false. The syntax to use while loop in java is given below.

```
while(condition)
{
Statement(s);
}
```

Example to Understand while Loop in Java:

```
class whileLoopDemo
{
public static void main(String args[])
{
int x=1:
// Exit when x becomes greater than 4
while (x <= 4)
{
System.out.println(x);
// Increment the value of x for
 // next iteration
x++:
}
}
}
```

Output:

12345

Do-while Loop in Java:

The difference between do-while and while is that do- while evaluates its expression at the bottom of the loop instead of the top. Therefore, the statements within the do block are always executed at least once.

Note that the do-while statement ends with a semicolon. The condition expression must be a boolean expression. The syntax to use the do-while loop is given below.

```
do{
Statement(s);
}
while(condition).
```

Example to Understand do-while Loop in Java:

```
class dowhileloopDemo
{
public static void main(String args[])
{
int x=21;
do
{
//The line will be printed even
//if the condition is false
System.out.println("Value of x:"+x);
x++;
while (x < 20);
}
}
```

Output: Value of x: 21

Q.35 How object are created In java? explain using method through the object. (RU BCA 2022)

Ans. The object is a basic building block of an OOPs language. In Java, we cannot execute any program without creating an object. There is various way to create an object in Java that we will discuss in this section, and also learn how to create an object in Java.

Java provides five ways to create an object.

Using new Keyword

Using clone() method

Using newInstance() method of the Class class

Using newInstance() method of the Constructor class

Using Deserialization

Example

```
Class sparkpublisher
{
Void show()
{
System.out.print(" wel come to spartkpublication");
}
}
public static void main(String args[]) (
{
sparkpublisher obj=new sparkpublisher()
Obj slow()
}
}
//inactive state until the init() method is invoked. stop0: The stopt) method stops the execution of the
```

Output: wel come to sparkpublication

Q.36. what is inner class in java. (RU BCA 2022)

Ans. java inner class or nested class is a class that is declared inside the class or interface. We use inner classes to logically group classes and interfaces in one place to be more readable and maintainable. Additionally, it can access all the members of the outer class, including private data members and methods.

1. Nested classes represent a particular type of relationship that is it can access all the members (data members and methods) of the outer class, including private
2. Nested classes are used to develop more readable and maintainable code because it logically group classes and interfaces in one place only.
3. Code Optimization: It requires less code to write

ONLINE RESOURCES

Practice Paper

Link: **https://forms.gle/Kg8gfDosAfYTNHiV6**

QR Code:

Video Content:

Link: **https://www.youtube.com/playlist?list=PLzlh_31VWEFoaNYQU5ofj-8LS23gOwTYt**

QR Code:

CHAPTER 4 - Multithreading and Generics

4.1 Multithreading and Synchronization

Multithreading and synchronization are fundamental concepts in Java that enable the concurrent execution of multiple threads of code. Multithreading allows your program to perform multiple tasks simultaneously, while synchronization ensures that threads access shared resources in a controlled and coordinated manner. Let's explore these concepts in detail:

1. Multithreading:

Multithreading is the concurrent execution of two or more threads within the same process. Threads are lightweight processes that share the same memory space, allowing them to communicate and interact efficiently. Here are key aspects of multithreading in Java:

a. Thread Creation: You can create threads in Java by extending the Thread class or implementing the Runnable interface.

Example –

```
class MyThread extends Thread {
  public void run() {
    // Code to run in this thread
  }
}

    // Create and start a thread
    MyThread thread = new MyThread();
    thread.start();
```

b. Runnable Interface: The Runnable interface provides a way to define the task a thread should execute.

Example –

```
    class MyRunnable implements Runnable {
      public void run() {
        // Code to run in this thread
      }
    }

    // Create a thread using Runnable
    Thread thread = new Thread(new MyRunnable());
    thread.start();
```

c. Thread States: Threads can be in various states, including NEW, RUNNABLE, BLOCKED, WAITING, TIMED_WAITING, and TERMINATED. You can manage thread states using methods like start(), sleep(), wait(), and notify().

d. Thread Synchronization: When multiple threads access shared resources concurrently, synchronization mechanisms are used to prevent data corruption and ensure thread safety.

2. Synchronization: Synchronization in Java is the process of controlling access to shared resources to avoid data inconsistency or race conditions. Synchronization can be achieved using various mechanisms:

a. synchronized Keyword: You can use the synchronized keyword to synchronize methods or blocks of code to ensure that only one thread can access them at a time.

Example –

```
    public synchronized void synchronizedMethod() {
      // Synchronized method code
    }
```

b. wait() and notify():

The wait() and notify() methods are used for inter-thread communication and synchronization.
wait() causes a thread to wait until another thread notifies it.
notify() wakes up a waiting thread, allowing it to continue execution.

c. Lock Interfaces (Java 5+): Java provides the java.util.concurrent.locks package, which includes lock interfaces such as Lock and classes like ReentrantLock for advanced synchronization.

d. volatile Keyword: The volatile keyword ensures that a variable's value is always read from and written to the main memory, preventing thread-specific caching.

Example –

```
    private volatile boolean flag = true;
```

e. Thread Safety: Ensuring thread safety is essential when working with shared data and resources.

Thread-safe data structures (e.g., ConcurrentHashMap, AtomicInteger) are provided in the Java API to facilitate thread-safe programming.

f. Deadlocks: Care must be taken to avoid deadlocks, where two or more threads are blocked indefinitely, waiting for each other to release a resource.

Java's multithreading and synchronization capabilities enable the efficient execution of concurrent tasks while ensuring data integrity and consistency. Proper synchronization techniques and careful thread management are crucial for building robust and scalable multithreaded Java applications.

4.2 File Handling and I/O Streams

File handling and I/O (Input/Output) streams are essential components in Java for reading from and writing to files, streams, and other data sources. These operations are crucial for working with external data, such as files and network connections. Let's explore file handling and I/O streams in Java in detail:

1. File Handling in Java: File handling in Java allows you to interact with files and directories on your file system. The java.io and java.nio packages provide classes and methods for file manipulation.

a. Reading and Writing Files: You can read from and write to files using various classes like FileInputStream, FileOutputStream, FileReader, and FileWriter. For efficient file operations, consider using buffered I/O classes like BufferedReader and BufferedWriter.

Example –

```
// Reading from a file using FileReader and BufferedReader
try (BufferedReader reader = new BufferedReader(new FileReader("example.txt"))) {
   String line;
   while ((line = reader.readLine()) != null) {
      System.out.println(line);
   }
} catch (IOException e) {
   e.printStackTrace();
}

// Writing to a file using FileWriter and BufferedWriter
try (BufferedWriter writer = new BufferedWriter(new FileWriter("output.txt"))) {
   writer.write("Hello, Java!");
} catch (IOException e) {
   e.printStackTrace();
}
```

b. File and Directory Operations: Java provides classes like File and Path to manipulate files and directories.
You can create, delete, rename, and check file and directory properties using these classes.

Example –

```
import java.io.File;

// Creating a directory
File directory = new File("my_directory");
directory.mkdir();

// Creating a file
File file = new File("my_directory/my_file.txt");
file.createNewFile();

// Checking if a file exists
boolean exists = file.exists();

// Renaming a file
File renamedFile = new File("my_directory/new_file.txt");
file.renameTo(renamedFile);

// Deleting a file
file.delete();
```

c. Exception Handling: File handling operations can throw IOException or related exceptions, so proper exception handling is essential.

2. I/O Streams in Java:

I/O streams are used for reading and writing data from/to various sources, including files, network sockets, and in-memory data structures. Java's I/O stream classes are categorized into two main types: byte streams and character streams.

a. Byte Strems: Byte streams are used for handling binary data. InputStream and OutputStream are the abstract classes for byte-oriented I/O operations.

Example –

```
// Reading from a binary file using FileInputStream
try (FileInputStream fis = new FileInputStream("data.dat")) {
   int data;
   while ((data = fis.read()) != -1) {
      // Process data
   }
} catch (IOException e) {
   e.printStackTrace();
}

// Writing to a binary file using FileOutputStream
try (FileOutputStream fos = new FileOutputStream("data.dat")) {
   fos.write(dataBytes);
} catch (IOException e) {
   e.printStackTrace();
}
```

b. Character Streams: Character streams are used for handling character data, making them suitable for text-based data. Reader and Writer are the abstract classes for character-oriented I/O operations.

Example –

```
// Reading from a text file using FileReader and BufferedReader
try (BufferedReader reader = new BufferedReader(new FileReader("text.txt"))) {
   String line;
   while ((line = reader.readLine()) != null) {
      // Process text data
   }
} catch (IOException e) {
   e.printStackTrace();
}

// Writing to a text file using FileWriter and BufferedWriter
try (BufferedWriter writer = new BufferedWriter(new FileWriter("text.txt"))) {
   writer.write("Hello, Java!");
} catch (IOException e) {
   e.printStackTrace();
}
```

c. Byte-to-Character Conversion: To convert bytes to characters and vice versa, you can use classes like InputStreamReader and OutputStreamWriter. Java's file handling and I/O stream capabilities are versatile and flexible, allowing you to interact with a wide range of data sources. Proper error handling and resource management, especially when working with files, are crucial to writing robust and reliable Java applications.

3. Benefits of Stream Classes

Stream classes offer several benefits that make them a valuable addition to the Java programming language:

Functional Programming Paradigm: Stream classes promote a more functional programming style in Java. They allow you to express data manipulation operations (e.g., filtering, mapping, and reduction) as a sequence of declarative and often more concise operations.

Code Clarity and Readability: Stream operations are typically more expressive and readable than equivalent iterative or imperative code. They enable you to write code that closely resembles the problem-solving steps, making it easier to understand and maintain.

Conciseness and Expressiveness: Streams allow you to chain multiple operations together, reducing the need for intermediate variables and nested loops. This results in shorter and more elegant code.

Lazy Evaluation: Streams support lazy evaluation, which means that elements are processed on-demand as they are needed. This can lead to improved performance, especially when dealing with large data sets.

Parallelism and Concurrency: Stream operations can be parallelized easily using parallel stream methods. This allows you to take advantage of multi-core processors and parallelize data processing tasks effortlessly.
Immutable Data: Stream operations do not modify the underlying data source. Instead, they create new streams or collections with transformed or filtered data. This immutability ensures data integrity and reduces the risk of unintended side effects.
Data Transformation: Streams provide a wide range of data transformation operations, including filtering, mapping, sorting, and reducing. These operations allow you to manipulate data in a clean and functional way.
Error Handling: Streams provide exception-handling mechanisms, such as try-catch blocks and methods like orElse or orElseThrow, which allow you to handle errors gracefully when working with optional data.
Integration with Collections and I/O: Streams seamlessly integrate with collections, arrays, and I/O streams, making it easy to apply stream operations to various data sources.
Standardization: The Java Standard Library includes many built-in stream operations for common tasks, reducing the need for custom code and promoting consistent coding practices.
Enhanced Debugging: Streams offer methods like peek that allow you to insert debugging statements into the stream processing pipeline, aiding in troubleshooting and debugging.
Reusability: Stream operations can be defined as reusable methods or lambdas, promoting code reuse and maintainability.

4.3 Generics and Collections

Generics and collections are two fundamental aspects of Java that enable you to write more flexible, type-safe, and reusable code for managing and manipulating data structures. Let's explore generics and collections in Java in detail:
1. Generics in Java: Generics in Java allow you to create classes, interfaces, and methods that operate on parameterized types. They provide type safety by allowing you to specify the type of data a class or method can work with at compile time.
a. Generic Classes: You can define a generic class by using angle brackets <T> to represent a type parameter.
Example –

```
public class Box<T> {
    private T value;

    public T getValue() {
        return value;
    }

    public void setValue(T value) {
        this.value = value;
    }
}
```

b. Generic Methods: You can also create generic methods within non-generic classes.
Example –

```
public <T> T getFirst(List<T> list) {
    if (list.isEmpty()) {
        return null;
    }
    return list.get(0);
}
```

c. Wildcards:

Wildcards (?) allow you to represent an unknown type within generics.
<?> represents an unknown type, while <? extends T> represents a bounded type.
java
Copy code

```
public void processList(List<?> list) {
    // Process the list without knowing its type
}
```

2. Collections Framework: Java's Collections Framework provides a comprehensive set of classes and interfaces for managing and manipulating collections of objects. Collections are widely used in Java for storing and working with groups of data.
a. Interfaces: The framework includes core interfaces such as List, Set, Map, and more, each with specific characteristics.

Example –

```
List<String> names = new ArrayList<>();
Set<Integer> numbers = new HashSet<>();
Map<String, Integer> ageMap = new HashMap<>();
```

b. Classes: Java provides various concrete collection classes that implement the core interfaces, including ArrayList, HashSet, HashMap, and many others.

Example –

```
List<String> names = new ArrayList<>();
names.add("Alice");
names.add("Bob");

Set<Integer> numbers = new HashSet<>();
numbers.add(1);
numbers.add(2);

Map<String, Integer> ageMap = new HashMap<>();
ageMap.put("Alice", 25);
ageMap.put("Bob", 30);
```

c. Iteration: You can iterate through collections using enhanced for loops or iterators.

Example –

```
List<String> names = new ArrayList<>();
// Add elements to the list

for (String name : names) {
   System.out.println(name);
}

Iterator<String> iterator = names.iterator();
while (iterator.hasNext()) {
   String name = iterator.next();
   System.out.println(name);
}
```

d. Generics in Collections: Generics are heavily used in the Collections Framework to ensure type safety.

Example –

```
List<String> names = new ArrayList<>();
Set<Integer> numbers = new HashSet<>();
```

e. Sorting and Searching: Collections Framework provides methods for sorting and searching collections.

Example –

```
List<Integer> numbers = new ArrayList<>();
// Add elements to the list

Collections.sort(numbers); // Sort the list
int index = Collections.binarySearch(numbers, 42); // Binary search
```

f. Thread Safety: Some collection classes are not thread-safe, while others, like Vector and ConcurrentHashMap, are designed for concurrent access.

Generics and the Collections Framework are integral to Java programming, enabling you to write more efficient, type-safe, and reusable code for managing and manipulating data structures. Understanding these concepts is crucial for effective Java development, as they play a significant role in everyday programming tasks.

4.4 Java Strings and String Handling

Strings and string handling are fundamental in Java and play a crucial role in text processing and manipulation. Java provides a rich set of features for working with strings. Let's explore Java strings and string handling in detail:

1. String Basics: In Java, strings are objects of the String class, and they represent sequences of characters. Here are some fundamental aspects of Java strings:

a. String Declaration: You can declare strings in Java using the String class.

Example –

```
String message = "Hello, Java!";
```

b. Immutable: Strings in Java are immutable, meaning their values cannot be changed once created. Operations that appear to modify strings actually create new string objects.

Example –

```
String original = "Hello";
String modified = original.concat(", Java!"); // Creates a new string
```
c. String Pool: Java maintains a string pool for literal strings (strings defined in source code). Repeated string literals are stored as references to the same string object.

Example –
```
String a = "Hello";
String b = "Hello"; // Both a and b reference the same "Hello" string
```
d. String Comparison: To compare strings for equality, you should use the equals() method rather than ==, which checks reference equality.

Example –
```
String str1 = "Hello";
String str2 = "Hello";
boolean isEqual = str1.equals(str2); // true
```
2. String Manipulation: Java provides various methods for manipulating strings:

a. Concatenation: You can concatenate strings using the + operator or the concat() method.

Example –
```
String firstName = "John";
String lastName = "Doe";
String fullName = firstName + " " + lastName;
```
b. Length and Substring: You can find the length of a string using the length() method and extract substrings using substring().

Example –
```
String text = "Hello, Java!";
int length = text.length(); // 12
String sub = text.substring(0, 5); // "Hello"
```
c. Searching and Replacing: You can search for substrings and replace them using methods like indexOf(), contains(), replace(), and replaceAll().

Example –
```
String text = "Java is great. Java is powerful.";
int index = text.indexOf("Java"); // 0 (first occurrence)
boolean contains = text.contains("powerful"); // true
String replaced = text.replace("Java", "Python");
```
d. Splitting and Joining: You can split a string into an array of substrings using split() and join an array of strings into a single string using join() (Java 8+).

Example –
```
String csvData = "John,Doe,30";
String[] parts = csvData.split(",");
String joined = String.join("-", parts); // "John-Doe-30"
```
3. String Formatting: Java provides various ways to format strings:

a. String.format(): You can use the String.format() method to create formatted strings.

Example –
```
String name = "John";
int age = 30;
String formatted = String.format("Name: %s, Age: %d", name, age);
```
b. printf(): The System.out.printf() method allows you to print formatted strings to the console.

Example –
```
String name = "John";
int age = 30;
System.out.printf("Name: %s, Age: %d", name, age);
```
c. StringBuilder and StringBuffer: For dynamic string construction, you can use StringBuilder (non-thread-safe) or StringBuffer (thread-safe).

Example –
```
StringBuilder builder = new StringBuilder();
builder.append("Hello");
builder.append(", ");
builder.append("Java!");
String result = builder.toString(); // "Hello, Java!"
```
4.4.2 Two commonly used methods of the StringBuffer class in Java:

1. append Method:

The append method is used to add (append) a specified value to the end of the StringBuffer object. It returns the modified StringBuffer object.

Syntax:

public StringBuffer append(String str);

Example usage:

StringBuffer sb = new StringBuffer("Hello");

sb.append(" World"); // Appends " World" to the existing string

2. insert Method:

The insert method is used to insert a specified value at a specified position in the StringBuffer object. It returns the modified StringBuffer object.

Syntax:

public StringBuffer insert(int offset, String str);

Example usage:

StringBuffer sb = new StringBuffer("Java");

sb.insert(1, "rocks"); // Inserts "rocks" at position 1

Both of these methods are commonly used for modifying the content of a StringBuffer object. The append method is used to add content to the end, while the insert method is used to insert content at a specific position within the StringBuffer.

Understanding Java strings and their handling is essential for text processing and manipulation in Java applications. It's crucial to be aware of the immutability of strings and choose appropriate methods for string manipulation and formatting to ensure efficient and correct code.

4.4.3 String manipulation functions of Java String class

The java.lang.String class in Java provides a wide range of methods for manipulating strings. Here are some of the commonly used string manipulation functions of the String class:

String Length:

int length(): Returns the length (number of characters) of the string.

Substring Extraction:

String substring(int beginIndex): Returns a substring starting from the specified index.

String substring(int beginIndex, int endIndex): Returns a substring from the beginIndex to the endIndex (exclusive).

Concatenation:

String concat(String str): Concatenates the specified string to the end of this string.

String + operator: The + operator can be used for string concatenation.

String Comparison:

boolean equals(Object obj): Compares the string with the specified object for equality.

boolean equalsIgnoreCase(String anotherString): Compares the string to another string, ignoring case.

int compareTo(String anotherString): Compares two strings lexicographically.

boolean startsWith(String prefix): Checks if the string starts with the specified prefix.

boolean endsWith(String suffix): Checks if the string ends with the specified suffix.

Character Extraction:

char charAt(int index): Returns the character at the specified index.

int codePointAt(int index): Returns the Unicode code point at the specified index.

Search and Replace:

int indexOf(String str): Returns the index of the first occurrence of the specified substring.

int indexOf(String str, int fromIndex): Searches for the specified substring starting from the given index.

int lastIndexOf(String str): Returns the index of the last occurrence of the specified substring.

int lastIndexOf(String str, int fromIndex): Searches for the specified substring backward from the given index.

String replace(char oldChar, char newChar): Replaces all occurrences of the oldChar with the newChar.

String replace(CharSequence target, CharSequence replacement): Replaces all occurrences of the target sequence with the replacement sequence.

Whitespace Trimming:

String trim(): Removes leading and trailing whitespace from the string.

Case Conversion:

String toLowerCase(): Converts all characters to lowercase.

String toUpperCase(): Converts all characters to uppercase.

String Splitting:

String[] split(String regex): Splits the string using the specified regular expression and returns an array of substrings.

String[] split(String regex, int limit): Splits the string using the specified regular expression, limiting the number of splits.

String Formatting:

static String format(String format, Object... args): Formats a string using a format string and a list of arguments.

Checking for Empty or Null:
boolean isEmpty(): Checks if the string is empty (length is 0).
static boolean isNullOrEmpty(String str): Checks if a string is null or empty.
String Comparison (Ignoring Locale):
boolean equalsIgnoreCase(String anotherString): Compares two strings for equality while ignoring case.
int compareToIgnoreCase(String str): Compares two strings lexicographically while ignoring case.

4.5 Java Exception Handling Best Practices

Exception handling is a critical aspect of writing robust and reliable Java code. It helps you handle unexpected situations and gracefully recover from errors. Here are some best practices for exception handling in Java:

1. Use Specific Exceptions: Catch and handle specific exceptions rather than catching the generic Exception class. This allows you to handle exceptions more effectively.

Example –

```
try {
  // Code that may throw specific exceptions
} catch (IOException e) {
  // Handle IOException
} catch (SQLException e) {
  // Handle SQLException
} catch (Exception e) {
  // Handle other exceptions
}
```

2. Handle Exceptions Appropriately: Handle exceptions at the appropriate level in your code. Avoid catching exceptions too early if they can be handled more effectively closer to the source of the problem.

3. Use the finally Block: The finally block is used to execute code that must run regardless of whether an exception was thrown or not. It's often used for resource cleanup, like closing files or database connections.

Example –

```
try {
  // Code that may throw exceptions
} catch (Exception e) {
  // Handle exceptions
} finally {
  // Cleanup code
}
```

4. Don't Swallow Exceptions: Avoid catching exceptions and doing nothing or logging insufficient information. Always log exceptions or rethrow them if they cannot be handled effectively.

Example –

```
try {
  // Code that may throw exceptions
} catch (Exception e) {
  log.error("An error occurred: " + e.getMessage());
  throw e; // Rethrow the exception
}
```

5. Log Exception Details: When logging exceptions, include as much relevant information as possible, such as the exception message, stack trace, and any contextual information that may help with debugging.

6. Use Try-With-Resources (Java 7+): When working with resources like files, streams, or database connections, use try-with-resources to automatically close them when they are no longer needed. This reduces resource leaks and the need for explicit cleanup in the finally block.

Example –

```
try (FileInputStream fis = new FileInputStream("example.txt")) {
  // Code that uses the resource
} catch (IOException e) {
  // Handle exceptions
}
```

7. Avoid Catching Throwable: Avoid catching the Throwable class or its subtypes like Error unless you have a specific and well-justified reason for doing so. These exceptions typically represent severe issues that are best left to the JVM to handle.

8. Document Exception Handling: Document your exception handling strategy in code comments or documentation, especially when working on code that may be maintained by others. Describe why specific exceptions are caught and how they are handled.

9. Use Checked and Unchecked Exceptions Wisely: Use checked exceptions for recoverable errors that can be handled gracefully by the calling code. Use unchecked exceptions (subclasses of Runtime Exception) for unrecoverable errors and programming errors (e.g., null pointer exceptions).

10. Keep Exception Handling Simple: Avoid complex exception handling logic that obscures the main purpose of the code. Make sure that the code remains readable and maintainable.

11. Test Exception Handling: Include tests that verify the correctness of your exception handling code. Test both the cases where exceptions are expected and where they are not expected.

Effective exception handling is crucial for writing reliable and maintainable Java applications. By following these best practices, you can ensure that your code is more robust, easier to maintain, and better equipped to handle unexpected situations gracefully.

4.6 Java Date and Time API

The Java Date and Time API, introduced in Java 8, provides a comprehensive set of classes for handling date and time operations. This API is part of the java.time package and addresses the shortcomings of the legacy java.util.Date and java.util.Calendar classes. Here's an overview of the Java Date and Time API:

1. Core Classes:

The Java Date and Time API introduces several core classes to represent dates, times, and durations. The most commonly used classes include:

- **LocalDate:** Represents a date without a time component, such as "2023-09-28."
- **LocalTime:** Represents a time without a date component, such as "14:30:45."
- **LocalDateTime:** Combines date and time, representing a point in time without a time zone, such as "2023-09-28T14:30:45."
- **ZonedDateTime: Represents a date and time with a time zone, such as "2023-09-28T14:30:45+02:00."**

2. Formatting and Parsing:

The API provides DateTimeFormatter for formatting dates and times as strings and parsing strings into date and time objects. It supports patterns and locale-specific formatting.

Example –

```
DateTimeFormatter formatter = DateTimeFormatter.ofPattern("yyyy-MM-dd HH:mm:ss");
String formattedDateTime = LocalDateTime.now().format(formatter);
LocalDateTime parsedDateTime = LocalDateTime.parse("2023-09-28 14:30:45", formatter);
```

3. Time Zones:

The Java Date and Time API allows you to work with time zones more effectively. You can create ZoneId objects to represent specific time zones and convert between different time zones using ZonedDateTime and OffsetDateTime.

Example –

```
ZoneId newYorkZone = ZoneId.of("America/New_York");
ZonedDateTime nyTime = ZonedDateTime.now(newYorkZone);
```

4. Date and Time Arithmetic:

You can perform arithmetic operations on date and time objects. For example, you can add or subtract days, hours, or other durations to a LocalDate, LocalTime, or LocalDateTime.

Example –

```
LocalDate tomorrow = LocalDate.now().plusDays(1);
LocalTime oneHourLater = LocalTime.now().plusHours(1);
```

5. Periods and Durations:

The Period class represents a period of time in years, months, and days, while the Duration class represents a duration in seconds and nanoseconds. These classes are useful for measuring and manipulating time intervals.

Example –

```
Period twoWeeks = Period.ofWeeks(2);
Duration threeHours = Duration.ofHours(3);
```

6. Temporal Adjusters:

Temporal adjusters allow you to perform various date and time adjustments, such as finding the first or last day of the month or finding the next or previous working day.

Example –

```
LocalDate firstDayOfMonth = LocalDate.now().with(TemporalAdjusters.firstDayOfMonth());
```

7. LocalDate vs. LocalDateTime:

When working with dates, prefer to use LocalDate to represent date-only values. Use LocalDateTime when you need to include time information. This helps avoid unintended side effects when working with dates.

8. Thread Safety:

The classes in the Java Date and Time API are designed to be thread-safe, which means you can safely use them in multithreaded applications without additional synchronization.

9. Handling Time Zones:

When dealing with time zones, always specify the desired time zone explicitly to avoid ambiguity. Be aware that not specifying a time zone may use the system's default time zone, which can lead to unexpected behaviour in different environments.

The Java Date and Time API provides a powerful and flexible way to work with dates and times in Java applications. It addresses many of the shortcomings of the older date and time classes and simplifies common date and time-related tasks. It's considered best practice to use this API for any new Java projects that require date and time handling.

Exercise

Exercise 1 – MCQ

Q 1. What is the purpose of synchronization in Java multithreading?
a) To prevent a thread from starting.
b) To allow multiple threads to execute a method simultaneously.
c) To ensure that only one thread can access a critical section of code at a time.
d) To force all threads to execute in a strict sequential order.

Q 2. Which of the following data structures in Java is NOT part of the Java Collections Framework?
a) ArrayList
b) HashSet
c) Array
d)HashMap

Exercise 2 – True/ False

Q 1. In Java, strings are mutable, which means you can change the content of a string after it is created.

Q 2. In Java, it is considered a best practice to catch and handle all exceptions, including the general "Exception" class, to ensure robust error handling.

Exercise 3 – Fill in the blanks

Q 1. To read text from a file in Java, you typically use the _______ class, which provides methods like readLine() for reading lines of text from a file.

Q 2. In Java, the Instant class represents a specific point in time, typically represented in _______ format, making it suitable for precise timestamp calculations.

Exercise 4 – Match case

Q 1. Match the Java exception handling keywords to their descriptions:
i. try
ii. catch
iii. finally
iv. throws

Descriptions:
a. Used to specify a block of code that may throw an exception.
b. Executes a block of code when an exception occurs.
c. Used to explicitly throw an exception within a method.
d. Used to define code that will always execute, regardless of whether an exception occurred or not.

Exercise 5 – One word answer

Q 1. What keyword is used to define a constant in Java?

Q 2. Which Java keyword is used to declare a method or variable that belongs to the class, not the instance of the class?

Exercise 6 – Small answer

Q 1. What is the purpose of the break statement in a Java loop?

Q 2. What is the difference between == and .equals() when comparing two objects in Java?

Exercise 7 – Long answer

Q 1. Explain the concept of multithreading in Java and provide an example of a scenario where multithreading is beneficial.

Q 2. Describe the principles of object-oriented programming (OOP) and provide an example of how they are applied in Java.

Answer:

Exercise 1. Q 1: C) To ensure that only one thread can access a critical section of code at a time. Q 2: c) Array
Exercise 2. Q 1: False Q 2: False
Exercise 3. Q 1: BufferedReader Q 2: Epoch (UNIX timestamp)

Exercise 4. Q 1: i. try – a ii. catch – b iii. finally - d iv. throw - c
Exercise 5. Q 1: final Q 2: static

Previous Year Questions

Q 1. Compare byte streams with character streams. (JNTU -B.Tech.- 2018)
Q 2. List string manipulation functions of Java String class. (SPPU – BCA - 2015)
Q 3. Give syntax of two methods of StringBuffer class? (SPPU – BCA - 2015)
Q 4. What is multithreading? Explain how does it help Java in its performance? (IGNOU MCA 2012)
Q 5. Briefly explain benefits of stream classes (IGNOU MCA 2012)
Q 6. Explain how exception handling is done in Java, with the help of an example. (IGNOU MCA 2012)
Q 7. What is String Buffer? How it is different from String? (IGNOU MCA 2012)
Q 8. Bring out the difference between the string and stringbuffer classes in Java. (IGNOU MCA 2013)
Q 9. What is Exception? Explain how exceptions are handled in Java. (IGNOU MCA 2014)
Q 10. What is String Class in Java? (IGNOU MCA 2014)
Q 11. What is String class? How is it different from StringBuffer class? (IGNOU MCA 2014)
Q 12. What is the use of Iterator class? (JNTU -B.Tech.- 2018)
Q 13. List the methods of Stack class. (Java collection framework) (JNTU -B.Tech.- 2016)
Q 14. Illustrate the use of static nested classes. (JNTU -B.Tech.- 2016)
Q 15. List the functions of Stack class. (JNTU -B.Tech. -2017)

Previous Year Solved Papers

Q. 1. What is multithreading programming? Explain how threads are created in Java. Explain the needs of thread synchronization, with an example. (RU BCA 2017)

Ans- Multithreading programming is the concurrent execution of multiple threads within the same process. It allows a program to perform multiple tasks concurrently, making more efficient use of the CPU and improving the overall performance of the application. In Java, multithreading is achieved by creating multiple threads that can execute concurrently, allowing for parallel processing and the execution of multiple tasks simultaneously.

Creating Threads in Java: Threads can be created in Java by extending the **Thread** class or by implementing the **Runnable** interface. Here's an example of both approaches:

1. Extending the **Thread** class:

```
class MyThread extends Thread {
  public void run() {
    System.out.println("Thread is running.");
  }
}
```

Implementing the **Runnable** interface:

```
class MyRunnable implements Runnable {
  public void run() {
    System.out.println("Thread is running.");
  }
}
```

Needs of Thread Synchronization: Thread synchronization is essential when multiple threads access shared resources concurrently. It ensures that only one thread can access the shared resource at a time, preventing data inconsistency and potential errors. Without proper synchronization, race conditions and data corruption may occur. Here's an example demonstrating the need for thread synchronization:

```
class Counter {
  private int count = 0;

  public synchronized void increment() {
    count++;
  }

  public int getCount() {
    return count;
  }
}
```

```
class MyThread implements Runnable {
    private Counter counter;

    public MyThread(Counter counter) {
        this.counter = counter;
    }

    public void run() {
        for (int i = 0; i < 1000; i++) {
            counter.increment();
        }
    }
}

public class ThreadSynchronizationExample {
    public static void main(String[] args) throws InterruptedException {
        Counter counter = new Counter();
        Thread thread1 = new Thread(new MyThread(counter));
        Thread thread2 = new Thread(new MyThread(counter));

        thread1.start();
        thread2.start();

        thread1.join();
        thread2.join();

        System.out.println("Final count: " + counter.getCount());
    }
}
```

In this example, the **Counter** class is shared between multiple threads, and the **increment** method is synchronized to ensure that only one thread can access it at a time. Without synchronization, the final count may not be accurate due to concurrent access. Synchronization prevents data corruption and ensures the correct count is maintained.

Q. 2. What do you mean by string handling? Explain various methods of string handling. (RU BCA 2017)

Ans- String handling refers to the manipulation and management of strings in a programming language. In Java, string handling involves various operations that can be performed on strings, such as creating, manipulating, and comparing strings. Java provides a rich set of methods and functionalities for handling strings efficiently. Some of the commonly used methods for string handling in Java include:

1. String Creation: Strings can be created in Java using the **String** class. They can be created either by direct assignment or using the **new** keyword. For example:

```
String str1 = "Hello";
String str2 = new String("World");
```

Concatenation: The **concat()** method is used to concatenate one string to the end of another. The + operator can also be used for concatenation. For example:

```
String str1 = "Hello";
String str2 = "World";
String result = str1.concat(str2); // or String result = str1 + str2;
```

Length: The **length()** method returns the length of the string. For example:

```
String str = "Hello World";
int len = str.length();
```

Comparison: The **equals()** method is used to check if two strings are equal. The **compareTo()** method compares two strings lexicographically. For example:

```
String str1 = "Hello";
String str2 = "Hello";
boolean isEqual = str1.equals(str2);
int compareResult = str1.compareTo(str2);
```

Substring: The **substring()** method is used to extract a substring from a string. For example:

```
String str = "Hello World";
String sub = str.substring(6);
```

Case Conversion: The **toUpperCase()** and **toLowerCase()** methods are used to convert the case of the characters in a string. For example:

```
String str = "Hello World";
String upper = str.toUpperCase();
String lower = str.toLowerCase();
```

Searching and Retrieval: The **indexOf()** method is used to find the index of a particular character or substring within a string. For example:

```
String str = "Hello World";
int index = str.indexOf('o');
```

These methods and functionalities facilitate efficient string handling in Java, allowing developers to manipulate and process strings effectively within their applications.

Q.3. What is Runnable in Java? (RU BCA 2017)

Ans- In Java, the **Runnable** interface is used to create a concurrent thread by defining the code that needs to be executed in a separate thread. It represents a task that can be executed concurrently by a thread. The **Runnable** interface must be implemented by any class whose instances are intended to be executed by a thread. The **Runnable** interface contains only one method, **run()**, which defines the code that will be executed when the thread is started.

Here is an example of implementing the **Runnable** interface:

```
public class MyRunnable implements Runnable {
    public void run() {
        System.out.println("Thread is running using Runnable interface.");
    }

    public static void main(String[] args) {
        MyRunnable myRunnable = new MyRunnable();
        Thread thread = new Thread(myRunnable);
        thread.start();
    }
}
```

In this example, the **MyRunnable** class implements the **Runnable** interface and provides an implementation for the **run()** method. The **run()** method contains the code that the thread will execute. The **Thread** class is then used to create a new thread and start its execution.

Implementing the **Runnable** interface is one way of creating a thread in Java. It allows for better design and object-oriented programming practices by separating the task from the thread logic. This approach is often preferred over directly extending the **Thread** class, as it enables better code reusability and flexibility in managing concurrent tasks in Java applications.

Q.4. What are the advantages of multithreading in java? (RU BCA 2017)

Ans- Multithreading in Java provides several advantages that contribute to the efficiency, responsiveness, and performance of Java applications. Some key advantages of multithreading in Java include:

Improved Performance: Multithreading allows tasks to be executed concurrently, utilizing the available CPU resources more efficiently. This leads to improved performance and faster execution of tasks, especially in applications that involve heavy computation or I/O operations.

Enhanced Responsiveness: Multithreading enables applications to remain responsive during time-consuming tasks by allowing background processes to execute concurrently with the main program. This ensures that the user interface remains interactive and responsive, providing a better user experience.

Resource Sharing: Multithreading facilitates the sharing of resources, such as memory and CPU time, among multiple threads within the same application. This leads to better utilization of resources and can result in overall improved system efficiency.

Simplified Design: Multithreading allows for the design of more efficient and streamlined applications by separating different tasks into individual threads. This leads to a more modular and maintainable codebase, making it easier to manage complex applications and improve overall code organization.

Concurrency Control: Multithreading provides mechanisms for controlling and synchronizing access to shared resources, preventing data inconsistencies and race conditions that may occur when multiple threads access and modify shared data simultaneously.

Asynchronous Programming: Multithreading enables the implementation of asynchronous programming, allowing tasks to run independently and concurrently without blocking the execution of the main program. This is particularly beneficial for applications that require parallel processing and real-time data handling.

By leveraging the advantages of multithreading, developers can create more efficient, responsive, and scalable Java applications that can perform complex tasks and operations concurrently, leading to improved overall performance and user experience.

Q. 5. What is Thread? Describe the life cycle of thread with the help of a diagram. Create any thread as an example. (RU BCA 2018)

Ans- A thread in Java represents an independent path of execution within a program. It allows concurrent execution of multiple tasks within the same program, enabling efficient utilization of CPU resources and facilitating the execution of multiple operations simultaneously.

The life cycle of a thread in Java consists of several stages, including the following:

- **New:** A thread is in the new state when it is created but has not yet started its execution.
- **Runnable:** After invoking the **start()** method on the thread, it enters the runnable state. In this state, the thread is ready to run, but the scheduler has not selected it to be the running thread.
- **Running:** The thread enters the running state when the CPU starts executing its **run()** method.
- **Blocked:** A thread can transition to the blocked state if it is waiting for a monitor lock to enter a synchronized block or method.
- **Waiting:** A thread enters the waiting state when it waits for another thread to perform a particular action.
- **Timed Waiting:** Threads enter the timed waiting state when they are waiting for another thread for a specified period.
- **Terminated:** A thread enters the terminated state when its **run()** method completes or when an uncaught exception occurs in the thread.

Here is a simple example of creating and starting a thread in Java:

```
public class MyThread extends Thread {
  public void run() {
    for (int i = 0; i < 5; i++) {
      System.out.println("Thread is running: " + i);
      try {
        Thread.sleep(1000);
      } catch (InterruptedException e) {
        e.printStackTrace();
      }
    }
  }

  public static void main(String[] args) {
    MyThread thread = new MyThread();
    thread.start();
  }
}
```

In this example, we create a thread by extending the **Thread** class and overriding the **run()** method. The **run()** method contains the code that the thread will execute. We then create an instance of **MyThread** and start the thread using the **start()** method.

This example demonstrates the creation, execution, and life cycle of a thread in Java, showing how a thread can perform a specific task independently while other parts of the program continue their execution.

Q. 6. Explain Exception handling and its types with example. (RU BCA 2018)

Ans- Exception handling in Java is a mechanism to handle runtime errors and exceptional situations that may occur during the execution of a program. It allows developers to gracefully manage and recover from unexpected situations, preventing the program from terminating abruptly. Java provides a robust and comprehensive exception handling framework that consists of several types of exceptions, each serving different purposes. Some common types of exceptions in Java include:

1. Checked Exceptions: These are the exceptions that are checked at compile time. The compiler checks whether the code that might throw a checked exception is enclosed within a try-catch block or whether the method throws the exception using the **throws** keyword. Examples of checked exceptions include **IOException**, **SQLException**, and **ClassNotFoundException**.

```
import java.io.FileReader;
import java.io.IOException;

public class CheckedExceptionExample {
```

```
  public static void main(String[] args) {
    FileReader file = null;
    try {
      file = new FileReader("file.txt");
    } catch (IOException e) {
      System.out.println("File not found or cannot be opened.");
      e.printStackTrace();
    }
  }
}
```

2. Unchecked Exceptions (RuntimeException): These are exceptions that are not checked at compile time. They occur during the execution of the program and are also known as runtime exceptions. Examples of unchecked exceptions include **NullPointerException**, **ArrayIndexOutOfBoundsException**, and **ArithmeticException**

```
public class UncheckedExceptionExample {
  public static void main(String[] args) {
    try {
      int result = 10 / 0; // ArithmeticException
    } catch (ArithmeticException e) {
      System.out.println("Cannot divide by zero.");
      e.printStackTrace();
    }
  }
}
```

Errors: These are exceptional conditions that are not expected to be caught or handled by the application. Examples include **OutOfMemoryError** and **StackOverflowError**. These errors are typically related to the environment in which the application is running.

```
public class ErrorExample {
  public static void main(String[] args) {
    try {
      throw new StackOverflowError();
    } catch (StackOverflowError e) {
      System.out.println("Stack overflow error occurred.");
      e.printStackTrace();
    }
  }
}
```

Exception handling in Java is implemented using the **try**, **catch**, **finally**, and **throw** keywords, allowing developers to catch and handle exceptions, perform cleanup operations, and throw custom exceptions when needed. By effectively implementing exception handling, developers can create more robust and reliable applications that can gracefully handle unforeseen errors and exceptional situations.

Q.7 What are the advantages of multithreading in java? (RU BCA 2018)

Ans- Multithreading in Java allows concurrent execution of two or more parts of a program for maximum utilization of CPU. It offers several advantages that make it a powerful tool in software development. Some of the key advantages of multithreading in Java include:

Improved Performance: Multithreading enables efficient utilization of CPU resources by executing multiple threads concurrently. This helps in speeding up the execution of tasks and maximizing the performance of the application.

Enhanced Responsiveness: Multithreading helps in keeping the application responsive by allowing it to perform multiple operations simultaneously. It ensures that the user interface remains interactive, even when the application is performing intensive tasks in the background.

Resource Sharing: Threads share the same address space, allowing them to access the same data and resources within the same process. This facilitates efficient communication and data sharing between different parts of the program, leading to effective resource utilization.

Economy of Scale: Multithreading enables the development of scalable applications that can handle multiple tasks concurrently. This helps in achieving better scalability and supporting the increasing demands of modern applications without significant performance degradation.

Simplified Complex Tasks: Multithreading simplifies the handling of complex tasks by allowing the decomposition of large tasks into smaller, more manageable threads. This makes it easier to handle intricate processes and enhances the overall maintainability and readability of the code.

Asynchronous Programming: Multithreading facilitates the implementation of asynchronous programming, allowing the execution of tasks without blocking the main program flow. This is particularly useful for handling I/O operations, network operations, and other time-consuming tasks without affecting the overall performance of the application.

Utilization of Multiprocessor Systems: Multithreading enables the effective utilization of multiprocessor systems by distributing the workload across multiple processors. This can result in significant performance improvements, especially in systems with multiple CPU cores.

While multithreading offers these advantages, it also introduces complexities such as thread synchronization, race conditions, and deadlock issues. Therefore, it is essential to handle these challenges effectively to ensure the stability and reliability of multithreaded Java applications.

Q. 8. Write a program in java to concatenate (merge) two string using array. (RU BCA 2019)

Ans. This example shows how to merge two arrays into a single array by the use of list Addall(array1 ast,ist(array2) method of List class and Arrays toString O method of Array class

Live Demo

```
import java.util.ArrayList;
import java.util.Arrays,
import java.util.List;
public class Main {
   public static void main(String args[]) {
   String a[]= {"A", "E", "I"};
   String b[]= {"0","U"};
   List list = new ArrayList(Arrays.asList(a)).
   list.addAll(Arrays.asList(b));
   Object[] c=list.toArray();
   System.out.println(Arrays.toString(c)).
  }
}
```

Result

The above code sample will produce the following result.

[A, E, I, O, U]

Q.9. What is string buffer objects in java? (RU BCA 2019)

Ans. StringBuffer is a peer class of String that provides much of the functionality of strings. String represents fixed-length, immutable character sequences while StringBuffer represents growable and writable character sequences.

StringBuffer may have characters and substrings inserted in the middle or appended to the end. It will automatically grow to make room for such additions and often has more characters preallocated than are actually needed, to allow room for growth.

Q.10. What is multithreading in java? (RU BCA 2019)

Ans. Multithreading in java is a process of executing multiple threads simultaneously. A thread is a lightweight sub-process, the smallest unit of processing. Multiprocessing and multithreading, both are used to achieve multitasking However, we use multithreading than multiprocessing because threads use a shared memory area. They don't allocate separate memory area so saves memory, and context-switching between the threads takes less time than process. Java Multithreading is mostly used in games, animation, etc.

Q.11. Explain synchronisation in respect to Multithreading in Java. (RU BCA 2020)

Ans- If you start with at least two threads inside a program, there might be a chance when multiple threads attempt to get to the same resource. It can even create an unexpected outcome because of concurrency issues.

Syntax:

```
synchronized(objectidentifier)
{
```

```
// Access shared variables and other shared resources;
}
```

For example, multiple threads attempt to write within an equivalent file. This may corrupt the data since one of the threads can override the data or when a thread is opening the same file at the same time, another thread might be closing the same file. There is a need to synchronize the action of multiple threads. This can be implemented using a concept called Monitors. Each object in Java is associated with a monitor, which a thread can lock or unlock. Only one thread at a time may hold a lock on a monitor. Java programming language provides a very handy way of creating threads and synchronizing their task by using the Synchronized blocks. It also keeps the shared resources within this particular block. Synchronized blocks in Java are marked with the Synchronized keyword. This block in Java is synchronized on some object. All blocks that are synchronized on the same object can only have one thread executing inside them at a time. All other threads attempting to enter the synchronized block are blocked until the thread inside the synchronized block exits the block

Types of Synchronization

There are basically two types of synchronization available. They are:

Process Synchronization: The simultaneous execution of multiple threads or processes to reach a state such that they commit to a certain sequence of actions.

Thread Synchronization: At times when more than one thread tries to access a shared resource, you need to ensure that resource will be used by only one thread at a time. Let's not get into the details of these types and try to understand what are locks in Java.

Locks in Java

As I mentioned earlier, Synchronization is built around an internal entity known as the lock or monitor. Each and every object has a lock associated with it. So a thread that needs consistent access to an object's fields needs to acquire the object's lock before accessing them, and then release the lock when the work is done.

Multi-threading with Synchronization

This is the same example as above but it prints the counter value in the sequence. Every time we run it, it produces the same result

```
class Multithread
{
public void printCount())
{
try
{
for(int i=5:i>0;i--)

System.out.println("Counter-"+i);
}
} catch (Exception e)
{
System.out.println(Thread interrupted");
}
}
}
class Thread extends Multithread
{
private Thread t;
private String threadName;
Multithread MT;
Thread(String name, Multithread mut)
{
threadName=name:
MT=mt;
}
public void run()
{
synchronized(MT)
{
MT.printCount();
}
System.out.println("Thread" + threadName + "exiting.");
}
```

```
public void start()
{
System.out.println("Starting"+threadName);
if (t=== null)
{
t=new Thread (this, threadName);
t.start():
}
}
}
public class TestThread
{
public static void main(String args[])
{
Multithread MT=new Multithread():
Thread T= new Thread("Thread-1", MT);
Thread T1 = new Thread("Thread - 2", MT);
T.start();
T1.start()://wait for threads to end
try
{
T.join();
T1.join();
} catch (Exception e)
{
System.out.println("Interrupted").
}
}
}
```

Q.12. Differentiate sleep(), suspend () and wait (). (RU BCA 2020)
sleep) is a static method that is used to send the calling thread into a non-runnable state for the given duration of time. The important part for this is recognizing the "calling thread, which is actually the thread in which the sleep() method is invoked rather than the thread object which may (which is essentially a violation of Java standards) invoke this method. What this means is, while calling Thread sleep duration in milliseconds) is appropriate and will send the invoking thread to non-runnable state, but calling t.sleep duration in milliseconds) is inappropriate as it would cause the thread in which this call appears to go to non-runnable state instead of the "T" thread whose object is invoking the method. While in "sleep", the thread will keep all the monitor locks which might be holding at the time of sleep invocation.
The t.suspend() method has been deprecated, as it is inherently deadlock-prone. It suspends the thread on which it is invoked. If the target thread holds a lock on the monitor protecting a critical system resource when it is suspended, no thread can access this resource until the target thread is resumed. If the thread that would resume the target thread attempts to lock this monitor prior to calling resume, deadlock results
t.wait() Causes current thread to wait until either another thread invokes the notify() method or the notify All method for this object, or a specified amount of time has elapsed. The difference between sleep) and wait() is that sleep() is called on a thread while wait() is called on an object (That's why it is part of Object class. The parent to all Java classes). The wait() method causes the current thread (call it T) to place itself in the wait set for this object and then to relinquish any and all synchronization claims on this object. Thread T becomes disabled for thread scheduling purposes. Later, another thread can synchronize on the same lock object and call lock.notify(). This wakes up the original, waiting thread T.

Q.13. Design a program using Java to perform the following operation (i) Count the numbers of vowels available in a string. (RU BCA 2020)
Ans.

```
public class Count {
  public static void main(String] args) {
  String line "This website is aw3som3."
  int vowels-0, consonants-0, digits 0, spaces-0.
  line-line.toLowerCase();
  for(int i=0;i<line.length(); ++i){
```

```
    char ch=line.charAt(i):
if( ch='a' || ch = = 'e' || ch = ="i " || ch= ="o"|| ch= ='u') {
++vowels
   }
  }
System.out.println("Vowels"+vowels);
 }
}
```

Output

Vowels: 6

Q.14 . Design a program using Java to reverse a string using user-defined function. (RU BCA 2020)

Ans

```
import java.util.Scanner
class ReverseStringExamplel
{
public static void main(String args[])
{
Strings:
Scanner sc=new Scanner(System.in);
System.out.print("Enter a String: ");
s=sc.nextLine(); //reading string from user
System.out.print("After reverse string is: ").
for(int i-s.length(),i>0;-i) // i is the length of the string
{
System.out.print(s.charAt(i-1)); //printing the character at indexi-1
}
}
}
```

Q.15. What is Runnable interface in Java? (RU BCA 2020)

Ans. The Runnable interface should be implemented by any class whose instances are intended to be executed by a thread. The class must define a method of no arguments called run. This interface is designed to provide a common protocol for objects that wish to execute code while they are active

Q. 16. What is the collection framework? Discuss the collection class hierarchy in java. (BCA-III Paper IV 2021)

Ans: The Collection in Java is a framework that provides an architecture to store and manipulate the group of objects. Java Collections can achieve all the operations that you perform on a data such as searching, sorting, insertion, manipulation, and deletion.

Java Collection means a single unit of objects. Java Collection framework provides many interfaces (Set, List, Queue, Deque) and classes (ArrayList, Vector, LinkedList, PriorityQueue, HashSet, LinkedHashSet, TreeSet).

Collection in Java:

A Collection represents a single unit of objects, i.e., a group.

Framework in Java:

It provides readymade architecture.

It represents a set of classes and interfaces.

It is optional.

Collection framework:

The Collection framework represents a unified architecture for storing and manipulating a group of objects.

It has:

1. Interfaces and its implementations, i.e.. classes
2. Algorithm

Hierarchy of Collection Framework

The java.util package contains all the classes and interfaces for the Collection framework.

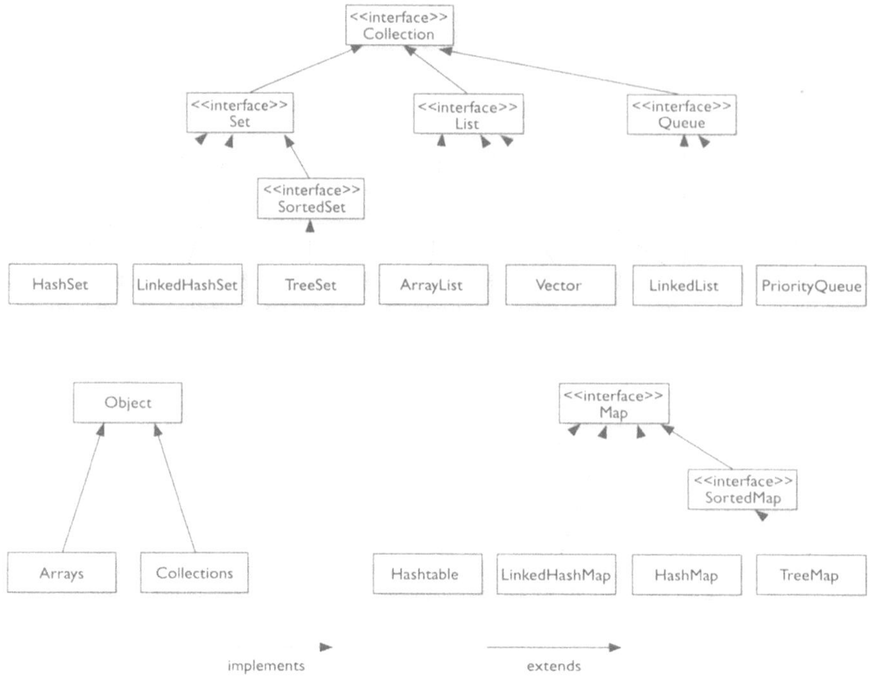

The **Collection** interface in Java is at the root of the Collection Framework. It represents a group of objects, known as its elements. Here are some of the important methods of the **Collection** interface in Java along with their short descriptions:

boolean add(E e):
Adds the specified element to the collection if it is not already present.

boolean remove(Object o):
Removes a single instance of the specified element from the collection, if it is present.

boolean contains(Object o):
Returns true if the collection contains the specified element.

int size():
Returns the number of elements in the collection.

boolean isEmpty():
Returns true if the collection contains no elements.

boolean containsAll(Collection<?> c):
Returns true if the collection contains all of the elements in the specified collection.

boolean addAll(Collection<? extends E> c):
Adds all of the elements in the specified collection to the collection.

boolean removeAll(Collection<?> c):
Removes all the elements from the collection that are also contained in the specified collection.

void clear():
Removes all of the elements from the collection.

Object[] toArray():
Returns an array containing all of the elements in the collection.

boolean retainAll(Collection<?> c):
Retains only the elements in the collection that are contained in the specified collection.

Iterator<E> iterator():
Returns an iterator over the elements in the collection.

Q. 17. Difference between: (RU BCA 2021)
(i) Character stream v/s byte stream
Ans-

Criteria	Character Streams	Byte Streams
Interpretation	Reads and writes data as a sequence of characters	Reads and writes data as a sequence of bytes
Encoding	Uses character encoding (e.g., UTF-8, UTF-16)	No encoding is performed on the data
Usage	Preferable when dealing with text-based data	Suitable for handling binary data or non-text data
Data Representation	Handles textual data and ensures proper character encoding	Treats data as raw bytes without interpretation
I/O Operations	Suitable for reading and writing textual information	Suitable for reading and writing binary data
Size	Larger in size due to encoding overhead	Smaller in size due to the absence of encoding overhead

Q. 18. How are 2D array declare and used in java. write program to input and sort array a name. (BCA-III Paper IV 2021)

Ans: 2D array can be defined as an array of arrays. The 2D array is organized as matrices which can be represented as the collection of rows and columns. However, 2D arrays are created to implement a relational database look alike data structure. It provides ease of holding bulk of data at once which can be passed to any number of functions wherever required. A multidimensional array is an array of arrays. Each element of a multidimensional array is an array itself. For example,

int a[0]=new int a[3][4]

Here, we have created a multidimensional array named a. It is a 2-dimensional array, that can hold a maximum of 12 elements,

```
import java.util.Scanner;
public class KboatArrangeNames
{
  public static void main(String args[]) {
        Scanner in = new Scanner(System.in);
        String names[] = new String[20];
        System.out.println("Enter 20 names:"};
        for (int i=0; i<names.length; i++) {
          names[i] in.nextLine()
        }
  //Bubble Sort
  for (int i = 0 i<names.length-1; i++){
     for (int j = 0; j names length-1-i: j++) {
       if (names[j].compareTolgnoreCase(names[j+
                                                  1]>0) {
        String temp names [j + 1];
        names[j+1]= names[j]:
        names[j]= temp;
        }
     }
  }

  System.out.println("\nSorted Names");
  for (int i = 0 ; i < names.length; i++) {
  System.out.println(names[i];
  }
 }
}
```

Q.19 How to Access Elements of an Array in Java? (RU BCA 2022)

Ans- We can access the element of an array using the index number. Here is the syntax for accessing elements of an array.

//access array elements

array[index]

Let's see an example of accessing array elements using index numbers.

Example: Access Array Elements

```
class Main {
public static void main(String[] args) {
// create an array
int[]age= {12,4,5,2,5};
// access each array elements
System.out.println("Accessing Elements of Array". System.out.println("First Element: "+age[0])..
System.out.println("Second Element: "+age[1]).
System.out.println("Third Element: "+age[2]).
System.out.println("Fourth Element: "+age[3]);
System.out.println("Fifth Element: "+age[4]).
}
}
```

Run Code

Output

```
Accessing Elements of Array:
First Element: 12
Second Element: 4
Third Element: 5
Fourth Element: 2
Fifth Element: 5
```

Q.20. How array is declared and used in java? Explain by given an example. In Java, here is how we can declare an array. (RU BCA 2022)

Ans. dataType[] arrayName;

datatype- it can be primitive types like int, char, double, byte, etc. or Java objects

arrayName - it is an identifier

For example,

```
double[] data;
```

Here, data is an array that can hold values of type double. But, how many elements can array this hold?

To define the number of elements that array can hold, we have to allocate memory for the array an in Java. For example,

```
// declare an array
 double[] data;
// allocate memory
data= new double[10]:
```

Here, the array can store 10 elements. We can also say that the size or length of the array is 10. In Java, we can declare and allocate the memory of an array in one single statement. For example,

```
double[] data = new double[10];
```

Q.21.How to Initialize Arrays in Java? (RU BCA 2022)

Ans- In Java, we can initialize arrays during declaration. For example,

```
//declare and initialize and array
int[] age (12, 4, 5, 2, 5);
```

Here, we have created an array named age and initialized it with the values inside the curly brackets.

Note that we have not provided the size of the array. In this case, the Java compiler automatically specifies the size by counting the number of elements in the array (i.e.5)In the Java array, each memory location is associated with a number. The number is known as an array index. We can also initialize arrays in Java, using the index number.

For example,

```
// declare an array
int[] age= new int[5]:
// initialize array
age[0] 12:
age[1]= 4:

age[2]=5:
```

Note:

Array indices always start from 0. That is, the first element of an array is at index 0. If the size of an array is n, then the last element of the array will be at index n-1.

Q.22 What is string buffer? (RU BCA 2022)
Ans. The java.lang.StringBuffer class is a thread-safe. mutable sequence of characters. Following are the important points about StringBuffer.
A string buffer is like a String, but can be modified.
It contains some particular sequence of characters, but the length and content of the sequence can be changed through certain method calls.
They are safe for use by multiple threads.
Every string buffer has a capacity

Q.23 Define implicit wait in thread. (RU BCA 2022)
Ans. The main function of implicit Wait is to tell the web driver to wait for some time before throwing a "No Such Element Exception". Its default setting is knocked at zero. Once the time is set, the driver automatically will wait for the amount of time defined by you before throwing the above- given exception.
Syntax: driver.manage().timeouts ().implicitly Wait (TimeOut, TimeUnit SECONDS).

ONLINE RESOURCES

Practice Paper
Link: https://forms.gle/qDU1c23eedSwydAj9
QR Code:

Video Content
Link: https://www.youtube.com/playlist?list=PLzlh_31VWEFqhMzp2tHykbBba3OwuUUjL
QR Code:

CHAPTER 5 - GUI & Applets

5.1 Introduction to GUI Programming

GUI (Graphical User Interface) programming in Java involves creating applications with graphical elements like windows, buttons, text fields, and menus to provide a user-friendly interface. Java offers several libraries and frameworks for GUI development, but the most common one is the Swing library, which is part of the Java Standard Library. Here's an introduction to GUI programming in Java:

1. Swing Library:

Swing is a powerful and flexible GUI toolkit for Java applications. It provides a rich set of components and containers for building graphical user interfaces. Swing components are lightweight, platform-independent, and highly customizable.

2. Key Concepts:

Before diving into GUI programming with Swing, it's essential to understand some key concepts:

- **Components**: Components are the building blocks of a GUI. Examples include buttons, labels, text fields, and panels.
- **Containers:** Containers are components that can hold other components. Common containers are frames, panels, and dialogs.
- **Layout Managers:** Layout managers control the arrangement and sizing of components within a container. Swing provides various layout managers like FlowLayout, BorderLayout, and GridLayout.
- **Event Handling:** GUI applications respond to user actions (events) like button clicks and mouse movements. Event handling involves registering event listeners and defining response logic.

3. Creating a Simple Swing Application:

Here's a basic outline of how to create a simple Swing application:

Import the necessary Swing classes:

Example-

```
import javax.swing.*;
```

Create a JFrame (window) to hold your GUI components:

Example-

```
JFrame frame = new JFrame("My Swing Application");
```

Create GUI components (buttons, labels, etc.):

Example-

```
JButton button = new JButton("Click Me");
JLabel label = new JLabel("Hello, Swing!");
```

Configure the layout manager for the frame and add components:

Example-

```
frame.setLayout(new FlowLayout());
frame.add(button);
frame.add(label);
```

Register event listeners and define event-handling code (e.g., button click):

Example-

```
button.addActionListener(e -> {
   label.setText("Button Clicked!");
});
```

Set the frame's size, visibility, and close operation:

Example-

```
frame.setSize(300, 150);
frame.setVisible(true);
frame.setDefaultCloseOperation(JFrame.EXIT_ON_CLOSE);
```

4. Swing Components:

Swing offers a wide range of components, including:

- **JButton:** A clickable button.
- **JLabel:** A non-editable text label.
- **JTextField:** A single-line text input field.
- **JTextArea:** A multi-line text input area.
- **JComboBox:** A drop-down selection list.
- **JCheckBox and JRadioButton**: Checkboxes and radio buttons for user choices.
- **JScrollPane:** A scrollable container for other components.
- **JFileChooser**: A dialog for file selection.

5. Advanced Features:

Swing provides advanced features such as:

- **Custom Components:** You can create custom Swing components by extending existing classes or implementing interfaces.
- **Custom Look and Feel:** You can customize the appearance of your GUI by creating custom look-and-feel (L&F) themes.
- **Dialogs and Popups:** Swing allows you to create dialog boxes, message boxes, and pop-up menus.

6. JavaFX (Optional):

While Swing is the traditional choice for Java GUI programming, JavaFX is a more modern and feature-rich framework for building rich client applications. JavaFX provides advanced features for multimedia, 2D/3D graphics, and more. Consider using JavaFX for new projects or when you need advanced graphical capabilities.

In summary, GUI programming in Java with Swing involves creating user interfaces by arranging and customizing Swing components within containers. Event handling and layout management are key aspects of building functional and user-friendly GUI applications in Java.

5.2 Swing Components and Layout Managers

Swing components and layout managers are crucial for designing user interfaces in Java Swing applications. Swing components are graphical elements like buttons, labels, and text fields, while layout managers control their placement and sizing within containers. Let's explore Swing components and layout managers in Java:

5.2.1. Swing Components:

Swing provides a wide range of components that you can use to create a user interface. Some of the commonly used Swing components include:

a. JButton: A clickable button that triggers an action when pressed.

Example-

```
JButton button = new JButton("Click Me");
```

b. JLabel: A non-editable text label used to display static text or information.

Example-

```
JLabel label = new JLabel("Welcome to Swing!");
```

c. JTextField: A single-line text input field for user input.

Example-

```
JTextField textField = new JTextField(20); // 20 characters wide
```

d. JTextArea: A multi-line text input area for longer text or paragraphs.

Example-

```
JTextArea textArea = new JTextArea(10, 30); // 10 rows, 30 columns
```

e. JComboBox: A drop-down selection list for choosing from a list of options.

Example-

```
String[] options = {"Option 1", "Option 2", "Option 3"};
JComboBox<String> comboBox = new JComboBox<>(options);
```

f. JCheckBox and JRadioButton: Checkboxes and radio buttons for user choices.

Example-

```
JCheckBox checkBox = new JCheckBox("Check me");
JRadioButton radioButton = new JRadioButton("Select one");
```

g. JScrollPane: A container for other components that provides scrollbars when the content exceeds the visible area.

Example-

```
JTextArea textArea = new JTextArea(10, 30);
JScrollPane scrollPane = new JScrollPane(textArea);
```

2. Layout Managers:

Layout managers are responsible for arranging and sizing components within a container. Swing offers several layout managers to suit different design needs. Some of the commonly used ones include:

a. FlowLayout: Components are laid out in a row or column, one after the other, like text in a paragraph.

Example-

```
JPanel panel = new JPanel(new FlowLayout());
```

b. BorderLayout: Components are placed in one of five regions: NORTH, SOUTH, EAST, WEST, and CENTER. Useful for building a simple page with distinct regions.

Example-

```
JPanel panel = new JPanel(new BorderLayout());
```

c. GridLayout: Components are arranged in a grid with specified rows and columns.

Example-

JPanel panel = new JPanel(new GridLayout(3, 2)); // 3 rows, 2 columns

d. GridBagLayout: Offers fine-grained control over component placement in a grid layout. It's more complex but highly flexible.

Example-

JPanel panel = new JPanel(new GridBagLayout());

e. BoxLayout: Components are arranged in a single row or column. Useful for creating vertical or horizontal layouts.

Example-

JPanel panel = new JPanel();
panel.setLayout(new BoxLayout(panel, BoxLayout.Y_AXIS)); // Vertical layout

f. CardLayout: Manages a stack of components where only one is visible at a time. Useful for creating wizard-like interfaces.

Example-

JPanel cardPanel = new JPanel(new CardLayout());

3. Choosing the Right Layout Manager:

Selecting the appropriate layout manager depends on your application's requirements and design. You can also combine different layout managers within nested containers to achieve complex layouts.

4. Adding Components to Containers:

After creating components and specifying a layout manager for a container, add the components to the container using the add() method.

Example-

panel.add(button);
panel.add(label);
panel.add(textField);
// ... add more components

5. Event Handling:

Once you've designed your user interface with Swing components, you can add event listeners to respond to user interactions, such as button clicks or text field input.

Swing components and layout managers provide the foundation for building rich graphical user interfaces in Java Swing applications. By selecting the appropriate components and layout managers and designing your user interface effectively, you can create intuitive and visually appealing applications.

5.2.2 Hierarchy for swing components

Swing is a graphical user interface (GUI) library in Java that provides a rich set of components for building desktop applications. Swing components are organized into a hierarchical structure. Below is a simplified hierarchy of some common Swing components:

1. java.awt.Component (Abstract Class)

Base class for all GUI components.

java.awt.Container
javax.swing.JComponent

Base class for all Swing components.

javax.swing.AbstractButton

Base class for buttons.

javax.swing.JButton
javax.swing.JCheckBox
javax.swing.JRadioButton
javax.swing.JToggleButton
javax.swing.JComboBox
javax.swing.JList
javax.swing.JSlider
javax.swing.JSpinner
javax.swing.JProgressBar
javax.swing.JTabbedPane
javax.swing.JToolBar
javax.swing.JMenuBar
javax.swing.JPopupMenu
javax.swing.JScrollPane
javax.swing.JViewport
javax.swing.JRootPane

javax.swing.JPanel
javax.swing.JLayeredPane
javax.swing.JDesktopPane
javax.swing.JInternalFrame

This hierarchy represents some of the key Swing components and their relationships. Swing provides a wide range of components for various GUI elements, including buttons, text fields, labels, containers, menus, and more. Each component has its own unique features and behavior. You can use these components to create sophisticated desktop applications with graphical user interfaces.

5.2.3 Containers available in swing

Swing, a GUI (Graphical User Interface) framework in Java, provides several types of containers that are used to organize and manage the placement of GUI components (such as buttons, text fields, and labels) within a graphical user interface. These containers help create the structure and layout of your GUI application. Here are the main containers available in Swing:

JFrame: JFrame is the top-level container for creating a windowed application. It represents the main application window that typically contains other Swing components.

JPanel: JPanel is a versatile container that is often used to group and organize components. It does not have a border or title bar and is commonly placed inside other containers like JFrame or other JPanels.

JDialog: JDialog is a top-level container that represents a dialog or pop-up window. It is typically used for secondary windows or user input forms.

JApplet: JApplet is a container used for creating Java applets, which are small, embedded Java applications typically run in web browsers.

JWindow: JWindow is a top-level container that represents a window without any decorations (no title bar or borders). It is often used for splash screens or custom windows.

JScrollPane: JScrollPane is a specialized container that provides scrolling capabilities for its child components. It is often used with components like JTextArea or JTable to display large amounts of data.

JTabbedPane: JTabbedPane is a container that allows you to create a tabbed interface, where each tab represents a different content panel. Users can switch between tabs to view different sections of your application.

JSplitPane: JSplitPane is a container that divides its content into two resizable panes with a divider in between. It is often used to create resizable split views or panes.

JLayeredPane: JLayeredPane is a container that allows you to layer components on top of each other. You can specify the depth or Z-order of components within the layered pane.

JDesktopPane and JInternalFrame: JDesktopPane is a container used for creating multiple document interface (MDI) applications, where multiple internal frames (child windows) can be displayed within the main application window.

These Swing containers provide a variety of options for organizing and structuring your GUI applications. You can use them to create complex and visually appealing user interfaces in Java. The choice of container depends on the specific requirements of your application and the desired layout and structure of your GUI.

5.2.4 Layout Manager

A layout manager is a component in graphical user interface (GUI) programming that is responsible for determining the size and position of GUI components (such as buttons, text fields, and labels) within a container (such as a window or panel). Layout managers are used to organize and control the layout of these components, ensuring that they are displayed correctly on the screen. The main purpose of layout managers is to create flexible and responsive user interfaces that can adapt to different screen sizes, resolutions, and user preferences.

Here are some key points about layout managers:

Automatic Arrangement: Layout managers automatically arrange GUI components based on certain rules or algorithms defined by the layout manager. This eliminates the need for developers to manually specify the exact position and size of each component.

Platform Independence: Layout managers help in creating platform-independent GUIs. They abstract away the specifics of component positioning, making the GUI consistent across different operating systems and devices.

Responsive Design: Layout managers enable the creation of responsive user interfaces that can adapt to changes in the size of the container or window. This is essential for ensuring that the GUI remains usable on different screen sizes and orientations.

Separation of Concerns: Layout managers promote a separation of concerns in GUI code. They separate the logic of how components should be arranged (handled by the layout manager) from the logic of what those components do (handled by event handlers and business logic).

Flexibility: Different layout managers offer different layout strategies, allowing developers to choose the one that best suits their application's requirements. For example, some layout managers arrange components in a grid, while others arrange them in a flow or along the edges of a container.

Localization and Internationalization: Layout managers can assist in accommodating different languages and text lengths by adjusting the size and position of components. This is important for creating applications that can be easily translated and localized for different regions and languages.

Accessibility: Properly designed layouts contribute to better accessibility for users with disabilities. Layout managers can help ensure that components are organized in a logical and accessible manner, benefiting users who rely on screen readers and assistive technologies.

Commonly used layout managers in various GUI frameworks include BorderLayout, FlowLayout, GridLayout, and GridBagLayout in Java Swing, and similar options exist in other programming languages and frameworks. Each layout manager has its own rules and behaviours for arranging components, and developers choose the one that best fits the design goals and requirements of their application.

5.2.5 Use of Layout Manager

Here's a detailed explanation of the use of layout managers in GUI design:

Dynamic Component Arrangement: Layout managers enable developers to design GUIs that can adapt to different screen sizes and resolutions. They automatically adjust the position and size of components based on the available space, ensuring that the interface remains functional and visually pleasing.

Platform Independence: Layout managers help in creating platform-independent GUIs. Since different operating systems and devices may have varying window sizes and user interface conventions, layout managers abstract away the specifics of component positioning, making the GUI consistent across platforms.

Responsive Design: Layout managers facilitate responsive design, ensuring that your GUI components respond gracefully to changes in the size of the container or window. This is critical for modern applications that need to work on various devices with varying screen sizes, including desktops, tablets, and smartphones.

Ease of Maintenance: Using layout managers makes your GUI code more maintainable. Separating the layout logic from the component functionality makes it easier to modify the interface without affecting the core functionality of the application. This separation of concerns enhances code readability and maintainability.

Localization and Internationalization: Layout managers can assist in accommodating different languages and text lengths by adjusting the size and position of components accordingly. This helps in creating applications that can be easily translated and localized for different regions and languages.

Consistency: Layout managers ensure that components are consistently aligned, spaced, and sized according to the chosen layout manager's rules. This consistency enhances the overall user experience and makes the interface more aesthetically pleasing.

Accessibility: Properly designed layouts contribute to better accessibility for users with disabilities. Layout managers can help ensure that components are organized in a logical and accessible manner, which benefits users who rely on screen readers and other assistive technologies.

Simplicity: Layout managers simplify the development process by automating the positioning and sizing of components. Developers don't need to manually calculate and specify the exact coordinates and dimensions of each component, reducing the potential for errors and saving development time.

Adaptability to Device Changes: In a world with diverse devices, layout managers enable applications to adapt seamlessly to different screen sizes and orientations. This adaptability is crucial for maintaining a consistent and user-friendly experience across devices.

Choice of Layout Managers: Developers can choose from a variety of layout managers, each with its own set of rules and behaviours. This flexibility allows them to select the most appropriate layout manager for the specific needs of their application.

5.2.6 The significance of layout managers

Platform Independence: Layout managers help ensure that your GUI components are positioned and sized correctly regardless of the platform or device on which your application runs. This platform independence is essential for creating cross-platform applications that work consistently across different operating systems.

Responsive Design: Layout managers allow GUI components to adapt dynamically to changes in the window size or screen resolution. This ensures that your application's interface remains usable and visually appealing on a wide range of devices, from small mobile screens to large desktop monitors.

Separation of Concerns: Layout managers promote a separation of concerns in your code. They separate the logic of how components should be arranged from the logic of what those components do. This makes your code more modular, maintainable, and easier to understand.

Localization and Internationalization: Layout managers can help accommodate different languages and text lengths by adjusting the size and position of components as needed. This is crucial for creating applications that can be easily localized and internationalized.

Consistency and Aesthetics: Layout managers help maintain a consistent and aesthetically pleasing appearance for your application's user interface. They ensure that components are aligned, spaced, and sized appropriately, enhancing the overall user experience.

Ease of Development: While manually positioning and sizing GUI components is possible, it can be error-prone and time-consuming. Layout managers simplify the development process by automating the placement and sizing of components, saving developers from having to calculate and specify every detail.

Accessibility: Properly designed layouts can improve accessibility for users with disabilities. Layout managers can help ensure that components are organized in a logical and accessible manner, making it easier for screen readers and assistive technologies to interpret and convey information.

Adaptability to Device Changes: With the proliferation of various devices, such as smartphones, tablets, and desktop computers, layout managers help applications adapt to different screen sizes and orientations, ensuring a consistent and user-friendly experience.

5.2.7 Common layout manager in Java Swing

One commonly used layout manager in Java Swing is the FlowLayout. It's straightforward and easy to understand, making it a good choice for simple layouts.

FlowLayout: FlowLayout is a layout manager that arranges components in a single row (or column, depending on the orientation) from left to right (or top to bottom) within a container. When one row (or column) is filled, the components automatically wrap to the next row (or column).

Here are some key characteristics and details about the FlowLayout:

Alignment: By default, components within a FlowLayout container are centered horizontally and vertically. You can specify different alignment options, such as left, right, or center, using constructor parameters or setter methods.

Resizing: FlowLayout does not resize components. Components are displayed at their preferred size, and the layout manager simply arranges them in rows or columns.

Responsive: FlowLayout is responsive to changes in the container's size. As the container's width (or height) changes, components wrap to the next row (or column) to accommodate the available space.

Simple to Use: FlowLayout is simple to use and suitable for situations where you want components to be arranged in a linear fashion, similar to a flow of text.

Here's a basic example of using FlowLayout in Java Swing:

```
import javax.swing.*;
import java.awt.*;

public class FlowLayoutExample {
    public static void main(String[] args) {
        // Create a JFrame
        JFrame frame = new JFrame("FlowLayout Example");
        frame.setDefaultCloseOperation(JFrame.EXIT_ON_CLOSE);

        // Create a JPanel with FlowLayout
        JPanel panel = new JPanel(new FlowLayout());

        // Add some components to the panel
        panel.add(new JButton("Button 1"));
        panel.add(new JButton("Button 2"));
        panel.add(new JButton("Button 3"));

        // Add the panel to the frame
        frame.add(panel);

        // Set frame size and make it visible
        frame.setSize(300, 100);
        frame.setVisible(true);
    }
}
```

In this example, a JFrame contains a JPanel with FlowLayout, and three buttons are added to the panel. When you run the application, you'll see that the buttons are arranged in a single row, and if you resize the window, they wrap to the next row as needed.

While FlowLayout is simple and easy to use, it may not be suitable for complex layouts with more specific alignment and sizing requirements. In such cases, other layout managers like BorderLayout, GridLayout, or GridBagLayout may be more appropriate.

5.3 Event Handling in Swing

Event handling in Swing is a crucial aspect of developing interactive graphical user interfaces (GUIs) in Java. Swing components generate events when users interact with them, such as clicking a button or typing text. These events need to be captured and processed by event listeners. Here's an overview of event handling in Swing:

1. Event Sources:

Swing components, such as buttons, text fields, and checkboxes, are event sources. They generate events when certain user actions occur. For example:

- A JButton generates an ActionEvent when clicked.
- A JTextField generates KeyEvent events when the user types into it.
- A JComboBox generates ItemEvent events when the user selects an item from the dropdown.

2. Event Listeners:

Event listeners are objects responsible for capturing and responding to events generated by event sources. In Swing, listeners are typically implemented as interfaces. Common Swing listener interfaces include:

- **ActionListener:** Listens for ActionEvent events, commonly used with buttons and menu items.
- **MouseListener:** Listens for MouseEvent events, used for mouse-related events like clicks and movements.
- **KeyListener:** Listens for KeyEvent events, used for keyboard input events.
- **ItemListener:** Listens for ItemEvent events, often used with components like JCheckBox and JComboBox.

3. Registering Event Listeners:

To handle events, you need to register event listeners with the relevant event sources. You can use methods like addActionListener(), addMouseListener(), and addKeyListener() to register listeners for specific event types.

For example, to register an action listener for a button:

Example-

```
JButton button = new JButton("Click Me");
button.addActionListener(new ActionListener() {
   @Override
   public void actionPerformed(ActionEvent e) {
      // Handle the button click event here
   }
});
```

4. Event Classes:

Swing defines various event classes to represent different types of user interactions. These classes provide information about the event, such as the source component and event-specific details. Common Swing event classes include:

- **ActionEvent**: Contains information about actions like button clicks.
- **MouseEvent:** Represents mouse events like clicks, movements, and drags.
- **KeyEvent:** Represents keyboard events like key presses and releases.
- **ItemEvent:** Represents item-related events, often used with checkboxes and combo boxes.

5. Event Dispatch Thread (EDT):

Swing components and event handling must occur on the Event Dispatch Thread (EDT) to ensure thread safety. The EDT is responsible for handling GUI events and updates. The main method of a Swing application runs on the EDT by default. To schedule tasks on the EDT, you can use SwingUtilities.invokeLater().

Example-

```
SwingUtilities.invokeLater(new Runnable() {
   @Override
   public void run() {
      // Create and display the GUI components
   }
});
```

6. Event Handling Flow:

When an event occurs, such as a button click, the event source generates the corresponding event object. This event object is then dispatched to the registered event listener(s). The listener's callback method (e.g., actionPerformed()) is invoked, and you can implement the desired behaviour in this method.

7. Anonymous Inner Classes and Lambdas:

In event handling, it's common to use anonymous inner classes or lambda expressions to implement event listeners concisely. For example, with Java 8 and later, you can use lambdas:

Example-

```
button.addActionListener(e -> {
   // Handle the button click event here
});
```

8. Custom Event Handling:

You can create custom event types by defining your event classes that extend java.util.EventObject. Implement custom listener interfaces for these events and register them with event sources to handle these custom events.

9. Event Propagation:

Swing components form a hierarchy, and events can propagate up or down this hierarchy. For example, mouse events can propagate from the top-level container down to the specific component that was clicked. Understanding event propagation is essential for handling events at the right level in the component hierarchy.

10. Event Handling Best Practices:

Keep event-handling code concise and focused on the specific action of interest.

Avoid blocking the EDT with long-running tasks; use worker threads for heavy processing.

When modifying Swing components in response to an event, use SwingUtilities.invokeLater() to ensure updates occur on the EDT.

Understanding event handling is vital for creating responsive and interactive GUI applications in Java Swing. By effectively registering event listeners, handling events, and ensuring proper thread safety, you can develop Java Swing applications that provide a seamless user experience.

5.4 Creating Simple Swing Applications

Creating simple Swing applications in Java involves designing a graphical user interface (GUI) with components like buttons, labels, and text fields. Here's a step-by-step guide in detail:

1. Import Swing Classes:

Start by importing the necessary Swing classes:

Example-

```
import javax.swing.*;
```

2. Create a JFrame:

A JFrame is the main window of a Swing application. Create a new JFrame object:

Example-

```
JFrame frame = new JFrame("Simple Swing Application");
```

You can set the title of the frame by passing it as an argument to the constructor.

3. Create Swing Components:

Create the GUI components you want to include in your application. Here are some common Swing components:

JButton for buttons.

JLabel for labels.

JTextField for single-line text input.

JTextArea for multi-line text input.

JComboBox for drop-down lists.

Example-

```
JButton button = new JButton("Click Me");
JLabel label = new JLabel("Hello, Swing!");
```

4. Configure Layout Manager:

Choose a layout manager to control how components are arranged within the frame. Common layout managers include FlowLayout, BorderLayout, and GridLayout. Set the layout manager for the frame:

Example-

```
frame.setLayout(new FlowLayout());
```

5. Add Components to the Frame:

Add the components to the frame using the add() method:

Example-

```
frame.add(button);
frame.add(label);
```

6. Register Event Listeners:

If your application includes buttons or other interactive elements, register event listeners to handle user actions. For example, to handle a button click:

Example-

```
button.addActionListener(e -> {
   label.setText("Button Clicked!");
});
```

7. Set Frame Properties:

Set properties for the frame, such as its size, default close operation, and visibility:

Example-

```
frame.setSize(300, 150); // Set the frame size (width x height)
frame.setDefaultCloseOperation(JFrame.EXIT_ON_CLOSE); // Close operation
frame.setVisible(true); // Make the frame visible
```

The setSize() method sets the initial dimensions of the frame.

setDefaultCloseOperation() specifies what should happen when the user closes the window. JFrame.EXIT_ON_CLOSE exits the application.

setVisible(true) makes the frame visible to the user.

8. Run on the Event Dispatch Thread (EDT):

Swing applications should be run on the Event Dispatch Thread (EDT) for thread safety. You can use SwingUtilities.invokeLater() to launch your GUI:

Example-

```
SwingUtilities.invokeLater(() -> {
   // Create and display the GUI components
});
```

9. Full Example:

Here's a complete example of a simple Swing application:

Code-

```
import javax.swing.*;
public class SimpleSwingApp {
   public static void main(String[] args) {
      SwingUtilities.invokeLater(() -> {
         JFrame frame = new JFrame("Simple Swing Application");

         JButton button = new JButton("Click Me");
         JLabel label = new JLabel("Hello, Swing!");

         button.addActionListener(e -> {
            label.setText("Button Clicked!");
         });

         frame.setLayout(new FlowLayout());
         frame.add(button);
         frame.add(label);

         frame.setSize(300, 150);
         frame.setDefaultCloseOperation(JFrame.EXIT_ON_CLOSE);
         frame.setVisible(true);
      });
   }
}
```

Compile and run this code, and you'll see a basic Swing application with a button that changes a label's text when clicked. This example provides a foundation for creating simple Swing applications. You can further enhance your application by adding more components, implementing additional event handling, and customizing the layout to meet your requirements.

5.5 Introduction to Applets

An applet is a small Java program that runs within a web browser. Applets were popular in the early days of the internet for adding interactive content to web pages. While they have been largely replaced by other technologies like JavaScript and HTML5, it's still valuable to understand the basics of Java applets. In this detailed introduction, we'll cover various aspects of Java applets:

1. Applet Basics:

Applet vs. Application: An applet is different from a standalone Java application. Applets are designed to be embedded within HTML pages and run in a web browser, while applications are standalone programs that run independently.

Applet Lifecycle: Applets have a well-defined lifecycle, consisting of methods like init(), start(), stop(), and destroy(). These methods are called by the browser at various stages of an applet's existence.

2. Embedding Applets:

To include an applet in an HTML page, you can use the <applet> or <object> tag. Here's an example:

Example-

```
<applet code="MyApplet.class" width="300" height="200">
  <!-- Alternative content if the applet doesn't run -->
</applet>
```

The code attribute specifies the name of the applet class file.

width and height specify the dimensions of the applet's display area.

3. Required Applet Methods:

init(): This method is called when the applet is first loaded. It's typically used for one-time initialization tasks, such as setting up variables or loading resources.

start(): The start() method is called when the applet is ready to begin execution. You can use it to start animations, initialize timers, or perform other tasks.

stop(): This method is called when the applet is temporarily stopped, such as when the user switches to another browser tab. You can use it to pause animations or release resources.

destroy(): The destroy() method is called when the applet is about to be unloaded. It's used for cleanup tasks like closing files or database connections.

4. Applet Communication:

Applets can communicate with their hosting HTML page and with other applets on the same page. Communication is typically done using parameters, JavaScript, or shared resources.

Parameters: You can pass parameters to an applet using the <param> tag in the HTML code. The applet can retrieve these parameters using the getParameter() method.

Example-

```
<applet code="MyApplet.class" width="300" height="200">
  <param name="message" value="Hello, Applet!">
</applet>
```

JavaScript: Applets can communicate with JavaScript code on the web page. JavaScript can call applet methods and retrieve values from the applet.

5. Applet Security:

Due to security concerns, modern web browsers have become increasingly restrictive about running applets. Applets are subject to various security restrictions and may require the user's permission to run. Applets can also be digitally signed to gain more privileges.

6. Applet Deprecated Status:

Java applets have become largely obsolete due to security issues, performance concerns, and the availability of more modern web technologies like JavaScript, HTML5, and WebAssembly. Major web browsers have deprecated or removed support for Java applets. As a result, they are no longer a recommended or practical choice for web development.

In summary, Java applets are small Java programs that can be embedded in web pages to provide interactive content. While they played a significant role in web development history, they have largely been replaced by other web technologies due to security and performance considerations. Understanding the basics of applets can be valuable for historical context but is not recommended for contemporary web development.

5.6 Applet Life Cycle and Parameters

In Java, an applet's life cycle and parameters are crucial aspects of its behavior and functionality when embedded within a web page. Understanding these concepts in detail is essential for developing Java applets. Let's explore the applet life cycle and parameters:

1. Applet Life Cycle:

The life cycle of a Java applet consists of several distinct stages that occur when the applet is loaded, started, stopped, and destroyed. The following methods are part of the applet's life cycle:

Initialization (init()):

The init() method is the first method called when the applet is loaded by the browser.

It's typically used for one-time initialization tasks, such as setting up variables, loading resources, or configuring the applet's initial state.

The init() method is called only once during the applet's lifetime.

Starting (start()):
The start() method is called after the init() method.
It's invoked when the applet is ready to begin execution, such as when the web page is first loaded or when the applet regains focus after being stopped.
You can use the start() method to start animations, initialize timers, or perform other tasks that should begin running when the applet becomes active.
The start() method may be called multiple times if the applet is stopped and restarted.
Stopping (stop()):
The stop() method is called when the applet is temporarily stopped, such as when the user switches to another browser tab or navigates away from the page containing the applet.
It is essential for pausing animations, releasing resources, or any cleanup tasks that should occur when the applet becomes inactive.
Like the start() method, stop() may be called multiple times during the applet's lifetime.
Destroying (destroy()):
The destroy() method is called when the applet is about to be unloaded, typically when the web page containing the applet is closed or refreshed.
It is used for cleanup tasks like closing files, database connections, or any resources that need to be released.
Similar to init(), the destroy() method is called only once during the applet's lifetime.
2. Applet Parameters:
Applet parameters are values that can be passed to an applet from the HTML code that embeds the applet. These parameters allow you to configure the applet's behaviour dynamically. To specify applet parameters in HTML, you use the <param> tag within the <applet> tag:
Example-
```
<applet code="MyApplet.class" width="300" height="200">
  <param name="paramName" value="paramValue">
</applet>
```
The code attribute specifies the name of the applet's class file.
width and height determine the applet's display size.
Applet parameters are retrieved within the applet using the getParameter() method:
Example-
```
String paramValue = getParameter("paramName");
```
Applet parameters are typically used to customize the applet's behavior or provide initial data. For example, you might use parameters to specify a configuration file, customize the applet's appearance, or pass user-specific information.
In summary, understanding the life cycle and parameters of a Java applet is essential for creating interactive applets that behave as expected when embedded within web pages. The life cycle methods (init(), start(), stop(), and destroy()) help manage the applet's behaviour at various stages of its execution, while parameters allow for dynamic configuration and customization of the applet's behaviour.

5.7 JButton

In Java, the JButton class is a part of the Swing library, which is used for creating graphical user interfaces (GUIs). While JButton itself is a class that represents a standard push-button component, there are no direct subclasses of JButton provided by the Swing library.
However, it's common to customize the appearance and behavior of buttons by extending the JButton class or by using custom components that are based on JButton. You can create subclasses of JButton to add custom functionality or styling to buttons in your Swing applications.
For example, you might create subclasses of JButton to implement specialized buttons like:

- **IconButton:** A button that displays an icon instead of text.
- **ColorButton:** A button that changes its background color when clicked.
- **ToggleButton:** A button that behaves as a toggle switch, staying pressed when clicked.
- **GradientButton**: A button with a gradient background.
- **Imagechapter 1Button:** A button that toggles between two different images.

These subclasses of JButton would extend the functionality of the base JButton class to meet specific requirements in your GUI application. While Swing itself doesn't provide these subclasses out of the box, you can easily create your own by extending JButton and customizing it according to your needs.

5.8 item event

In Java, the ItemEvent is an event class used to handle events related to components that allow user selection of items, such as Checkbox, Choice, List, and CheckboxMenuItem. The ItemEvent class provides information about the source of the event, the selected item, and its state change (selected or deselected).

The sources for ItemEvent typically include components that allow the user to interact with and select items. Here are some common sources for ItemEvent:

- **Checkbox:** The Checkbox component is a user interface element that allows the user to select or deselect an option. When the state of a checkbox changes (e.g., from selected to deselected or vice versa), it generates an ItemEvent.
- **Choice:** The Choice component, also known as a dropdown or combo box, allows the user to select one option from a list of choices. When the user selects an item from the dropdown list, it generates an ItemEvent.
- **List:** The List component presents a list of items from which the user can select one or more items. When the user clicks an item in the list, it generates an ItemEvent.
- **CheckboxMenuItem:** The CheckboxMenuItem is a menu item in a menu that can be checked or unchecked by the user. When the user checks or unchecks a CheckboxMenuItem, it generates an ItemEvent.
- **PopupMenu:** Pop-up menus, often used in combination with components like CheckboxMenuItem, can generate ItemEvent when their menu items are selected or deselected.

To handle ItemEvent for these sources, you typically implement an ItemListener interface, which defines the itemStateChanged method. This method is called when an item's state changes, and it receives an ItemEvent object that contains information about the event, such as the source of the event, the selected item, and its state (selected or deselected).
Here's an example of how you might implement an ItemListener to handle ItemEvent for a Checkbox:

```
import java.awt.*;
import java.awt.event.*;

public class CheckboxExample extends Frame implements ItemListener {
  private Checkbox checkbox;

  public CheckboxExample() {
    checkbox = new Checkbox("Check Me");
    checkbox.addItemListener(this);
    add(checkbox);
    setSize(300, 200);
    setVisible(true);
  }

  public void itemStateChanged(ItemEvent e) {
    if (e.getSource() == checkbox) {
      if (checkbox.getState()) {
        System.out.println("Checkbox is selected");
      } else {
        System.out.println("Checkbox is deselected");
      }
    }
  }

  public static void main(String[] args) {
    new CheckboxExample();
  }
}
```

In this example, the Checkbox generates ItemEvent when it is checked or unchecked, and the itemStateChanged method is called to handle these events.

5.8 Usage of Flow Layout and Card Layout in Java Applet

1. FlowLayout in Java Applet:

FlowLayout is a layout manager in Java that arranges components in a linear fashion, flowing from left to right (or top to bottom) within a container. It's suitable for creating simple, flowing layouts. Here's how you can use FlowLayout in a Java applet:

Example-

```
import java.applet.Applet;
import java.awt.*;

public class FlowLayoutExample extends Applet {
  public void init() {
```

```
        setLayout(new FlowLayout());

        add(new Button("Button 1"));
        add(new Button("Button 2"));
        add(new Button("Button 3"));
        add(new Button("Button 4"));
        add(new Button("Button 5"));
    }
}
```

In the code above, we create a Java applet and set its layout manager to FlowLayout using setLayout(new FlowLayout()). We then add five buttons to the applet. When you run this applet, the buttons will be arranged horizontally in a flow from left to right, like this:

Example-

[Button 1] [Button 2] [Button 3] [Button 4] [Button 5]

If you resize the applet's window, the buttons will wrap to the next row as needed to fit the available space.

2. CardLayout in Java Applet:

CardLayout is a layout manager in Java that allows you to manage multiple components as if they were stacked on top of each other like a deck of cards. Only one component is visible at a time, and you can switch between components programmatically. It's useful for creating wizard-style interfaces or tabbed views. Here's how you can use CardLayout in a Java applet:

Example-

```
import java.applet.Applet;
import java.awt.*;
import java.awt.event.ActionEvent;
import java.awt.event.ActionListener;

public class CardLayoutExample extends Applet implements ActionListener {
    CardLayout cardLayout;

    public void init() {
        cardLayout = new CardLayout();
        setLayout(cardLayout);

        Button button1 = new Button("Card 1");
        Button button2 = new Button("Card 2");
        Button button3 = new Button("Card 3");

        button1.addActionListener(this);
        button2.addActionListener(this);
        button3.addActionListener(this);

        add(button1, "Card 1");
        add(button2, "Card 2");
        add(button3, "Card 3");
    }

    public void actionPerformed(ActionEvent e) {
        cardLayout.next(this);
    }
}
```

In the code above, we create a Java applet and set its layout manager to CardLayout using setLayout(cardLayout). We then add three buttons with labels "Card 1," "Card 2," and "Card 3" to the applet. These buttons are associated with different cards. When a button is clicked, the actionPerformed method is called, which uses cardLayout.next(this) to switch to the next card in the layout.

Initially, only the "Card 1" button is visible. Clicking it will switch to "Card 2," and so on. This behavior is similar to flipping through cards in a deck.

5.9 AWT

AWT, which stands for Abstract Window Toolkit, is one of the foundational libraries in Java for creating graphical user interfaces (GUIs). AWT provides a set of classes and methods that allow developers to build cross-platform, platform-independent graphical applications in Java. It is part of the Java Standard Library and has been a core component of Java since its early versions.

Here are some key features and components of AWT in Java:

Components: AWT provides a wide range of GUI components, such as buttons, labels, text fields, checkboxes, radio buttons, lists, and more. These components are represented by classes like Button, Label, TextField, Checkbox, and List.

Layout Managers: AWT includes layout managers (e.g., FlowLayout, BorderLayout, GridLayout, GridBagLayout) that help organize and arrange GUI components within containers. Layout managers provide flexibility in designing the visual layout of the GUI.

Event Handling: AWT supports event-driven programming, allowing you to define event listeners and handle events generated by GUI components. Events include mouse clicks, keyboard input, window actions, and more. Event handling in AWT involves implementing listener interfaces like ActionListener, MouseListener, and KeyListener.

Graphics and Drawing: AWT provides a Graphics class for drawing shapes, text, and images on GUI components. You can customize the appearance of components and create custom graphics using methods like drawLine(), drawRect(), drawString(), and more.

Containers: AWT includes container classes like Frame, Panel, Window, and Dialog that serve as containers for organizing and managing GUI components. The top-level container is typically a Frame, which represents the main window of an application.

Platform Independence: AWT is designed to be platform-independent, allowing you to write GUI code once and run it on various operating systems without modification. AWT components and layouts adapt to the native look and feel of the underlying platform.

Event Dispatch Thread (EDT): AWT applications run on a single thread known as the Event Dispatch Thread (EDT). All GUI-related events and updates are processed on the EDT to ensure thread safety.

Swing (JFC): While AWT provides basic GUI components and functionality, Swing (part of the Java Foundation Classes or JFC) is an extension of AWT that offers a more advanced set of GUI components and a more modern look and feel. Swing is built on top of AWT but provides additional features.

Despite the availability of Swing and more modern GUI libraries like JavaFX, AWT remains a fundamental part of Java's GUI capabilities and can still be used for building simple graphical applications or for scenarios where platform independence is crucial.

It's important to note that AWT's appearance may not be as modern as more recent GUI libraries, but it remains a valuable choice for specific use cases and legacy applications. For more advanced and feature-rich GUI applications, Swing or JavaFX is often preferred.

5.10 Merits of Swing over AWT

Swing components in Java offer several advantages over the older AWT (Abstract Window Toolkit) components. Here are some of the key merits of Swing components compared to AWT:

Platform Independence: Swing components are implemented entirely in Java and do not rely on platform-specific code or native libraries. This makes Swing applications highly platform-independent, allowing them to run consistently across different operating systems without modification.

Rich Look and Feel: Swing provides a pluggable look and feel (PLAF) mechanism, allowing developers to customize the appearance and behaviour of their applications. This results in a more modern and aesthetically pleasing user interface compared to AWT, which uses the native platform's appearance.

Lightweight Rendering: Swing components are lightweight in terms of memory usage and rendering performance. They are not based on heavyweight native components, which consume more system resources. This makes Swing more efficient for creating complex and interactive user interfaces.

Double Buffering: Swing components support double buffering by default, which reduces flickering when components are repainted. This results in smoother and more visually appealing animations and updates.

Accessibility: Swing components provide better support for accessibility features, making them more accessible to users with disabilities. Features like keyboard navigation and screen reader compatibility are easier to implement in Swing.

Rich Component Set: Swing offers a broader and more versatile set of components than AWT. It includes advanced components like tables, trees, tabbed panes, sliders, spinners, text components, and more, making it easier to create feature-rich GUIs.

Customization and Extensibility: Swing components are highly customizable and extensible. Developers can easily create custom components and behaviours by subclassing Swing classes or by implementing custom rendering and event handling.

Layout Managers: Swing provides a range of layout managers that make it easier to design complex and resizable user interfaces. Layout managers help ensure that components are positioned and sized correctly as the window is resized.
Advanced Controls: Swing components offer advanced controls like tables and trees, which are crucial for creating data-intensive applications, such as spreadsheet programs and file explorers. These controls are not available in AWT.
Internationalization and Localization: Swing components provide better support for internationalization and localization. They handle text rendering and bidirectional text more effectively, making it easier to create applications for a global audience.
Consistency Across Platforms: Swing components offer a consistent behaviour and appearance across different platforms, which is not always the case with AWT components. This ensures that the user experience remains consistent regardless of the underlying operating system.
Advanced Event Handling: Swing provides a more robust event handling mechanism, allowing developers to register event listeners for fine-grained control over user interactions and component behaviours.

While Swing has many advantages over AWT, it's worth noting that Swing applications may have slightly higher memory overhead due to the additional framework code and the Swing component architecture. However, the benefits in terms of flexibility, look and feel, and cross-platform compatibility make Swing a preferred choice for modern Java GUI development.

Exercise

Exercise 1 – MCQ

Q 1. Which of the following is NOT a layout manager in Swing for organizing components?
a) FlowLayout
b) BorderLayout
c) GridLayout
d) TextLayout

Q 2. In Java applets, what method is called when an applet is initialized and should be used for one-time setup tasks?
a) start()
b) init()
c) stop()
d) destroy()

Exercise 2 – True/ False

Q 1. In Swing, event handling is primarily accomplished by directly implementing event listener interfaces such as ActionListener for handling button clicks.

Q 2. The stop() method in a Java applet is always called before the init() method during the applet's life cycle

Exercise 3 – Fill in the blanks

Q 1. To create a graphical user interface (GUI) in Java, you can use Swing components such as _______, _______, and _______ to build the user interface elements.

Q 2. In Java applets, the _______ method is automatically called when the applet is first loaded into a web browser, making it suitable for initialization tasks.

Exercise 4 – Match case

Q 1. Match the Java Swing components with their primary usage:
i. JButton ()
ii. JTextField ()
iii. JLabel ()
iv. JPanel ()

Descriptions:
a. Provides a container for other components with flexible layout.
b. Used to display and handle button clicks.
c. Used to display text or image, often with descriptions.
d. Allows users to input single-line text.

Exercise 5 – One word answer

Q 1. What is the primary purpose of the JTextArea component in Java Swing?

Q 2. Which Java Swing component is commonly used for selecting items from a dropdown list?

Exercise 6 – Small answer

Q 1. What is the primary purpose of the ActionListener interface in Java Swing?

Q 2. Which layout manager in Swing is commonly used for arranging components in a single row or column?

Exercise 7 – Long answer

Q 1. Explain the concept of event handling in Java Swing. Provide an example of a Swing component and how you would attach an event listener to it.
Q 2. Describe the purpose and use cases of the JScrollPane component in Java Swing. Provide an example scenario where using JScrollPane would be beneficial.

Answer:

Exercise 1. Q 1: d) TextLayout Q 2: b) init ()
Exercise 2. Q 1: True Q 2: False
Exercise 3. Q 1: JButton, JTextField, JLabel Q 2: init ()
Exercise 4. Q 1: i JButton () – b ii. JTextField () - a iii. JLabel() – d iv. JPanel () - b
Exercise 5. Q 1: Text Q 2: JComboBox

Previous Year Questions

Q 1. What is the role of event listeners in event handling? List the Java event listeners (JNTU -B.Tech.- 2018)
Q 2. Write an applet to display the mouse cursor position in that applet window. (JNTU -B.Tech.- 2018)
Q 3. Give the subclasses of JButton class. (JNTU -B.Tech.- 2018)
Q 4. What are the sources for item event? (JNTU -B.Tech. -2017)
Q 5. Give the hierarchy for swing components. (JNTU -B.Tech. -2017)
Q 6. Explain the life cycle of an applet. (JNTU -B.Tech. -2017)
Q 7. Why swing components are preferred over AWT components? (JNTU -B.Tech. -2017)
Q 8. Is Applet more secure than application program? Justify your answer. (JNTU -B.Tech.- 2016)
Q 9. What are the merits of swing components over AWT? (JNTU -B.Tech.- 2016)
Q 10. Differentiate between Swing and AWT. (SPPU – BCA - 2015)
Q 11. What are the containers available in swing? (SPPU – BCA - 2015)
Q 12. Compare Applets with application programs. (SPPU – BCA - 2015)
Q 13. What is an Applet? Explain its Lifecycle. (SPPU – BCA - 2015)
Q 14. What are applets? (Punjab Technical University MCA -2015)
Q 15. Explain in detail the lifecycle of applet. (Punjab Technical University MCA -2015)
Q 16. Which method is used to specify containers layout? Write its syntax. (SPPU – BCA - 2015)
Q 17. What is Layout Manager? Explain any one in detail. (SPPU – BCA - 2015)
Q 18. What is the significance of layout managers? Discuss briefly various layout managers. (SPPU – BCA - 2015)
Q 19. Give an overview of JButton class. (SPPU – BCA - 2015)
Q 20. Explain the use of layout managers. (JNTU -B.Tech.- 2016)
Q 21. What is a layout managers? Explain layouts with example. (IGNOU MCA 2011)
Q 22. What is layout manager? Which is the default layout manager? Differentiate among the way of managing components by different layouts. (IGNOU MCA 2011)
Q 23. Compare the different layout managers in briefs. (IGNOU MCA 2012)
Q 24. What do you mean by an event? Explain different components of an event. (IGNOU MCA 2012)
Q 25. Explain the difference between application and applet? (IGNOU MCA 2012)
Q 26. What are Java controls and containers? (IGNOU MCA 2013)
Q 27. What is Java applet? How is it different from Java application program? (IGNOU MCA 2014)
Q 28. Explain the usage of Flow Layout and Card Layout in Java Applet with diagram. (IGNOU MCA 2016)

Previous Year Solved Papers

Q. 1. Explain how to set font of an applet using font class. Give suitable code segment to demonstrate. (RU BCA 2017)
Ans- To set the font of an applet using the **Font** class in Java, you can create a new **Font** object with the desired font type, style, and size, and then use it to set the font for specific components within the applet. Here is a simple code segment demonstrating how to set the font of an applet using the **Font** class:

```
import java.applet.Applet;
import java.awt.*;

public class FontApplet extends Applet {

    public void paint(Graphics g) {
        // Create a Font object with desired font type, style, and size
        Font font = new Font("Arial", Font.BOLD, 20);
```

```
        // Set the font for the Graphics context
        g.setFont(font);

        // Draw text using the set font
        g.drawString("Hello, this is a custom font!", 20, 40);
    }
}
```

In this example, the **FontApplet** class extends the **Applet** class and overrides the **paint** method to set the font using the **Font** class. The **Font** object is created with the font type "Arial", bold style, and size 20. The **setFont** method of the **Graphics** object **g** is used to set the font for the applet. Finally, the **drawString** method is used to display text using the set font at the specified coordinates (20, 40) within the applet. You can run this applet to see the text rendered with the specified font.

Q. 2. What are the different types or layout managers? Explain. (RU BCA 2017)

Ans- In Java, layout managers are used to determine the position and size of components within a container. They help in arranging and organizing the graphical components in a user interface. There are several types of layout managers available in Java, each with its own approach to managing the layout of components. Some of the commonly used layout managers include:

FlowLayout: It arranges components in a left-to-right flow, moving to the next line if the horizontal space is insufficient. It is simple and easy to use but may not be suitable for complex layouts.

BorderLayout: It divides the container into five regions: north, south, east, west, and center. Components can be added to each region, and the layout manager determines their positions and sizes accordingly.

GridLayout: It arranges components in a grid of rows and columns. All components are of equal size, and the layout adjusts the size of each component to fit the grid cells.

CardLayout: It allows multiple components to be stacked on top of each other, like a deck of cards. Only one component is visible at a time, and the layout manager provides methods to switch between the components.

GridBagLayout: It is a flexible and powerful layout manager that allows components to be arranged in a grid-like fashion. It supports specifying constraints for each component, such as minimum and maximum sizes, alignment, and padding.

BoxLayout: It arranges components either vertically or horizontally in a single row or column. It is useful for creating simple, linear layouts without the complexity of other layout managers.

GroupLayout: It is a versatile and powerful layout manager that allows developers to create complex and dynamic layouts. It provides extensive support for creating group-based layouts and managing the alignment and sizing of components.

Each layout manager has its own strengths and is suitable for different types of user interfaces. The choice of a layout manager depends on the specific requirements of the graphical interface and the desired arrangement of components within the container.

Q.3. What is AWT? Explain AWT package in brief. (RU BCA 2017)

Ans- AWT (Abstract Window Toolkit) is a set of classes and APIs in Java that provides the foundation for creating graphical user interfaces (GUIs) for Java applications. It is the original GUI toolkit for the Java programming language and is part of the Java Foundation Classes (JFC). AWT provides a collection of components and classes that allow developers to create and manage user interface elements such as windows, buttons, menus, and other graphical components.

Some key features and components of the AWT package include:

Components: AWT provides a variety of components such as buttons, labels, text fields, checkboxes, and menus that can be used to build the graphical interface of an application.

Layout Managers: AWT includes layout managers that help in arranging and organizing the components within containers, enabling developers to create flexible and dynamic layouts for their applications.

Event Handling: AWT supports event-driven programming, allowing developers to handle user interactions and events generated by the graphical components. It provides mechanisms to capture and process events such as mouse clicks, key presses, and window events.

Graphics and Fonts: AWT provides a set of classes for rendering graphics, drawing shapes, and displaying text, allowing developers to create custom graphics and visual elements within their applications.

Platform Independence: AWT components are designed to be platform-independent, providing a consistent look and feel across different operating systems and environments.

While AWT was the first GUI toolkit in Java, it has certain limitations and is considered less powerful compared to its successor, Swing. Swing, which is built on top of AWT, provides a more extensive set of components and features for creating modern and sophisticated GUIs. However, AWT remains an essential part of Java's GUI capabilities and is still used in some scenarios where lightweight components and platform independence are crucial.

Q.4. What is the order of method invocation in an Applet? (RU BCA 2017)

Ans- In an applet, the methods are invoked in a specific order during its life cycle. The life cycle of an applet is controlled by the browser or applet viewer, and several methods are called at different stages of the applet's existence. Here is the typical order of method invocation in an applet:

init(): This method is called when the applet is first created. It is used for applet initialization tasks such as initializing variables, setting up the UI components, and performing other one-time setup operations.

start(): The start method is called after the init method and whenever the applet is revisited or the web browser returns to the page containing the applet. It is used to start or resume the applet's execution after it has been initialized.

paint(Graphics g): The paint method is called when the applet needs to be rendered or repainted. It is automatically called by the system whenever the applet needs to redraw itself, such as when it is first displayed or when it is uncovered after being minimized.

stop(): The stop method is called when the applet is stopped or when the user navigates away from the web page containing the applet. It is used to stop or pause the applet's execution temporarily.

destroy(): The destroy method is called when the applet is about to be destroyed. It is used for cleanup tasks and releasing resources held by the applet before it is removed from memory.

The specific order of these method invocations forms the life cycle of the applet, ensuring that the applet is properly initialized, executed, and cleaned up according to its state and the user's interaction with the web page containing the applet.

Q.5. What is the difference between Swing and AWT components? (RU BCA 2017)

Ans-

Feature	AWT (Abstract Window Toolkit)	Swing
Platform	AWT components are platform-dependent and use native controls.	Swing components are lightweight and are not dependent on native controls, ensuring a consistent look and feel across different platforms.
Look and feel	AWT components inherit the look and feel of the underlying platform.	Swing components provide a pluggable look and feel, allowing developers to choose different styles and themes for the application.
Customisation	AWT components have limited customisation options.	Swing components offer extensive customisation options, including colours, fonts, borders, and other properties.
Complexity	AWT is relatively more straightforward and has a smaller set of components.	Swing is more complex and provides a richer set of components and functionalities.
Availability	AWT is part of the Java API and is available by default.	Swing is built on top of AWT and is available as an extension of the AWT library.
Examples	AWT components include **Button**, **Label**, **Checkbox**, and **TextField**.	Swing components include **JButton**, **JLabel**, **JCheckBox**, **JTextField**, and more advanced components such as **JTable**, **JTree**, and **JComboBox**.

Q.6 What is swing? (RU BCA 2017)

Ans- Swing is a powerful GUI (Graphical User Interface) toolkit for Java. It is part of the Java Foundation Classes (JFC) and is used for creating a rich set of user interfaces for Java applications. Swing provides a comprehensive set of GUI components that are lightweight, customizable, and platform-independent, making it one of the most popular choices for building desktop applications in Java. Some key features and components of Swing include:

Rich Set of Components: Swing provides a wide range of components, including buttons, labels, text fields, lists, tables, menus, and more, enabling developers to create interactive and feature-rich user interfaces.

Customization: Swing components are highly customizable, allowing developers to modify the appearance and behavior of components according to specific requirements. Customization options include setting colors, fonts, sizes, and various other properties.

Platform Independence: Swing is built on top of the Java AWT (Abstract Window Toolkit) and provides a consistent look and feel across different platforms, ensuring that Swing-based applications have a uniform appearance on various operating systems.

Event Handling: Swing supports event-driven programming, allowing developers to handle user interactions and system events efficiently. It provides a robust event handling mechanism that enables the creation of responsive and interactive applications.

Layout Managers: Swing provides a set of layout managers that help in arranging components within containers, enabling developers to create flexible and dynamic layouts for their applications.
Graphics and 2D API: Swing includes a powerful graphics and 2D API that allows developers to create and manipulate graphics, draw shapes, and render images, providing a rich and interactive visual experience for users.
Accessibility: Swing supports accessibility features, making it possible to create applications that are accessible to users with disabilities. It includes support for assistive technologies and adherence to accessibility standards.

Swing remains a popular choice for developing desktop applications in Java, offering a comprehensive set of components and functionalities that enable the creation of sophisticated and user-friendly graphical interfaces for various types of applications.

Q.7 Describe the Applet with example and also explain life cycle of applet (RU BCA 2018)

Ans- An applet in Java is a small program that is designed to be transmitted over the internet and executed within a web browser. It is a type of Java program that runs in a restricted environment called the "sandbox," which provides security and prevents the applet from accessing the local file system without explicit permission. Applets were commonly used to provide interactive features to web applications that couldn't be provided by HTML alone, although their usage has significantly declined due to security concerns and the advancement of web technologies.

Here's an example of a simple applet in Java:

```
import java.applet.Applet;
import java.awt.Graphics;

public class SimpleApplet extends Applet {
   public void paint(Graphics g) {
      g.drawString("Welcome to Applet", 20, 20);
   }
}
```

The applet's life cycle in Java consists of the following stages:

Initialization (init): The **init** method is called when the applet is initialized. It is invoked only once during the applet's life cycle. This method is used for initialization tasks such as setting up the UI components and initializing variables.
Start (start): The **start** method is called when the applet is started or when the web browser returns to the page containing the applet. It is used to start or resume the applet's execution after it has been initialized.
Stop (stop): The **stop** method is called when the applet is stopped or when the user navigates away from the web page containing the applet. It is used to stop or pause the applet's execution temporarily.
Destroy (destroy): The **destroy** method is called when the applet is about to be destroyed. It is used to perform cleanup tasks and release resources held by the applet before it is removed from memory.
Painting (paint): The **paint** method is called when the applet needs to be rendered or repainted. It is used to draw graphics and display visual elements on the applet's surface.

Understanding the life cycle of an applet in Java is essential for implementing the necessary logic and behaviors at each stage of the applet's execution, ensuring proper initialization, execution, and cleanup of resources.

Q. 8. Give difference between AWT and Swing package in details. (RU BCA 2018)

Ans-

Feature	AWT (Abstract Window Toolkit)	Swing
Level of Abstraction	AWT is the original set of Java classes for creating GUI components, providing a lower level of abstraction.	Swing is built on top of AWT and provides a higher level of abstraction with a richer set of GUI components and functionalities.
Look and Feel	AWT components use the look and feel of the underlying native platform, resulting in a less consistent appearance across different platforms.	Swing components have a consistent look and feel across different platforms, providing a more uniform appearance for GUI components.
Customization	AWT components have limited customization options, making it difficult to modify the appearance and behaviour of components.	Swing components offer extensive customization options, allowing developers to modify the appearance, behaviour, and functionality according to specific requirements.
Features and Components	AWT provides a basic set of GUI components, including buttons, labels, and menus, with limited functionality.	Swing offers an extended, more affluent set of GUI components, including advanced components like tables, trees, and scroll panes, with enhanced functionality and flexibility.
Performance	AWT is relatively lightweight and performs better for simple applications requiring essential GUI components.	Due to its high-level abstraction, Swing is relatively heavier, which can result in slightly slower performance compared to AWT for complex applications.
Popularity	AWT was the original Java GUI toolkit but has become less popular compared to Swing and other modern GUI libraries.	Swing gained popularity due to its rich set of components, customizable look and feel, and cross-platform compatibility, making it the preferred choice for building modern Java GUI applications.

Q. 9. What is Event Handling in java? Explain it with an example. (RU BCA 2018)

Ans- Event handling in Java refers to the mechanism of capturing and processing events, such as user actions (mouse clicks, keyboard inputs) or system-generated events, in a graphical user interface (GUI) application. It involves the use of event listeners and handlers to respond to user interactions or system events and perform specific actions based on those events.

Here's an example of event handling in Java using the **ActionListener** interface to handle button click events:

```
import java.awt.*;
import java.awt.event.*;
import javax.swing.*;

public class EventHandlingExample {
  public static void main(String[] args) {
    JFrame frame = new JFrame("Event Handling Example");
    JPanel panel = new JPanel();
    JButton button = new JButton("Click Me");

    button.addActionListener(new ActionListener() {
      public void actionPerformed(ActionEvent e) {
        JOptionPane.showMessageDialog(frame, "Button Clicked!");
      }
    });

    panel.add(button);
    frame.add(panel);
    frame.setSize(300, 200);
    frame.setDefaultCloseOperation(JFrame.EXIT_ON_CLOSE);
    frame.setVisible(true);
  }
}
```

In this example:

- We create a simple Swing application with a **JFrame** that contains a **JPanel**.
- A **JButton** is added to the panel.
- We attach an **ActionListener** to the button using an anonymous inner class. This listener listens for the button click event.
- When the button is clicked, the **actionPerformed** method of the **ActionListener** is triggered, displaying a message using **JOptionPane**.

This example demonstrates the handling of a button click event in a graphical user interface. Event handling in Java enables developers to create interactive applications where different actions can be triggered by user interactions or system events. By implementing event handling effectively, developers can create responsive and user-friendly applications that cater to user actions and provide dynamic feedback based on those actions.

Q.10. What is java AWT? (RU BCA 2018)

Ans- In Java, AWT (Abstract Window Toolkit) is a set of application programming interfaces (APIs) used for creating and managing graphical user interfaces (GUIs) in a Java application. AWT provides a collection of classes and methods that enable the creation of windows, buttons, menus, and other GUI components. It forms the foundation for creating simple and basic GUI-based applications in Java.

Key features and components of AWT include:

- **Components:** AWT provides a variety of components, such as buttons, labels, text fields, checkboxes, and more, that can be used to create a user interface for a Java application.
- **Layout Managers:** AWT includes layout managers that help to arrange the components within containers. Layout managers determine the position and size of components based on predefined rules, allowing for consistent and dynamic GUI design.
- **Event Handling:** AWT supports event handling for user interactions, such as mouse clicks, keyboard input, and window events. Developers can implement event listeners to respond to user actions and create interactive applications.
- **Graphics and Fonts:** AWT provides basic graphics and font capabilities for drawing simple shapes, images, and text on the screen.
- **Platform Independence:** AWT is designed to provide a platform-independent way of creating GUIs, ensuring that the appearance and behavior of the user interface remain consistent across different operating systems.

While AWT is a fundamental GUI toolkit in Java, it has some limitations, such as its relatively simple and less customizable appearance compared to modern GUI frameworks. As a result, Swing, a more advanced and customizable GUI toolkit built on top of AWT, became more popular for developing rich and complex GUI-based applications. Additionally, JavaFX, introduced later, further expanded the capabilities of Java for creating modern and visually appealing user interfaces. Despite these advancements, AWT remains an essential part of Java's GUI programming heritage.

Q.11. What is java Applet? (RU BCA 2018)

Ans- In Java, an applet is a small application that is designed to be transmitted over the Internet and executed within a web browser. Applets were primarily used to provide interactive features to web applications that could not be provided by HTML alone. However, their usage has significantly decreased over the years due to security concerns and the advancement of web technologies.

Key features of Java applets include:

- **Embeddable:** Applets can be embedded within an HTML page and executed within a web browser using the Java plugin.
- **Security Restrictions:** Applets run in a restricted environment known as the "sandbox," which imposes certain security restrictions to prevent them from accessing the local file system and other resources on the user's computer without permission.
- **Rich GUI:** Applets can provide a rich graphical user interface (GUI) by using the AWT (Abstract Window Toolkit) or Swing libraries to create interactive and visually appealing components.
- **Network Communication:** Applets can communicate with web servers and other resources over the network, enabling them to fetch and display dynamic content from the internet.
- **Lifecycle Methods:** Applets have several lifecycle methods, such as **init**, **start**, **stop**, and **destroy**, which allow developers to initialize resources, start and stop execution, and clean up resources when the applet is no longer needed.

While Java applets were popular in the past for creating interactive web content, their usage has significantly declined due to various factors, including security vulnerabilities, the rise of alternative web technologies like JavaScript and HTML5, and the deprecation of support for Java applets in many modern web browsers. As of my knowledge cutoff date in

September 2021, most web browsers have dropped support for Java applets due to security concerns and the shift towards more secure and efficient web technologies.

Q.12.Write a program using java to illustrate the applet with suitable example. (RU BCA 2019)

An applet in a Java program that runs in a Web browser. An applet can be a fully functional Java application because it has the entire Java API at its disposal. There are some important differences between an applet and a standalone Java application, including the following

Applets are designed to be embedded within an HTML page. When a user views an HTML page that contains an applet, the code for the applet is downloaded to the user's machine.

AJVM is required to view an applet. The JVM can be either a plug-in of the Web browser or a separate runtime environment.

The JVM on the user's machine creates an instance of the applet class and invokes various methods during the applet's lifetime.

Applets have strict security rules that are enforced by the Web browser. The security of an applet is often referred to as sandbox security, comparing the applet to a child playing in a sandbox with various rules that must be followed.

Other classes that the applet needs can be downloaded in a single Java Archive (JAR) file.

```
import java.applet.*;
import java.awt.*;
public class Main extends Applet {
  public void paint(Graphics g){
  g.draw String("Welcome in Java Applet.",40,20).
  }
}
```

Now compile the above code and call the generated class in your HTML code as follows"

```
<HTML>
<HEAD>
</HEAD>

<BODY>
<div>
   <APPLET CODE-"Main.class" WIDTH="800" HEIGHT="500"></APPLET>
</div>
</BODY>
</HTML>
```

Result

The above code sample will produce the following result in a java enabled web browser.

Welcome in Java Applet.Q. How do we manage Thread in java? Also explain Thread synchronization and inter-thread communication with suitable example?

Ans- Inter-thread communication or Co-operation is all about allowing synchronized threads to communicate with each other. Cooperation (Inter-thread communication) is a mechanism in which a thread is paused running in its critical section and another thread is allowed to enter (or lock) in the same critical section to be executed. It is implemented by following methods of

Object class

wait()

notify()

notify All()

(1) wait() method

Causes current thread to release the lock and wait until either another thread invokes the notify() method or the notify All() method for this object, or a specified amount of time has elapsed.

The current thread must own this object's monitor, so it must be called from the synchronized method only otherwise it will throw exception.

Method	Description
public final void wait(long timeout) throws InterruptedException	waits for the specified amount of time
public final void wait throws	InterruptedException

(2) notify() method

Wakes up a single thread that is waiting on this object's monitor. If any threads are waiting on this object, one of them is chosen to be awakened. The choice is arbitrary and occurs at the discretion of the implementation Syntax

```
public final void notify
(3) notify All() method
Wakes up all threads that are waiting on this object's monitor Syntax
public final void notifyAllO
class Customer(
int amount = 10000,
synchronized void withdraw(int amount){
System.out.println ("going to withdraw...")
if this amount-<amount){
System.out println()("Less balance, waiting for deposit...").
try (wait)catch(Exception e){}
System.out println() ("withdraw completed.....")
}

synchronized void deposit (int amount){

System.out.println("going to deposit.");
this amount+=amount;
System.out.println("deposit completed...");
notify():
}
}
class Test(
public static void main(String args[]){
final Customer c= new Customer();
new Thread(){
public void run()(c. withdraw(15000);}
}start();
new Thread(){
public void run(){c. deposit(10000);}
}start();
}}
Output: going to withdraw...
Less balance, waiting for deposit...
going to deposit....
deposit completed...
withdraw completed
```

Q.13. Why swing is called light weight. (RU BCA 2019)

Ans- Swing components depend less on the target platform and use less of the native GUI resource. Hence the Swing components that don't rely on native GUT are referred to as lightweight components. Swing is considered lightweight because it is fully implemented in Java, without calling the native operating system for drawing the graphical user interface components. As Swing is implemented in Java, it does have some performance disadvantage, however, I hear that performance has improved incest releases of Java.

The advantage of Swing is that it has many more components available such as JTable and JList which are more graphical and extensible than the components provided in AWT, allowing for more graphics-rich applications to be developed.

Q.14. Explain border layout and grid layout. (RU BCA 2019)

Ans. Java BorderLayout

The BorderLayout is used to arrange the components in five regions: north, south, east, west and center. Each region (area) may contain one component only. It is the default layout of frame or window. The BorderLayout provides five constants for each region:

1. public static final int NORTH
2. public static final int SOUTH
3. public static final int EAST
4. public static final int WEST

5. public static final int CENTER

Constructors of BorderLayout class

BorderLayout(): creates a border layout but with no gaps between the components.

JBorderLayout(int hgap, int vgap): creates a border layout with the given horizontal and vertical gaps between the components

Java GridLayout- The GridLayout is used to arrange the components in rectangular grid. One component is displayed in each rectangle.

Constructors of GridLayout class

1. GridLayout(): creates a grid layout with one column per component in a row.
2. GridLayout(int rows, int columns): creates a grid layout with the given rows and columns but no gaps between the components
3. GridLayout(int rows, int columns, int bgap, int vgap): creates a grid layout with the given rows and columns alongwith given horizontal and vertical gaps.

Q.15. Differentiate paint and repaint in java swing. (RU BCA 2019)

Ans-

Criteria	**paint ()**	**repaint ()**
Definition	It is used for initial rendering and manual redrawing of Swing components.	This method requests a component to be repainted on the screen.
Invocation	Called implicitly by the system or manually for initial rendering or redrawing.	I called explicitly to request a component to be repainted at the next available opportunity.
Arguments	Takes a single argument of type Graphics.	Takes no arguments.
Use Case	Used for performing the actual painting of the component and its children.	Used to request the repainting of a component, triggering the subsequent invocation of the paint method.
Direct Control	Provides direct control over the painting process and is used for custom drawing.	It does not directly control the painting process but schedules a repaint request to be executed by the system.
Performance	Directly affects the performance due to the direct rendering on the screen.	Triggers a repaint operation that may be optimized by the Swing framework for better performance.

Q.17. Explain Applet life cycle? (RU BCA 2019)

Ans. The life cycle of an applet is as shown in the figure below: 149094

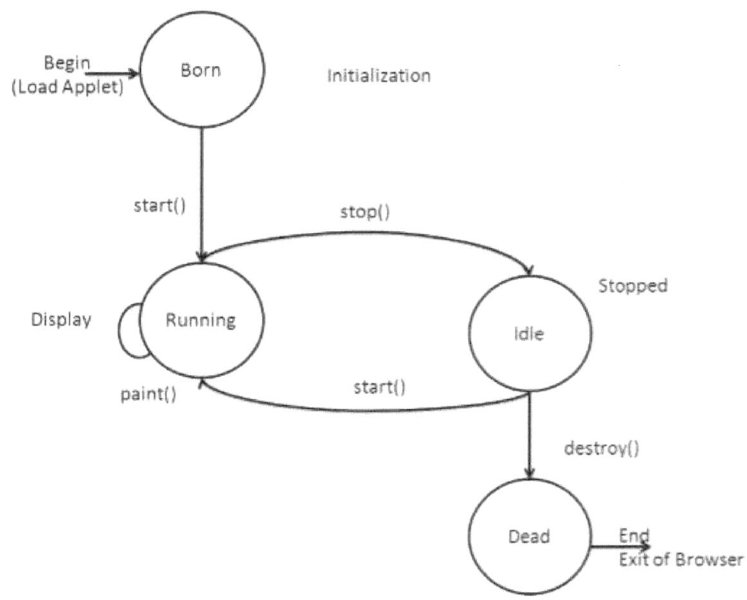

As shown in the above diagram, the life cycle of an applet starts with init method and ends with destroy method. Other life cycle methods are start, stop and paint. The methods to execute only once in the applet life cycle are init() and destroy(). Other methods execute multiple times.

Below is the description of each applet life cycle method:

init(): The inito method is the first method to execute when the applet is executed. Variable declaration and initialization operations are performed in this method.

start(): The start method contains the actual code of the applet that should run. The start) method executes immediately after the inir method. It also executes whenever the applet is restored, maximized or moving from one tab to another tab in the browser
stop(): The stop() method stops the execution of the applet. The stop() method executes when the applet is minimized or when moving from one tab to another in the browser.
destroy(): The destroy method executes when the applet window is closed or when the tab containing the webpage is closed step method executes just before when destroy() method is invoked. The destroy method removes the applet object from memory.
paint(): The paint() method is used to redraw the output on the applet display area. The paint() method executes after the execution of start method and whenever the applet or browser is resized.

Q.18. Discuss some of event handling mechanism in java? (RU BCA 2019)
Ans. Event Handling is the mechanism that controls the event and decides what should happen if an event occurs. This mechanism have the code which is known as event handler that is executed when an event occurs. Java Uses the Delegation Event Model to handle the events. This model defines the standard mechanism to generate and handle the events. Let's have a brief introduction to this model.
The Delegation Event Model has the following key participants namely:

Source-The source is an object on which event occurs. Source is responsible for providing information of the occurred event to it's handler. Java provide as with classes for source object.

Listener. It is also known as event handler Listener is responsible for generating response to an event. From java implementation point of view the listener is also an object. Listener waits until it receives an event. Once the event is received, the listener process the event an then returns.

The benefit of this approach is that the user interface logic is completely separated from the logic that generates the event. The user interface element is able to delegate the processing of an event to the separate piece of code. In this model. Listener needs to be registered with the source object so that the listener can receive the event notification. This is an efficient way of handling the event because the event notifications are sent only to those listener that want to receive them.

Q.19. What is the use of applet in java? (RU BCA 2019)
Ans. An applet is a small Internet-based program written in Java, a programming language for the Web, which can be downloaded by any computer. The applet is also able to run in HTML. The applet is usually embedded in an HTML page on a Web site and can be executed from

Q.20. What is AWT class? (RU BCA 2019)
Ans. Abstract Window Toolkit (AWT) is a set of application program interfaces (API) used by Java programmers to create graphical user interface (GUI) objects, such as buttons, scroll bars, and windows AWT is part of the Java Foundation Classes (JFC from Sun Microsystems, the company that originated Java. The JFC are a comprehensive set of GUI class libraries that make it easier to develop the user interface part of an application program
A more recent set of GUI interfaces called Swing extends the AWT so that the programmer can create generalized GUI objects that are independent of a specific operating system's windowing system.

Q.21. What do you understand by swing in java? (RU BCA 2019)
Ans. Java Swing is a lightweight Java graphical user interface (GUT) widget toolkit that includes a rich set of widgets. It is part of the Java Foundation Classes (IFC) and includes several packages for developing rich desktop applications in Java. Swing includes built-in controls such as trees, image buttons, tabbed panes, sliders, toolbars, color choosers, tables, and text areas to display HTTP or rich text format (RTF). Swing components are written entirely in Java and thus are platform-independent.
within a browser.

Q.22. Explain some of the important drawbacks of Applet and design the code in Java to explain the Applet viewer tool by Applet. (RU BCA 2020)
Ans- Disadvantage of applets
Applet conjoins some disadvantage, these are given beneath
Some browsers especially mobile browsers which are running on Apple 105 or Android don't support applets run.
If a proxy server is applied to web access, than automatically installation and update of Java can be failed, that's why applets can't run with specific requirements unless Java is manually installed or updated.
Applets don't access client-side resources, like-
Files
Operating system
Apples have to tag as trusted applets and they must be registered to APS (Applet Security Manager)

Applet cannot work with native methods.
Applet can only extract information about client-machine is its name, java version, OS, version etc.

Applet by appletviewer tool:
To execute the applet by appletviewer tool, create an applet that contains applet tag in comment and compile it. After that run it by: appletviewer First java. Now Huml file is not required but it is for testing purpose only.

```
//First java
import java applet. Applet;
import java.awt.Graphics,
public class First extends Applet
public void paint(Graphics g)
g.drawString("welcome to applet",150,150),
}
}
/*
<applet code="First.class" width="300" height="300">
<applet>
*/
```

To execute the applet by applerviewer tool, write in command prompt
c:\javacFirst.java
c:\appletviewerFirst.java

Q.23 How to create instance of frame class using AWT. (RU BCA 2020)
Ans-

```
import java.awt.*;
class First extends Frame{
First(){
Button b-new Button("click me),
b.setBounds(30,100,80,30);// setting button position
add(b)//adding button into frame
setSize(300,300)//frame size 300 width and 300 height
setLayout(null);//no layout manager
setVisible(true);//new frame will be visible, by default not visible
}
public static void main(String args[]){
First f=new First();
}}
```

Q.24. Java AWT Hierarchy (RU BCA 2020)
Ans- The hierarchy of Java AWT classes are given below.
The Java Abstract Window Toolkit (AWT) provides a set of graphical user interface (GUI) components for building a Java application's user interface. The AWT hierarchy consists of various classes and interfaces that form the foundation of the AWT framework. Here's an overview of the Java AWT hierarchy:

java.awt.Component:
The base class for all AWT components.
It provides the foundation for all UI elements.

java.awt.Container:
A subclass of Component that can contain other AWT components.
Examples include windows, panels, and frames.

java.awt.Panel:
A container that can group multiple components.
It is used for organizing and managing groups of components.

java.awt.Window:
Represents a top-level window with no borders or decorations.
It can be used as the primary application window.

java.awt.Frame:
An extended version of the Window class that adds support for decorations and controls.
It represents a window with a title bar, border, and buttons for closing, minimizing, and maximizing.

java.awt.Canvas:
A component that can be used as a custom area for drawing graphics.
It provides a space for low-level graphics.
java.awt.Graphics:
An abstract class that provides the capability to draw on components.
It is used in conjunction with the Canvas class for custom rendering.

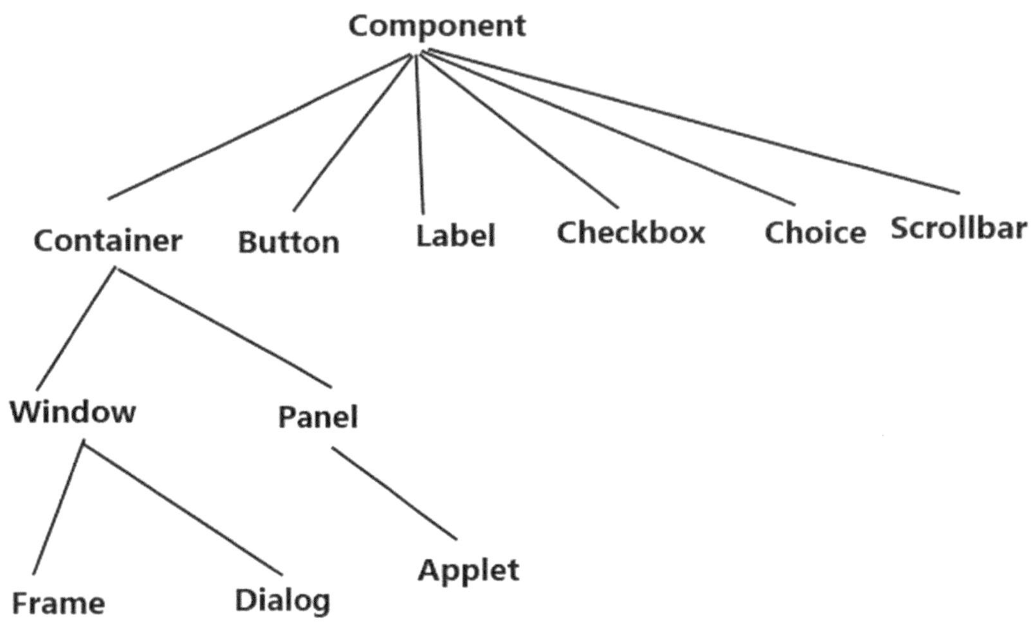

Q.25. What is the life cycle of Applet in Java, explain. (RU BCA 2020)
Ans-These are the different stages involved in the life cycle of an applet:
Initialization State
Running state
Idle or stopped state
Dead state
Display state
Initialization State: This state is the first state of the applet life cycle. An applet is created by the method init(). This method initializes the created applet. It is Called exactly once in an applet's life when applet is first loaded, which is after object creation, eg. when the browser visits the web page for the first time. Used to read applet parameters, start downloading any other images or media files, etc. Init() method should be overridden in our applet.

```
Public void init()
{
    bgColor-Color.cyan,
    setBackground(bgColor),
}
```

Running State: This state is the second stage of the applet life cycle. This state comes when starto method is called. Called at least once. Called when an applet is started or restarted, ie, whenever the browser visits the web page.

```
Public void start()
{
   super start(),
}
```

Idle or Stopped State: This state is the third stage of the applet life cycle. This state comes when stop() method is called implicitly or explicitly stop() method is called implicitly. It is called at least once when the browser leaves the web page when we move from one page to another. This method is called only in the running state and can be called any number of times. It should be overridden in our applet.

```
Public void stop()
```

```
{
    super.stop();
}
```

Dead State: This state is the fourth stage of the applet life cycle. This state comes when destroy() method is called. In this state the applet is completely removed from the memory. It called exactly once when the browser unloads the applet. Used to perform any final clean-up. It occurs only once in the life cycle. It should be overridden in our applet.

```
Public void destroy
{
    super destroy();
}
```

Display State: This state is the fifth stage of the applet life cycle. This state comes when uses the applet displays something on the screen. This is achieved by calling paint method. Paint() method can be called any number of times. This can be called only in the running state. This method is a must in all applets. It should be overridden in our applet.

```
Public void paint(Graphics obj)
{
    super paint(g).
}
```

Q.26.Discuss any 2 features of Swings in Java. (RU BCA 2020)

Ans. 1. Lightweight components

2. Pluggable look and feel

Q.27. Why is the need of Applet in Java? (RU BCA 2020)

Ans. The applets are used to provide interactive features to web applications that cannot be provided by HTML alone. They can capture mouse input and also have controls like buttons or check boxes. In response to user actions, an applet can change the provided graphic content.

Q. 28. Discuss about different layout manger available in java. (BCA 2021)

Ans: In Java, various layout managers are used to arrange GUI components within a container. Each layout manager has its own unique way of arranging components, providing flexibility and control over the positioning of GUI elements. Here are some of the commonly used layout managers in Java:

FlowLayout:

Arranges components in a left-to-right flow, wrapping to the next line as necessary.

Useful for arranging components in a single row.

Components are centered by default.

BorderLayout:

Divides the container into five regions: North, South, East, West, and Center.

Each component can be placed in one of these regions.

Useful for creating simple and basic layouts.

GridLayout:

Divides the container into a grid of rows and columns where each cell can contain one component.

Components are laid out in a row-major order, filling each row before moving to the next.

Useful for creating uniformly spaced layouts with a fixed number of rows and columns.

CardLayout:

Allows multiple components to be stacked on top of each other, with only one component visible at a time.

Useful for creating wizard-style interfaces or panels that switch between different views.

GridBagLayout:

Provides the most flexible and complex layout manager in the Java AWT toolkit.

Allows components to be arranged in a grid with different constraints on each component, such as resizing, alignment, and anchoring.

Useful for creating complex and customizable layouts.

BoxLayout:

Arranges components in a single row or column.

Supports both horizontal and vertical arrangements.

Useful for creating simple and flexible layouts that require components to be aligned in a single direction.

GroupLayout:

Enables the creation of complex layouts by grouping components and aligning them based on their logical structure.

Provides support for creating user interfaces that adjust well to different screen sizes and localization.

These layout managers provide different ways to organize the components within a container, allowing developers to create visually appealing and user-friendly GUI applications in Java. Choosing the right layout manager depends on the specific requirements and design of the GUI application.

Q. 29. Difference between: (RU BCA 2021)
(i) Character stream v/s byte stream
Ans-

Criteria	Character Streams	Byte Streams
Interpretation	Reads and writes data as a sequence of characters	Reads and writes data as a sequence of bytes
Encoding	Uses character encoding (e.g., UTF-8, UTF-16)	No encoding is performed on the data
Usage	Preferable when dealing with text-based data	Suitable for handling binary data or non-text data
Data Representation	Handles textual data and ensures proper character encoding	Treats data as raw bytes without interpretation
I/O Operations	Suitable for reading and writing textual information	Suitable for reading and writing binary data
Size	Larger in size due to encoding overhead	Smaller in size due to the absence of encoding overhead

Q.30. What is delegation event model. (RU BCA 2021)
Ans: The Delegation Event model is defined to handle events in GUI programming languages. The GUI stands for Graphical User Interface, where a user graphically/visually interacts with the system.
The GUI programming is inherently event-driven; whenever a user initiates an activity such as a mouse activity, clicks, scrolling, etc., each is known as an event that is mapped to a code to respond to functionality to the user. This is known as event handling.

Q.31. Relationship between Listener & Adapter Class. (RU BCA 2022)
Ans- When a programmer plans to use the majority of the methods specified under the interface, listeners are employed. If a class implements a listener interface directly, it must implement all of the interface's methods, which makes the code excessively big. The use of an adapter class in java can help to fix this problem. When an event just requires a few specialized methods, an adapter class comes in handy.
Example of window adapter class AdapterExample()

```
f= newFrame("Hello World");
f.addWindowListener(new WindowAdapter()
public void windowClosing(WindowEvent e)
{
f.close();
}
}
```

Example of action listener

```
import java.awt.*;
import java.awt.event.*;
public class ActionListenerExample {
public static void main(String[] args) {
        Frame f=new Frame("ActionListener Example");
        final TextField tf-new TextField(); 150,20);
        tf.setBounds(50,50, Button b-new Button("Click Here");
        b.setBounds(50,100,60,30);
        b.addActionListener(new ActionListener(){ public void actionPerformed(ActionEvent e) {
        tf.setText("Welcome to Javatpoint.");
}
});
f.add(b);f.add(f);
f.setSize(400,400);
f.setLayout(null);
f.setVisible(true);
}
}
```

Q.32. discuss" applet life cycle. (RU BCA 2022)

init(): The init() method is the first method to run that initializes the applet. It can be invoked only once at the time of initialization. The web browser creates the initialized objects, ie, the web browser (after checking the security settings) runs the init() method within the applet.

start(): The start() method contains the actual code of the applet and starts the applet. It is invoked immediately after the init() method is invoked. Every time the browser is loaded or refreshed, the start() method is invoked. It is also invoked whenever the applet is maximized, restored, or moving from one tab to another in the browser. It is in an inactive state until the init() method is invoked.

stop(): The stop() method stops the execution of the applet. The stop () method is invoked whenever the applet is stopped, minimized, or moving from one tab to another in the browser, the stop() method is invoked. When we go back to that page, the start() method is invoked again.

destroy(): The destroy() method destroys the applet after its work is done. It is invoked when the applet window is closed or when the tab containing the webpage is closed. It removes the applet object from memory and is executed only once. We cannot start the applet once it is destroyed.

paint(): The paint() method belongs to the Graphics class in Java. It is used to draw shapes like circle, square. trapezium, etc., in the applet. It is executed after the start() method and when the browser or applet windows are resized.

//applet. The stop () method is invoked whenever the applet is stopped, minimized, or moving from one tab to another in the browser, the stop() method is imoked. When we go back to that page, the start() method is invoked again

Q.33 Describe" delegation event model" by providing suitable example. (RU BCA 2022)

Ans. The Delegation Event model is defined to handle events in GUI programming languages. The GUI stands for Graphical User Interface, where a user graphically/visually interacts with the system. The GUI programming is inherently event-driven. whenever a user initiates an activity such as a mouse activity, clicks, scrolling, etc, each is known as an event that is mapped to a code to respond to functionality to the user. This is known as event handling. Event handling is a mechanism to control the events and to decide what should happen after an event occur. To handle the events, Java follows the Delegation Event model

Source: Events are generated from the source. There are various sources like buttons, checkboxes, list, menu-item, choice, scrollbar, text components, windows, etc., to generate events

Listeners: Listeners are used for handling the events generated from the source. Each of these listeners represents interfaces that are responsible for handling events. To perform Event Handling, we need to register the source with the Listener

Registering the Source With Listener

Different Classes provide different registration methods.

Syntax:

addTypeListener()

.

Q.34 What is AWT in java? (RU BCA 2022)

Ans. AWT stands for Abstract window toolkit is an Application programming interface (API) for creating Graphical User Interface (GUI) in Java. It allows Java programmers to develop window-based applications.

AWT provides various components like button, label. checkbox, etc. used as objects inside a Java Program AWT components use the resources of the operating system, i.e. they are platform-dependent, which means, component's view can be changed according to the view of the operating system. The classes for AWT are provided by the Java.awt package for various AWT components.

Q.35 Define applet? (RU BCA 2022)

Ans. An applet is a Java program that runs is a Web browser. An applet can be a fully functional because it has the entire Java API as its disposal. There are some important differences and a standalone Java application, An applet is a Java class that extends the java applet. Applet class.

A main() method is not invoked on an applet class will not define main().

Applets are designed to be embedded within an HTML page

When a user views an HTML page that contains an applet, the code for the applet is downloaded to the user's machine.

ONLINE RESOURCES

Practice Paper
Link: https://forms.gle/XSzkGQJS6VrjzKm27
QR Code:

Video Content
Link: https://www.youtube.com/playlist?list=PLzlh_31VWEFoUtTRRmg89RrahGM58tcGA
QR Code:

CHAPTER 6 - Networking in Java

6.1 Networking in Java

Networking in Java allows you to create networked applications that can communicate over the internet or a local network. Java provides a comprehensive set of classes and libraries for network programming. In this detailed overview, we'll explore networking in Java, covering topics such as sockets, protocols, client-server communication, and more.

Networking Fundamentals:

Sockets: At the heart of Java networking is the concept of sockets. A socket is an endpoint for sending or receiving data across a computer network. Java provides classes like Socket and ServerSocket to work with sockets.

Protocols: Networking in Java is based on various networking protocols, such as TCP (Transmission Control Protocol) and UDP (User Datagram Protocol). TCP provides a reliable, connection-oriented communication, while UDP offers a lightweight, connectionless protocol.

Client-Server Communication:

Client: In a client-server model, a client is an application that initiates a connection to a server to request services or data.

Server: The server is an application that listens for incoming connections from clients and provides requested services.

Socket Programming:

Socket Creation: To create a socket in Java, you can use the Socket class for clients and the ServerSocket class for servers. For example, to create a client socket:

Example-

```
Socket clientSocket = new Socket("server_address", port);
```

ServerSocket: On the server side, you use a ServerSocket to listen for incoming client connections:

Example-

```
ServerSocket serverSocket = new ServerSocket(port);
Socket clientSocket = serverSocket.accept();
```

4. Data Transfer:

Input and Output Streams: Java's networking API works seamlessly with input and output streams. You can use InputStream and OutputStream to read and write data over sockets.

Example-

```
InputStream inputStream = clientSocket.getInputStream();
OutputStream outputStream = clientSocket.getOutputStream();
```

5. URL Handling:

Java's java.net package includes classes like URL and URLConnection for handling URLs. You can use these classes to retrieve data from web servers or other online resources.

Example-

```
URL url = new URL("http://example.com");
URLConnection connection = url.openConnection();
```

6. HTTP Client and Server:

Java includes an HTTP client library in the form of the java.net.http package (available in Java 11 and later). It allows you to send HTTP requests and receive responses from web servers.

Example-

```
import java.net.http.HttpClient;
import java.net.http.HttpRequest;
import java.net.http.HttpResponse;

HttpClient httpClient = HttpClient.newHttpClient();
HttpRequest request = HttpRequest.newBuilder()
        .uri(new URI("http://example.com"))
        .build();
HttpResponse<String> response = httpClient.send(request, HttpResponse.BodyHandlers.ofString());
```

For creating an HTTP server, you can use third-party libraries like Apache Tomcat or Jetty, which provide Java Servlet support.

7. Socket-Level Security:

Java allows you to secure your network communication using encryption and authentication. The Java Secure Socket Extension (JSSE) provides support for SSL/TLS, enabling secure socket communication.

8. Multithreading and Networking:

Multithreading is often essential in networking applications. You can create a new thread to handle each client connection, allowing your server to handle multiple clients simultaneously.

9. Error Handling:

Proper error handling is crucial in network programming. You need to handle exceptions, such as IOException, SocketException, and SecurityException, gracefully to ensure the stability of your networked applications.

10. Networking Best Practices:

- Always close sockets and resources when you're done with them using close(), try-with-resources, or similar methods.
- Implement robust error handling and graceful recovery mechanisms to handle network failures.
- Consider network timeouts to prevent blocking indefinitely.
- Be aware of security considerations when transferring sensitive data over the network.

In conclusion, networking in Java is a powerful and versatile capability that allows you to create networked applications for various purposes, from simple client-server communication to complex web services. By understanding the fundamentals of socket programming, protocols, and the Java networking API, you can develop robust and efficient networked applications.

6.1.1 DatagramPacket:

The DatagramPacket class is part of Java's support for UDP (User Datagram Protocol) communication and is found in the java.net package. It plays a key role in sending and receiving data in a connectionless manner over a network. Here's a brief explanation of the role of the DatagramPacket class:

- **Data Container:** DatagramPacket is a container that holds data to be sent or received over a UDP socket. It encapsulates both the data itself and information about its source and destination.
- **Sending Data:** To send data using UDP, you create a DatagramPacket containing the data and specify the destination IP address and port number. Then, you use a DatagramSocket to send the packet to the specified destination.
- **Receiving Data:** When receiving UDP data, you create a DatagramPacket and use a DatagramSocket to receive incoming data. The received data is stored in the DatagramPacket, along with information about the sender (source IP address and port).
- **Connectionless Communication:** UDP is connectionless, meaning that there is no formal connection setup as in TCP. Each DatagramPacket is independent, and the sender and receiver do not maintain any state information about each other.

Lightweight and Low Overhead: UDP is often used for tasks where low overhead and minimal latency are crucial, such as real-time multimedia streaming, online gaming, and network discovery protocols like DHCP and DNS.

6.2 Database Connectivity with JDBC

Java Database Connectivity (JDBC) is a Java-based API that allows Java applications to interact with relational databases. It provides a standard interface for connecting to databases, executing SQL queries, and processing results. In this detailed overview, we'll explore database connectivity with JDBC:

1. JDBC Architecture:

The JDBC architecture consists of three main components:

- **JDBC API:** This includes the classes and interfaces provided by Java for database connectivity. Key classes include DriverManager, Connection, Statement, and ResultSet.
- **JDBC Driver Manager:** The DriverManager class manages a list of database drivers. It is responsible for establishing database connections. Developers can register and unregister drivers with the DriverManager.
- **Database-Specific JDBC Drivers:** These are platform-specific implementations provided by database vendors. They translate JDBC calls into database-specific calls.

2. Establishing Database Connection:

To connect to a database using JDBC, follow these steps:

- **Load JDBC Driver:** Load the appropriate JDBC driver using Class.forName() or rely on the service provider mechanism (JDBC 4.0 or later).

Example-

```
Class.forName("com.mysql.cj.jdbc.Driver"); // Load MySQL driver
```

- **Create a Connection**: Use the DriverManager.getConnection() method to establish a connection to the database. Provide the database URL, username, and password.

Example-

```
String url = "jdbc:mysql://localhost:3306/mydatabase";
String username = "myuser";
String password = "mypassword";
Connection connection = DriverManager.getConnection(url, username, password);
```

3. Executing SQL Queries:

Once you have a database connection, you can execute SQL queries using JDBC Statement objects. There are three types of statements:

Statement: Used for executing simple SQL queries with no parameters.

Example-

```
Statement statement = connection.createStatement();
```

```
ResultSet resultSet = statement.executeQuery("SELECT * FROM employees");
```

PreparedStatement: Used for executing precompiled SQL queries with parameters, providing better performance and security.

Example-

```
String sql = "INSERT INTO employees (id, name) VALUES (?, ?)";
PreparedStatement preparedStatement = connection.prepareStatement(sql);
preparedStatement.setInt(1, 101);
preparedStatement.setString(2, "John Doe");
int rowsAffected = preparedStatement.executeUpdate();
```

CallableStatement: Used for calling stored procedures in the database.

4. Processing Query Results:

JDBC ResultSet objects are used to retrieve query results:

Example-

```
ResultSet resultSet = statement.executeQuery("SELECT * FROM employees");
while (resultSet.next()) {
   int id = resultSet.getInt("id");
   String name = resultSet.getString("name");
   // Process the data
}
```

5. Exception Handling:

Proper error handling is crucial in database connectivity. Handle exceptions like SQLException and resource management (closing connections, statements, and result sets) gracefully.

Example-

```
try {
   // JDBC code
} catch (SQLException e) {
   e.printStackTrace();
} finally {
   try {
      if (resultSet != null) resultSet.close();
      if (statement != null) statement.close();
      if (connection != null) connection.close();
   } catch (SQLException e) {
      e.printStackTrace();
   }
}
```

6. Transactions:

JDBC allows you to manage database transactions using the commit() and rollback() methods of the Connection object. Transactions ensure that a series of database operations are executed as a single, atomic unit.

Example-

```
try {
   connection.setAutoCommit(false); // Start a transaction
   // Execute multiple SQL statements
   connection.commit(); // Commit the transaction
} catch (SQLException e) {
   connection.rollback(); // Rollback the transaction in case of an error
}
```

7. DataSource and Connection Pooling:

In production applications, it's common to use DataSource and connection pooling libraries like Apache DBCP or HikariCP to efficiently manage database connections and improve performance.

8. Best Practices:

Use PreparedStatement to prevent SQL injection and improve performance.

Close resources (connections, statements, result sets) in finally blocks to ensure resource cleanup.

Use connection pooling for improved resource utilization.

Handle exceptions gracefully and log them for debugging and monitoring.

Avoid executing long-running queries on the main application thread.

In conclusion, JDBC is a fundamental technology for Java developers working with relational databases. It provides a standardized and efficient way to connect to databases, execute SQL queries, and process results. By following best practices and handling resources and exceptions correctly, you can build robust and efficient database-driven Java applications.

6.2.1 Types of JDBC drivers

JDBC (Java Database Connectivity) drivers are essential components for connecting Java applications to databases. They facilitate communication between Java code and different database systems. There are four main types of JDBC drivers, each with its own characteristics and use cases:

Type-1: JDBC-ODBC Bridge Driver (Bridge Driver):

Description: The Type-1 driver is a bridge driver that acts as an intermediary between JDBC and ODBC (Open Database Connectivity). It uses the ODBC driver provided by the database system to connect to the database.

Pros:

Easy to set up and configure.

Can connect to multiple databases through ODBC.

Cons:

Limited platform independence because it relies on ODBC, which is typically available only on Windows.

Performance overhead due to the translation between JDBC calls and ODBC calls.

Use Cases: The Type-1 driver is suitable for prototyping and testing but is not recommended for production use due to its limitations and performance issues.

Type-2: Native-API Driver (Thin Driver):

Description: The Type-2 driver uses a database-specific native library to connect to the database. It communicates directly with the database system's native API.

Pros:

Provides better performance than the Type-1 driver.

Platform independence to some extent because it relies on Java code and a native library.

Cons:

Not fully platform-independent since it depends on the availability of a native library.

Requires the installation of a database-specific native library on the client machine.

Use Cases: The Type-2 driver is suitable for applications where performance is critical, and platform independence is not a strict requirement.

Type-3: Network Protocol Driver (Middleware Driver):

Description: The Type-3 driver, also known as the network protocol driver or middleware driver, communicates with a middleware server using a database-independent protocol. The middleware server then interacts with the database using a Type-4 or Type-2 driver.

Pros:

Platform-independent because the middleware server abstracts the database-specific details.

Allows multiple clients to connect to the same middleware server.

Cons:

Requires the installation and configuration of a middleware server.

Slightly slower than Type-4 drivers due to the additional network layer.

Use Cases: The Type-3 driver is suitable for applications where platform independence and centralized connection management are important.

Type-4: Thin Driver (Direct-to-Database Driver):

Description: The Type-4 driver, also known as the thin driver, communicates directly with the database using a database-specific protocol. It does not require any native libraries or middleware servers.

Pros:

High performance because it communicates directly with the database.

Full platform independence as it relies solely on Java code.

Cons:

May not support all database systems (depends on driver availability).

Network configuration might be needed to establish a connection.

Use Cases: The Type-4 driver is widely used in production applications where performance and platform independence are crucial. It is the preferred choice for modern JDBC development.

6.3 Java Servlets and JSP

Java Servlets and JSP are essential technologies for building dynamic web applications in Java. Servlets handle the server-side logic, while JSPs help create dynamic web pages. In this detailed overview, we'll explore Java Servlets and JSPs, covering their concepts, architecture, usage, and best practices.

1. Java Servlets:

Java Servlets are Java classes that extend the javax.servlet.Servlet interface. They run on the server-side and handle client requests, processing data, and generating dynamic responses. Here's how servlets work:

Lifecycle: Servlets have a well-defined lifecycle with methods like init(), service(), and destroy(). The service() method handles HTTP requests (GET, POST, etc.) and generates responses.

Request and Response: Servlets receive HTTP requests as HttpServletRequest objects and send responses as HttpServletResponse objects.

Mapping: Servlets are mapped to URLs using servlet mappings defined in the web.xml configuration file or annotations.

2. JavaServer Pages (JSP):

JSP is a technology used to create dynamic web content. JSP pages are text-based and combine HTML or XML with Java code to generate dynamic web pages. Key aspects of JSP include:

JSP Tags: JSP provides custom tags, called JSP tags or JSTL (JavaServer Pages Standard Tag Library), for embedding Java code and performing actions like loops, conditionals, and database operations within HTML-like templates.

Expression Language (EL): EL is a simplified scripting language used in JSP pages to access and manipulate data stored in JavaBeans, session attributes, and other scopes.

Lifecycle: JSP pages are compiled into servlets by the web container at runtime, allowing them to participate in the servlet lifecycle.

3. MVC Architecture with Servlets and JSP:

Servlets and JSPs are often used in the Model-View-Controller (MVC) design pattern:

Model: The model represents the application's data and business logic. It's typically implemented as JavaBeans or POJOs.

View (JSP): JSP pages act as the view layer, responsible for rendering the user interface and displaying data to users.

Controller (Servlets): Servlets serve as the controller, handling user requests, invoking model operations, and forwarding data to the view.

4. Session Management:

Servlets and JSPs can manage user sessions, typically using HTTP session objects. Sessions enable the server to maintain state information across multiple requests from the same client.

Session Creation: When a user accesses a web application, a session can be created for that user. Typically, a unique session ID (also known as a session token) is generated and associated with the user.

Storing Data: Servlets can store user-specific data in the HttpSession object, such as user preferences, shopping cart items, or login information. This data can persist throughout the user's interaction with the application.

Accessing the Session: To access the session associated with a user, servlets use the getSession() method of the HttpServletRequest object. If a session does not exist for the user, a new one is created.

Example-

```
// Setting a session attribute in a servlet
HttpSession session = request.getSession();
```

Storing Data in the Session: Servlets can store data in the session using the setAttribute() method. For example, to store a user's name:

Example-

```
session.setAttribute("username", "John");
```

Retrieving Data from the Session: Servlets can retrieve data from the session using the getAttribute() method:

// Retrieving a session attribute in a JSP

Example-

```
String username = (String) session.getAttribute("username");
```

Session Timeout: Sessions typically have a timeout period, after which they are considered inactive and may be invalidated to free up server resources. The timeout period can be configured in the web application's deployment descriptor (web.xml).

Invalidating a Session: When a user logs out or the session is no longer needed, servlets can invalidate the session using the invalidate() method

Example-

session.invalidate();

Session Management Across Requests: The session ID is often stored in cookies or appended to URLs to enable the web server to associate subsequent requests with the correct session.

Security: Session management also plays a crucial role in web application security. Developers must protect against session hijacking and other security threats by implementing best practices, such as using secure (HTTPS) connections, employing strong session ID generation techniques, and validating session data.

5. Form Handling:

Servlets and JSPs are commonly used for handling HTML forms. They receive form data as HTTP request parameters and process or validate it on the server.

Example-

```
<form action="processFormServlet" method="post">
   <input type="text" name="username">
   <input type="submit" value="Submit">
</form>
```

6. Error Handling

Servlets and JSPs can handle errors and exceptions gracefully, providing custom error pages and logging for debugging.

Example-

```
<!-- Error page configuration in web.xml -->
<error-page>
   <exception-type>java.lang.Exception</exception-type>
   <location>/error.jsp</location>
</error-page>
```

7. Security:

Servlets and JSPs can enforce security by configuring authentication, authorization, and access control using servlet filters and security constraints in web.xml.

8. Best Practices:

- Separate business logic from presentation logic by using servlets as controllers and JSPs as views.
- Use JSTL and EL to minimize Java code in JSPs.
- Validate user input and sanitize data to prevent security vulnerabilities.
- Implement error handling for graceful failure recovery.
- Minimize session usage for scalability and consider stateless approaches when applicable.
- Follow coding standards and naming conventions to improve code readability.

In conclusion, Java Servlets and JSPs are fundamental technologies for building dynamic web applications in Java. They provide a powerful combination for handling HTTP requests, generating dynamic web pages, and implementing MVC architecture. By understanding their concepts, architecture, and best practices, you can develop robust and maintainable web applications in Java.

6.4 Get Method and Post Method in Servlet.

Aspect	Get Method	Post Method
Purpose	Primarily used for data retrieval.	Used for submitting data for processing.
Data in URL	Appends data as query parameters in the URL, making it visible.	Sends data in the request body, not visible in the URL.
Usage	It is commonly used for fetching web pages, images, or data from a server.	Typically used for submitting forms, file uploads, or data to be processed on the server.
Visibility	Data is visible in the URL, which may be a security concern for sensitive information.	Data is not visible in the URL, providing better security for sensitive data.
Data Size	Limited by the URL length, which may restrict the amount of data that can be sent.	Can handle larger amounts of data as it's sent in the request body, without URL length limitations.
Caching	Responses can be cached by browsers and proxy servers, potentially exposing sensitive data.	Responses are not cached by default, reducing exposure of sensitive data.
Idempotent	Generally considered idempotent, meaning repeated "Get" requests do not have side effects on the server.	Not considered idempotent, meaning repeated "Post" requests may have side effects on the server (e.g., creating multiple records).

6.5 Introduction to JavaFX

JavaFX is a modern, versatile framework for building rich desktop and web applications in Java. It provides a set of tools and libraries for creating interactive and visually appealing user interfaces. In this detailed overview, we'll explore JavaFX, covering its key concepts, architecture, components, and best practices.

1. Key Concepts:

Rich User Interfaces: JavaFX is designed for building visually stunning and responsive user interfaces (UIs) with support for animations, graphics, and multimedia.

FXML: FXML is an XML-based markup language used for defining the UI structure in a declarative manner, separating the UI layout from the application's logic.

Scene Graph: JavaFX applications are built on a hierarchical scene graph, representing the UI components and their relationships. This allows for efficient rendering and manipulation of UI elements.

CSS Styling: JavaFX supports CSS for styling UI components, making it easy to customize the appearance of your application.

Event Handling: JavaFX provides a comprehensive event handling system for responding to user input and interactions.

2. Architecture:

JavaFX follows a modular architecture that includes various components:

Scene Graph: At the core of JavaFX is the scene graph, which represents the UI hierarchy. It consists of nodes, where each node can be a UI control, layout container, or a shape.

Stage: A JavaFX application typically has one primary stage that represents the main window. You can create additional stages for pop-up windows or dialog boxes.

Scenes: Stages are composed of scenes. A scene defines the content to be displayed within a stage and contains a reference to the root node of the scene graph.

UI Controls: JavaFX includes a rich set of UI controls like buttons, labels, text fields, tables, and more. These controls are highly customizable and can be used to build complex UIs.

Layout Containers: Layout containers, such as VBox, HBox, and GridPane, help organize and position UI components within a scene.

3. Building a JavaFX Application:

To create a JavaFX application, you typically follow these steps:

Create a JavaFX Project: Set up a JavaFX project using a build tool like Gradle or Maven or an integrated development environment (IDE) like IntelliJ IDEA or Eclipse.

Design the UI: Use FXML or Java code to define the UI layout and components.

Event Handling: Implement event handlers to respond to user interactions, such as button clicks or mouse events.

CSS Styling: Apply CSS styles to customize the appearance of UI components.

Running the Application: Launch the JavaFX application by running the main class or the JavaFX Application class.

4. Scene Builder:

Scene Builder is a visual layout tool provided by Oracle (now part of Gluon) for designing JavaFX UIs using FXML. It allows you to drag and drop UI controls onto a canvas and visually design your application's UI.

5. Best Practices:

Use FXML for UI design to separate UI structure from application logic.

Follow the Model-View-Controller (MVC) or Model-View-ViewModel (MVVM) architectural patterns for organizing code.

Utilize CSS for consistent and customizable UI styling.

Use appropriate layout containers to achieve desired UI layouts.

Optimize the scene graph for performance by minimizing node traversal and updates.

Implement proper exception handling and debugging techniques.

Leverage JavaFX concurrency utilities for responsive applications.

6. Deployment:

JavaFX applications can be deployed as standalone desktop applications, web applets, or as part of a web page. Deployment options include packaging as a JAR file, native installer, or using Java Web Start.

7. Integration:

JavaFX can be integrated with other Java technologies, such as JDBC for database access, RESTful web services for data retrieval, and external libraries for additional functionality.

In conclusion, JavaFX is a powerful framework for building modern and interactive Java applications with rich user interfaces. It provides a robust architecture, comprehensive UI controls, styling options, and event handling capabilities. By understanding its key concepts and following best practices, you can create visually appealing and responsive desktop and web applications in Java.

6.6 Introduction to Java Beans

JavaBeans, often referred to simply as "beans," are reusable software components in Java that follow specific coding conventions and design patterns. They are used to encapsulate and manage data and behaviour within Java applications, making it easier to create, maintain, and extend software. In this detailed overview, we'll explore JavaBeans, covering their key concepts, characteristics, usage, and best practices.

1. Key Concepts:

Encapsulation: JavaBeans are designed to encapsulate data and functionality into self-contained, reusable components. This encapsulation helps ensure data integrity and simplifies code maintenance.

Properties: JavaBeans expose their state (data) as properties, which are accessed through getter and setter methods. Properties are essential for providing controlled access to bean attributes.

Events: JavaBeans can raise and handle events. Event handling in beans allows them to respond to changes in state or user interactions.

Serializability: JavaBeans are serializable, which means they can be converted into a format suitable for storage or transmission and later reconstructed.

2. Characteristics of JavaBeans:

JavaBeans adhere to specific conventions and characteristics:

Public Default Constructor: JavaBeans have a public no-argument constructor, allowing them to be easily instantiated using the Class.newInstance() method or other mechanisms.

Properties: JavaBeans define properties with getter and setter methods. Property names follow the convention of getPropertyName() for getters and setPropertyName() for setters.

Serializable: Beans implement the java.io.Serializable interface to support serialization. This allows them to be saved to a file or transmitted over a network.

Custom Events: JavaBeans can define custom events and event listeners, allowing them to participate in event-driven programming.

3. Usage of JavaBeans:

JavaBeans are widely used in various contexts:

Graphical User Interfaces (GUIs): JavaBeans are used to create user interface components like buttons, text fields, and checkboxes. These beans encapsulate the UI behavior and properties.

Enterprise Applications: In Java EE (Enterprise Edition), Enterprise JavaBeans (EJBs) are a type of JavaBean used to implement business logic in distributed enterprise applications.

Serialization: JavaBeans are used for data serialization and deserialization, enabling data exchange and persistence.

Event Handling: In event-driven applications, JavaBeans raise events and handle them, allowing for loosely coupled, responsive systems.

4. Best Practices:

To create effective JavaBeans, consider the following best practices:

Follow the Naming Conventions: Adhere to the naming conventions for getters and setters, such as getPropertyName() and setPropertyName().

Provide a Default Constructor: Ensure that your JavaBean has a public no-argument constructor for easy instantiation.

Make Properties Private: Encapsulate properties by making them private and providing getter and setter methods.

Implement Serializable: If necessary, implement the Serializable interface to support serialization.

Define Clear Contracts: Clearly document the properties, methods, and events of your JavaBeans.

Test and Validate: Thoroughly test your JavaBeans to ensure they function as expected.

5. Bean Development Tools:

Several development tools and frameworks, such as JavaBeans Development Kit (BDK) and JavaBeans Activation Framework (JAF), assist in bean development and integration.

In conclusion, JavaBeans are reusable software components in Java that encapsulate data and behaviour, following specific conventions and design patterns. They are a fundamental building block in Java development, enabling modular and maintainable code. By adhering to JavaBean conventions and best practices, developers can create robust and reusable components for a wide range of applications.

6.7 Introspection in JavaBeans

Introspection is a mechanism used in JavaBeans to examine and analyse the properties, methods, and events of a bean at runtime. It allows tools, like visual development environments and libraries, to discover and manipulate the attributes and behaviours of JavaBeans dynamically.

The JavaBeans Introspector, a built-in Java class, provides a standard way to perform introspection on JavaBeans. Here are some key aspects of introspection in JavaBeans:

Property Discovery: Introspection helps discover the properties of a bean, including their names, types, and access methods (getters and setters).

Event Discovery: It also enables the discovery of events supported by a bean, including the event listener registration methods.

Method Discovery: Introspection allows you to find methods defined by the bean, such as action methods.

Customization: Tools and libraries can use introspection to provide customizable interfaces for JavaBeans, allowing users to interactively configure beans.

6.8 Overview of Design Patterns in Java

Design patterns are fundamental templates for solving common software design problems in a reusable and efficient way. They provide proven solutions to recurring design challenges, fostering maintainable, flexible, and scalable software systems. In this detailed overview, we'll explore design patterns in Java, covering their key concepts, types, and examples.

1. What Are Design Patterns:

Design patterns are general, reusable solutions to common problems that occur during software design and development. They offer a structured approach to solving design challenges, making it easier to create robust, maintainable, and flexible software.

2. Benefits of Design Patterns:

Design patterns offer several advantages:

Reusability: Patterns encapsulate best practices and can be applied across different projects and domains.

Maintainability: Patterns provide a clear structure that makes code easier to understand and maintain.

Scalability: Patterns promote the development of scalable and extensible software.

Communication: Patterns facilitate communication among developers by providing a common design vocabulary.

3. Types of Design Patterns:

Design patterns are typically categorized into three main groups:

Creational Patterns: These patterns deal with object creation mechanisms, trying to create objects in a manner suitable to the situation. Examples include Singleton, Factory Method, and Builder patterns.

Structural Patterns: These patterns focus on object composition to form larger structures while keeping them flexible and efficient. Examples include Adapter, Decorator, and Bridge patterns.

Behavioural Patterns: These patterns deal with object collaboration and responsibilities, defining how objects interact and distribute tasks. Examples include Observer, Strategy, and Command patterns.

4. Common Java Design Patterns:

Let's look at a few common design patterns in Java:

Singleton Pattern: Ensures a class has only one instance and provides a global point of access to it. Useful for scenarios like configuration managers or logging.

Example-

```
public class Singleton {
  private static Singleton instance;

  private Singleton() {}

  public static Singleton getInstance() {
    if (instance == null) {
      instance = new Singleton();
    }
    return instance;
  }
}
```

Factory Method Pattern: Defines an interface for creating an object but allows subclasses to alter the type of objects that will be created.

Example-

```
interface Product {
  void create();
}

class ConcreteProductA implements Product {
  @Override
  public void create() {
    // Implementation for Product A creation
  }
}

class ConcreteProductB implements Product {
  @Override
  public void create() {
    // Implementation for Product B creation
```

```
    }
}

abstract class Creator {
    abstract Product factoryMethod();
}

class ConcreteCreatorA extends Creator {
    @Override
    Product factoryMethod() {
        return new ConcreteProductA();
    }
}
```

Observer Pattern: Defines a one-to-many dependency between objects, where one object (the subject) maintains a list of its dependents (observers) and notifies them of changes.

Example-

```
import java.util.ArrayList;
import java.util.List;

class Subject {
    private List<Observer> observers = new ArrayList<>();
    private int state;

    public void attach(Observer observer) {
        observers.add(observer);
    }

    public int getState() {
        return state;
    }

    public void setState(int state) {
        this.state = state;
        notifyAllObservers();
    }

    private void notifyAllObservers() {
        for (Observer observer : observers) {
            observer.update();
        }
    }
}

class Observer {
    private String name;
    private Subject subject;

    public Observer(String name, Subject subject) {
        this.name = name;
        this.subject = subject;
        this.subject.attach(this);
    }

    public void update() {
        System.out.println(name + " received an update. New state: " + subject.getState());
    }
}
```

5. Best Practices for Using Design Patterns:

Understand the problem before applying a design pattern. Not every problem requires a pattern.

Follow naming and coding conventions related to the pattern you're using.
Document your design decisions and the patterns you apply.
Be aware of the trade-offs associated with patterns, such as increased complexity.
Use patterns to address specific issues in your design, not as a one-size-fits-all solution.

In summary, design patterns are essential tools for improving the quality, maintainability, and scalability of software in Java and other programming languages. By understanding the various types of design patterns and how they are implemented, developers can make informed design decisions and create more robust and flexible software systems.

6.9 Introduction to Java Security

Java places a strong emphasis on security, allowing developers to create secure and reliable applications. Java's security model includes features like bytecode verification, access control, and cryptography to protect against a wide range of threats. In this detailed overview, we'll explore Java security, covering its key concepts, mechanisms, and best practices.

1. Key Concepts:

Bytecode Verification: Java's bytecode verifier checks class files for invalid code that could harm the JVM or the host system. This verification step ensures that classes loaded by the JVM are safe to execute.

Access Control: Java's security model enforces access control mechanisms that restrict what code can do. Access control includes controlling access to classes, methods, and resources.

Classloaders: Java uses classloaders to load classes into the JVM. Classloaders can define different security domains, allowing applications to have different levels of trust.

Security Managers: Java applications can have a security manager that defines a security policy. The security manager enforces security restrictions on code execution, such as access to system resources.

2. Java Security Mechanisms:

Sandboxing: Java applets and untrusted code are executed within a secure sandbox. The sandbox restricts access to system resources, preventing malicious code from harming the host system.

Code Signing: Code signing allows developers to sign their code with a digital signature. Users can then decide whether to trust the code based on the signature's source.

Cryptography: Java provides robust cryptographic libraries for encryption, decryption, hashing, and secure communication. This is essential for protecting sensitive data.

Security Providers: Java's security architecture supports security providers that implement cryptographic algorithms and services. Providers can be added or replaced to customize security features

3. Java Security APIs:

Java provides a range of security-related APIs:

Java Security API: The java.security package contains core classes and interfaces for Java security, including the SecurityManager class.

Java Cryptography Architecture (JCA): The JCA is a framework for cryptographic operations. It provides the javax.crypto package for encryption and decryption.

Java Authentication and Authorization Service (JAAS): JAAS provides a way to establish user identities and control access to resources based on authentication and authorization.

Java Secure Socket Extension (JSSE): The JSSE library offers secure network communication through SSL/TLS protocols.

Java Authentication Service Provider Interface for Containers (JASPIC): JASPIC defines an SPI for pluggable authentication modules in Java EE containers.

4. Best Practices for Java Security:

Keep Software Updated: Regularly update your Java runtime environment (JRE) to receive security patches and updates.

Avoid Unsafe Practices: Avoid using deprecated or unsafe classes and methods, especially those related to cryptography and random number generation.

Follow Secure Coding Practices: Adhere to secure coding practices, such as input validation, to prevent common vulnerabilities like injection attacks.

Use Strong Passwords: When implementing authentication mechanisms, ensure the use of strong password policies and secure storage.

Minimize Privileges: Limit the privileges of code running in your applications, especially in applets and untrusted code.

Code Reviews and Testing: Perform code reviews and security testing, such as penetration testing, to identify and address vulnerabilities.

Implement Access Controls: Use appropriate access controls to restrict access to sensitive resources and data.

5. Security Challenges:

Zero-Day Vulnerabilities: New security vulnerabilities can emerge, and attackers may exploit them before patches are available.

Social Engineering: Attackers may use social engineering techniques to trick users into executing malicious code or revealing sensitive information.

Legacy Code: Legacy code may contain security vulnerabilities that are challenging to mitigate.

Complexity: As software systems become more complex, ensuring security becomes increasingly challenging.

In conclusion, Java's security model provides robust mechanisms for securing applications and protecting against various threats. By understanding the key concepts, best practices, and available security APIs, developers can create secure Java applications that safeguard sensitive data and prevent unauthorized access. Regular updates and adherence to security guidelines are essential for maintaining the security of Java applications in an evolving threat landscape.

Exercise

Exercise 1 – MCQ

Q 1. Which Java class is commonly used for creating server socket objects and listening for client connections?
a) Socket
b) DatagramSocket
c) ServerSocket
d) HttpURLConnection

Q 2. In JavaFX, which class represents the main application window and serves as the entry point for a JavaFX application?
a) JavaFXWindow
b) Scene
c) Stage
d) ApplicationWindow

Exercise 2 – True/ False

Q 1. Java Servlets and JavaServer Pages (JSP) are used primarily for client-side scripting in web development.

Q 2. Design patterns in Java are specific implementations of code that are unique to each project and cannot be reused in other software development projects.

Exercise 3 – Fill in the blanks

Q 1. To establish a connection to a database using JDBC, you need to load the appropriate database driver using the Class.forName("_________") method.

Q 2. In Java, the ______________ class is used to securely manage and store sensitive information such as passwords and encryption keys.

Exercise 4 – Match case

Q 1. Match the Java design patterns with their descriptions:
i. Singleton Pattern ()
ii. Factory Method Pattern ()
iii. Observer Pattern ()
iv. Strategy Pattern ()

Descriptions:

a. Ensures a class has only one instance and provides a global point of access to it.
b. Defines an interface for creating an object but let's subclasses alter the type of objects that will be created.
c. Allows an object to alter its behaviour when its internal state changes.
d. Defines a one-to-many dependency between objects so that when one object changes state, all its dependents are notified and updated.

Exercise 5 – One word answer

Q 1. What is the purpose of the ClassLoader in Java?

Q 2. Which Java keyword is used for inheritance between classes?

Exercise 6 – Small answer

Q 1. What is the primary role of the ResultSet object in Java Database Connectivity (JDBC)?

Q 2. In JavaFX, what is the purpose of the FXML file?

Exercise 7 – Long answer

Q 1. Explain the concept of a Java Bean and provide an example of a situation where using Java Beans would be advantageous.

Q 2. Describe the concept of design patterns in Java and provide an example of a commonly used design pattern along with its benefits.

Answer:

Exercise 1. Q 1: c) ServerSocket Q 2: c) Stage
Exercise 2. Q 1: False Q 2: False

Exercise 3. Q 1: JDBC driver class name Q 2: KeyStore
Exercise 4. Q 1: i Singleton Pattern ()- a ii. Factory Method Pattern () -b
iii. Observer Pattern ()- c iv. Strategy Pattern ()-d
Exercise 5. Q 1: Loading Q 2: extends

Previous Year Questions

Q 1. Describe different types of JDBC drivers. (JNTU -B.Tech.- 2018)
Q 2. What is the need of JDBC type 3, type 4 drivers? (JNTU -B.Tech. -2017)
Q 3. Write about driver manager class for database connectivity. (JNTU -B.Tech. -2017)
Q 4. Discuss the four types of JDBC driver with suitable diagrams. (SPPU – BCA - 2015)
Q 5. Briefly explain role of following classes in Java Network programming (i) Socket (ii) Datagrams Packet (SPPU – BCA – 2015)
Q 6. What is Java Bean? What are its advantages. (IGNOU MCS 2010)
Q 7. What is Introspection in Java Beans? Illustrate with a code fragment. (IGNOU MCS 2010)
Q 8. What are the characteristics of JDBC? What are the various types of JDBC? (IGNOU MCA 2012)
Q 9. Why we use Java Beans in Java? Explain features of Java Beans. (IGNOU MCA 2012)
Q 10. What is Servlet? Explain how session handling is performed in Servlet programming. (IGNOU MCA 2015)
Q 11. Distinguish between the following terms : Get Method and Post Method in Servlet. (IGNOU MCA 2016)

Previous Year Solved Papers

Q. 1. What is a TCP/IP socket? Explain basic networking features of Java. (RU BCA 2017)
Ans- A TCP/IP socket is an endpoint for sending and receiving data across a computer network using the TCP/IP protocol suite. It provides a mechanism for communication between two nodes over a network, allowing processes on different devices to establish a connection and exchange data. The TCP/IP socket is identified by an IP address and a port number, enabling the network communication between different applications and systems.
Basic networking features of Java include:

java.net package: Java provides the **java.net** package, which includes classes and interfaces for networking, such as **Socket**, **ServerSocket**, and **InetAddress**, enabling network communication and manipulation of network resources.
Socket: The **Socket** class represents a client-side socket that allows for the establishment of a connection to a server. It provides input and output streams for sending and receiving data over the network.
ServerSocket: The **ServerSocket** class represents a server-side socket that listens for incoming connections from clients. It enables the server to accept and handle client connections.
InetAddress: The **InetAddress** class encapsulates an IP address and provides methods for resolving hostnames to IP addresses and vice versa.

URL and URLConnection: Java provides the **URL** class for working with URLs, allowing the opening of connections to the resource specified by the URL. The **URLConnection** class provides methods for establishing a connection to the URL and retrieving data from the resource.

Q. 2. Explain Datagram. Explain the classes for implementing it. (RU BCA 2017)
Ans- In Java, Datagram is a part of the User Datagram Protocol (UDP) communication protocol, which is a connectionless protocol used for sending and receiving datagrams between applications over an IP network. Datagram communication is often preferred for applications that require fast and efficient communication with no guarantee of data delivery.
Java provides several classes for implementing Datagram functionality, primarily through the **java.net** package. Some of the key classes for implementing Datagram functionality in Java are:

DatagramSocket: The **DatagramSocket** class represents a connectionless, point-to-point communication link for sending and receiving datagram packets. It allows applications to send and receive datagrams over the network.
DatagramPacket: The **DatagramPacket** class represents a datagram packet that can be sent or received. It encapsulates the data to be sent or received, along with information about the target or source address and port.

Here is a simple example demonstrating the use of DatagramSocket and DatagramPacket in Java:

```
import java.net.*;

public class DatagramExample {
  public static void main(String[] args) {
    try {
      DatagramSocket socket = new DatagramSocket(); // Create a DatagramSocket

      String message = "Hello, this is a datagram message.";
```

```
            InetAddress address = InetAddress.getByName("localhost");
            int port = 12345;

            // Create a DatagramPacket for sending the message
            DatagramPacket packet = new DatagramPacket(message.getBytes(), message.length(), address, port);

            // Send the packet
            socket.send(packet);

            // Receive the packet
            byte[] buffer = new byte[1024];
            DatagramPacket receivedPacket = new DatagramPacket(buffer, buffer.length);
            socket.receive(receivedPacket);

            String receivedMessage = new String(receivedPacket.getData(), 0, receivedPacket.getLength());
            System.out.println("Received message: " + receivedMessage);

            socket.close(); // Close the socket
        } catch (Exception e) {
            e.printStackTrace();
        }
    }
}
```

In this example, a **DatagramSocket** is created, and a message is sent as a **DatagramPacket**. The program then waits to receive a response from the same port and prints the received message.

Q.3. What does JDBC do? (RU BCA 2017)

Ans- JDBC (Java Database Connectivity) is an API (Application Programming Interface) in Java that provides a standard way for Java applications to interact with relational databases. It enables developers to perform various database operations, such as connecting to a database, sending SQL queries, and processing the results. JDBC acts as a middle layer between the Java application and the database, providing a uniform interface for database access across different database management systems. Some key functions of JDBC include:

Connection Establishment: JDBC enables Java applications to establish connections to various types of databases, including MySQL, Oracle, PostgreSQL, and many others, by providing the necessary drivers for each database.

SQL Execution: JDBC allows developers to execute SQL statements, such as SELECT, INSERT, UPDATE, and DELETE, on the connected database. It provides methods to create and execute SQL queries and updates, and to retrieve and manipulate data from the database.

Result Processing: JDBC enables the processing of query results returned from the database. It provides methods for iterating through the result sets, accessing and manipulating the data, and handling metadata associated with the result sets.

Transaction Management: JDBC supports transaction management, allowing developers to control and manage transactions involving multiple SQL statements. It enables the execution of transactional operations, such as committing or rolling back changes to the database, ensuring data integrity and consistency.

Error Handling: JDBC provides mechanisms for handling database-related errors and exceptions, such as connection failures, SQL syntax errors, and data retrieval issues. It allows developers to handle errors gracefully and take appropriate actions based on the type of error encountered.

By providing a standardized API for database access, JDBC simplifies the process of integrating Java applications with various relational databases, making it easier for developers to build robust, data-driven applications that interact seamlessly with back-end databases.

Q.4. Which class is used by server applications to obtain a port and listen for client requests? (RU BCA 2017)

Ans- The class used by server applications in Java to obtain a port and listen for client requests is the **ServerSocket** class. This class is available in the **java.net** package and provides the functionality to create a server socket that listens for incoming client connections on the specified port. It is a fundamental component for building server applications that need to accept client connections and enable communication over a network.

Here's an example of how the **ServerSocket** class can be used:

```
import java.io.IOException;
import java.net.ServerSocket;
```

```java
import java.net.Socket;

public class ServerExample {
    public static void main(String[] args) {
        try {
            int port = 12345; // Specify the port number
            ServerSocket serverSocket = new ServerSocket(port); // Create a ServerSocket
            System.out.println("Server is listening on port: " + port);

            // Server is ready to accept client connections
            Socket clientSocket = serverSocket.accept();
            System.out.println("Client connected: " + clientSocket);

            // Perform operations with the client
            // ...

            // Close the server socket
            serverSocket.close();
        } catch (IOException e) {
            e.printStackTrace();
        }
    }
}
```

In this example, the **ServerSocket** is created on port 12345, and the **accept()** method is used to listen and accept incoming client connections. Once the client is connected, further operations can be performed. Finally, the **ServerSocket** is closed to release the port and free up system resources.

The **ServerSocket** class is a critical component for implementing server applications in Java and is essential for handling client connections and enabling communication between the server and clients over a network.

Q.5. What is socket? (RU BCA 2017)

Ans-A socket is a software endpoint that establishes a bidirectional communication link between a client and a server over a network. The **java.net.Socket** class in Java provides the mechanism for creating client sockets that can connect to server sockets, allowing for data transmission and communication between different machines. Sockets in Java are used for implementing various network protocols and building network-based applications.

Q.6 Java Networking (RU BCA 2018)

Ans- Java Networking refers to the set of functionalities and APIs provided by the Java platform for developing networked applications. Java provides comprehensive support for networking, allowing developers to create client-server applications, communicate over various network protocols, and transfer data between different machines. Some key components and features of Java Networking include:

Network Classes and Interfaces: Java provides a rich set of classes and interfaces, such as **Socket**, **ServerSocket**, and **DatagramSocket**, for establishing connections and communicating over different network protocols like TCP (Transmission Control Protocol) and UDP (User Datagram Protocol).

URL Handling: Java supports the **URL** and **URLConnection** classes for working with URLs, enabling developers to retrieve data from web servers and open connections to various web resources.

Sockets and Server Sockets: Java allows the creation of client-server applications using sockets. Sockets enable bidirectional communication between client and server applications over the network, facilitating the exchange of data and information.

Datagrams: Java supports the use of datagrams for connectionless communication between hosts. Datagram sockets allow the sending and receiving of datagrams, making it suitable for applications that require low-latency and quick data transmission, such as real-time systems and online gaming.

Networking Protocols: Java supports various networking protocols, including HTTP, HTTPS, FTP, and SMTP, allowing developers to build applications that can communicate over different protocols and perform tasks such as sending emails, downloading files, and accessing web resources.

Networking Security: Java provides extensive security features for networking, including support for secure communication protocols, digital certificates, and encryption, ensuring secure data transmission and protecting sensitive information during network communication.

Q. 7. Explain the JDBC and Jar files. (RU BCA 2018)

Ans- **JDBC (Java Database Connectivity):** JDBC is a Java API that allows Java programs to interact with databases. It provides a set of classes and interfaces that enable developers to connect to and execute SQL queries on a database. JDBC acts as a middle layer between the Java application and the database, providing a standard way to access various relational databases. It enables tasks such as establishing connections, sending queries, and retrieving results from a database in a platform-independent manner. JDBC provides drivers for different databases, allowing Java applications to connect to a wide range of database systems.

JAR (Java Archive) Files: JAR files are archive files that allow multiple Java class files and associated metadata and resources (such as images, sound files, and text files) to be bundled together into a single file. They are compressed and use the ZIP file format. JAR files are used to distribute Java libraries, applications, or components, making it easier to manage and deploy Java applications. JAR files are commonly used for packaging Java applets and applications that can be easily downloaded and run on any system with Java support. They simplify the distribution of Java programs by providing a convenient way to package all the necessary files into a single archive.

Understanding JDBC enables developers to interact with various databases using Java, while understanding JAR files helps in packaging and distributing Java applications and libraries efficiently. Both are essential components in the development and deployment of Java applications, especially those that require database connectivity and distribution across different platforms.

Q.8. What is URL Class and usage through connection? (RU BCA 2018)

Ans- In Java, the **URL** class represents a Uniform Resource Locator, which is a pointer to a "resource" on the World Wide Web. This resource can be any file or a document that can be identified by a unique address. The **URL** class provides various methods to retrieve information about the resource, such as the protocol, host name, file name, and port number.

Here is an example of using the **URL** class to establish a connection:

```
import java.net.URL;
import java.net.HttpURLConnection;
import java.io.BufferedReader;
import java.io.InputStreamReader;

public class URLConnectionExample {
  public static void main(String[] args) {
    try {
      URL url = new URL("https://www.example.com"); // Create a URL object

      // Open a connection to the specified URL
      HttpURLConnection connection = (HttpURLConnection) url.openConnection();

      // Set request method
      connection.setRequestMethod("GET");

      // Get the input stream and read the response
      BufferedReader in = new BufferedReader(new InputStreamReader(connection.getInputStream()));
      String inputLine;
      StringBuilder content = new StringBuilder();
      while ((inputLine = in.readLine()) != null) {
        content.append(inputLine);
      }
      in.close();

      // Print the response
      System.out.println(content.toString());

      // Disconnect the connection
      connection.disconnect();

    } catch (Exception e) {
      e.printStackTrace();
    }
  }
```

}

In this example, the **URL** class is used to create a URL object that points to the specified web address. The **openConnection** method is used to establish a connection to the URL, and the **HttpURLConnection** class is used to handle the HTTP-specific connection. The example then reads the response from the URL and prints it to the console.

The **URL** class in Java is a fundamental part of network programming, allowing developers to establish connections to various resources on the internet and retrieve the data associated with those resources. It is commonly used in scenarios where data needs to be fetched from a specific web address or when network operations are required for the functioning of the application.

Q.8. Why do we use JDBC? Explain by writing the code java with example? (RU BCA 2019)

Ans. JDBC stands for Java Database Connectivity JDBC is a Java API to connect and execute the query with the database. It is a part of JavaSE (Java Standard Edition). JDBC API uses JDBC drivers to connect with the database. There are four types of JDBC drivers

JDBC-ODBC Bridge Driver,
Native Driver,
Netwerk Protocol Driver, and
Thin Driver

We have discussed the above four drivers in the next chapter. We can use JDBC API to access tabular data stored in any relational database. By the help of JDBC API, we can save, update, delete and fetch data from the database. It is like Open Database Connectivity (ODBC) provided by Microsoft

A list of popular interfaces of JDBC API are given below:
Driver interface
Connection interface
Statement interface

Q.9. What is the use of jar file? (RU BCA 2019)

Ans. A Java Archive, or JAR file, contains all of the various components that make up a self-contained, executable Java application, deployable Java applet er, most commonly, a Java library to which any Java Runtime Environment can link. There are two key benefits of using a JAR file. The first is the ability to aggregate hundreds, if not thousands, of different files that make up an application. The second is the means to compress all of the contained files, greatly reducing the size of the application, and making it easier to move the JAR file over a network and between environments.

Q.10. Explain the types of Result sets in JDBC. (RU BCA 2020)

Ans- The type of a ResultSet object determines the level of its functionality in two areas: the ways in which the cursor can be manipulated, and how concurrent changes made to the underlying data source are reflected by the ResultSet object. The sensitivity of a ResultSet object is determined by one of three different ResultSet types:

TYPE FORWARD_ONLY:

The result set cannot be scrolled, its cursor moves forward only, from before the first row to after the last row. The rows contained in the result set depend on how the underlying database generates the results. That is, it contains the rows that satisfy the query at either the time the query is executed or as the rows are retrieved.

TYPE SCROLL INSENSITIVE:

The result can be scrolled; its cursor can move both forward and backward relative to the current position, and it can move to an absolute position. The result set is insensitive to changes made to the underlying data source while it is open. It contains the rows that satisfy the query at either the time the query is executed or as the rows are retrieved.

TYPE SCROLL SENSITIVE:

The result can be scrolled; its cursor can move both forward and backward relative to the current position, and it can move to an absolute position. The result set reflects changes made to the underlying data source while the result set remains open.

The default ResultSet type is TYPE FORWARD_ONLY.

Q.11. Explain Socket Class and Server Socket Class and their important methods by taking a program as an example.(RU BCA 2020)

Ans- Sockets are the endpoints of a bidirectional communication channel. They may communicate within a process, between processes on the same machine or between processes on different machines. On a similar note, a network socket is one endpoint in a communication flow between two programs running over a computer network such as the Internet. It is purely a virtual thing and does not mean any hardware. Network socket can be identified by a unique combination of an IP address and port number Network sockets may be implemented over a number of different channel types like TCP, UDP, and so on.

The different terms related to socket used in network programming are as follows
Domain- Domain is the family of protocols that is used as the transport mechanism. These values are constants such as AF_INET, PF_INET, PF_UNIX, PF X25, and so on.
Type-Type means the kind of communication between two endpoints, typically SOCK STREAM for connection-oriented protocols and SOCK DGRAM for connectionless protocols.
Protocol - This may be used to identify a variant of a protocol within a domain and type. Its default value is 0. This is usually left out
Hostname -This works as the identifier of a network interface. A hostname nay be a string a dotted quad address, or an IPV6 address in colon (and possibly dot) notation.
Port - Each server listens for clients calling on one or more ports. A port may be a Fixnum port number, a string containing a port number, or the name of a service.
Python's Socket Module for Socket Programming
To Implement socket programming in python, we need to use the Socket module. Following is a simple syntax to create a Socket
import socket
s=socket.socket (socket_family, socket type, protocol = 0)
Here, we need to import the socket library and then make a simple socket. Following are the different parameters used while making socket"
socket family" This is either AF UNIX or AF_INET, as explained earlier
socket type "This is either SOCK STREAM or SOCK_DGRAM.
protocol This is usually left out, defaulting to 0.
Socket Methods
In this section, we will learn about the different socket methods. The three different set of socket methods are described below

Server Socket Methods
Client Socket Methods
General Socket Methods
Server Socket Methods

In the client-server architecture, there is one centralized server that provides service and many clients receive service from that centralized server. The clients also do the request to server. A few important server socket methods in this architecture are as follows"
socket.bind() This method binds the address (hostname, port number) to the socket socketlisten("This method basically listens to the connections made to the socket It starts TCP listener. Backlog is an argument of this method which specifies the maximum number of queued connections. Its minimum value is 0 and maximum value is 5.
socket.accept("This will accept TCP client connection. The pair (conn, address) is the return value pair of this method Here, conn is a new socket object used to send and receive data on the connection and address is the address bound to the socket. Before using this method, the socket bind and socket listen() method must be used Client Socket Methods
The client in the client-server architecture requests the server and receives services from the server. For this, there is only one method dedicated for clients"
socket.connect(address)" this method actively intimate server connection or in simple words this method connects then client to the server. The argument address represents the address of the server.
General Socket Methods
Other than client and server socket methods, there are some general socket methods, which are very useful in socket programming. The general socket methods are as follows"
Socket.recv(bufsize)" As name implies, this method receives the TCP message from socket. The argument bufsize stands for buffer size and defines the maximum data this method can receive at any one time. Socket.send(bytes) "This method is used to send data to the socket which is connected to the remote machine. The argument bytes will gives the number of bytes sent to the socket
Socket.recvfrom(data, address)"This method receives data from the socket. Two pair (data, address) value is returned by this method. Data defines the received data and address specifies the address of socket sending the data.
Socket.sendto(data, address)"As name implies, this method is used to send data from the socket. Two pair (data, address) value is returned by this method Data defines the number of bytes sent and address specifles the address of the remote machine.
socket.close()"This method will close the socket
socket.gethostname()"This method will return the name of the host
socket.sendall(data) "This method sends all the data to the socket which is connected to a remote machine. It will carelessly transfers the data until an error occurs and if it happens then it uses socket close() method to close the socket.

Q.12 Explain TCP/IP socket in Java. (RU BCA 2020)

Ans. A socket in Java is one endpoint of a two-way communication link between two programs running on the network. A socket is bound to a port number so that the TCP layer can identify the application that data is destined to be sent to. An endpoint is a combination of an IP address and a port number.

Q.13.Discuss any 2 usages of Socket Programming. (RU BCA 2020)
Ans. 1. Program A program is an executable file residing on a disk in a directory. A program is read intomemory and is executed by the kernel as ad result of an exec() function. The exec() has six variants, but we only consider the simplest one (exec()) in this course.
2. Process An executing instance of a program is called a process. Sometimes, task is used instead of process with the same meaning. UNIX guarantees that every process has a unique identifier called the process ID. The process ID is always a non-negative integer

Q.14. List out any of the 2 importance of Threading in Java. (RU BCA 2020)
Ans. 1. The main purpose of multithreading is to provide simultaneous execution of two or more parts of a program to maximum utilize the CPU time. A multithreaded program contains two or more parts that can run concurrently. Each such part of a program called thread.
2. Threads are lightweight sub-processes, they share the common memory space, In Multithreaded environment, programs that are benefited from multithreading, utilize the maximum CPU time so that the idle time can be kept to minimum.

Q.15. What is socket programming in java and what classes are used for it. (RU BCA 2021)
Ans: Java Socket programming is used for communication between the applications running on different JRE. Java Socket programming can be connection-oriented or connection-less. Socket and Server Socket classes are used for connection-oriented socket programming and Datagram Socket and Datagram Packet classes are used for connection-less socket programming.
The client in socket programming must know two information:
1. IP Address of Server, and
2. Port number.
Here, we are going to make one-way client and server communication. In this application, client sends a message to the server, server reads the message and prints it. Here, two classes are being used: Socket and Server Socket. The Socket class is used to communicate client and server. Through this class, we can read and write message. The Server Socket class is used at server-side. The accept() method of Server Socket class blocks the console until the client is connected. After the successful connection of client, it returns the instance of Socket at server-side.
Example of Java Socket Programming
Creating Server:
To create the server application, we need to create the instance of Server Socket class. Here, we are using 6666 port number for the communication between the client and server. You may also choose any other port number. The accept() method waits for the client. If clients connects with the given port number, it returns an instance of Socket.
1. ServerSocket ss= new Server Socket(6666);
2. Socket s-ss.accept();//establishes connection and waits for the client
Creating Client:
To create the client application, we need to create the instance of Socket class. Here, we need to pass the IP address or hostname of the Server and a port number. Here, we are using "localhost" because our server is running on same system.
1. Socket s-new Socket("localhost",6666);
Let's see a simple of Java socket programming where client sends a text and server receives and prints it.
Socket class
A socket is simply an endpoint for communications between the machines. The Socket class can be used to create a socket. Here are some important methods of the **Socket** class:
getInputStream():
Returns an input stream for this socket.
Used to read data from the server.
getOutputStream():
Returns an output stream for this socket.
Used to write data to the server.
connect(SocketAddress endpoint):
Connects this socket to the server.
The **endpoint** is the IP address and port of the server.
close():
Closes the socket.

Releases the socket and its resources.

getInetAddress():

Returns the remote IP address to which the socket is connected.
Useful for identifying the remote server's address.

getPort():

Returns the remote port number to which this socket is connected.
Helpful for identifying the port number of the remote server.

setSoTimeout(int timeout):

Sets the timeout in milliseconds for blocking socket operations.
If the timeout expires, a **SocketTimeoutException** is raised.

isConnected():

Returns the connection state of the socket.
Useful for checking if the socket is currently connected to a server.

isClosed():

Returns the closed state of the socket.
Useful for checking if the socket has been closed.

setKeepAlive(boolean on):

Enables or disables the TCP keep-alive mechanism.
Useful for ensuring that the connection is maintained.

Server Socket Class

The ServerSocket class in Java is used for implementing server applications. It provides the necessary functionality to listen for and accept incoming client connections.

Here are some important methods of the **Server Socket class**:

1) public Socket accept()- returns the socket and establish a connection between client. server and
2) public synchronized void close()- closes the server socket

Q. 16. What is multi-threading and what are its advantages? How is multi-threading support by java programming language. (RU BCA 2021)

Ans: Multi-threading refers to the ability of a CPU or a single core in a multi-core processor to provide multiple threads of execution concurrently. In the context of programming, multi-threading allows a single program to perform multiple tasks concurrently. Each of these tasks is known as a thread. These threads can run independently, sharing the same resources such as memory, while executing different parts of the program simultaneously.

Advantages of Multi-threading:

Improved Performance: Multi-threading can lead to better performance by efficiently utilizing the available CPU resources, especially in multi-core systems, enabling parallel processing of tasks.

Responsiveness: It enhances the user experience by ensuring that the user interface remains responsive even when performing intensive tasks in the background.

Resource Sharing: Threads can share resources such as memory, files, and other I/O devices, enabling efficient communication and coordination between different parts of the program.

Simplified Design: Complex applications can be simplified by breaking them into multiple threads, each responsible for a specific task, leading to a more manageable and structured design.

Concurrency: It enables the execution of multiple parts of a program concurrently, allowing for the seamless execution of tasks that are independent of each other.

Java has built-in support for multi-threading through the use of the **java.lang.Thread** class and the **java.lang.Runnable** interface. Additionally, the **java.util.concurrent** package provides a rich set of utilities and classes to support concurrent programming. Java's support for multi-threading includes features such as thread synchronization, locking mechanisms, and higher-level concurrency utilities such as **ExecutorService** and **ThreadPoolExecutor**. Java's multi-threading capabilities allow developers to create robust and efficient applications that can take advantage of modern multi-core processors and improve overall application performance. However, the handling of concurrent programming in Java requires careful consideration of potential issues such as race conditions, deadlocks, and thread synchronization to ensure the reliability and stability of the application.

Q.17. What is multi-threading and how is it beneficial? (RU BCA 2021)

Ans: Multithreading in Java is a process of executing multiple threads simultaneously. A thread is a lightweight sub-process, the smallest unit of processing Multiprocessing and multithreading, both are used to achieve multitasking. However, we use multithreading than multiprocessing because threads use a shared memory area. They don't allocate separate memory area so saves memory, and context- switching between the threads takes less time than process.

Advantages of Java Multithreading.

(1) It doesn't block the user because threads are
(2) Independent and you can perform multiple operations at the same time. You can perform many operations together, so it saves time.
(3) Threads are independent, so it doesn't affect other threads if an exception occurs in a single thread. A Multithreading is mostly used in games, animation, etc.

Q.18. Differentiate between AWT and swing. (RU BCA 2021)
Ans:

Aspect	AWT	Swing
Platform Dependency	Heavily dependent on the underlying platform's windowing toolkit.	Platform-independent, as it is entirely written in Java and not dependent on the underlying platform.
Look and feel	Uses the native platform's look and feel, providing a native appearance.	Provides a consistent look and feel across all platforms, offering a unified appearance.
Components	Provides a basic set of GUI components.	Provides an extensive set of rich, customizable, and lightweight GUI components.
Features	Relatively limited in terms of features and customization options.	Offers a wide range of features, including customizable components, better event handling, and more advanced layout options.
Performance	Generally, less efficient in terms of performance due to platform dependency.	More efficient than AWT as it uses lightweight components and is not dependent on the platform's windowing system.
Extensibility	Less extensible compared to Swing.	More extensible, allowing developers to create custom components and extend existing ones more easily.

Q.19. what are different categories of jdbc drivers. (RU BCA 2021)
Ans: There are five types of JDBC drivers in use:
Type 1: JDBC-ODBC bridge.
Type 2: partial Java driver.
Type 3: pure Java driver for database middleware.
Type 4: pure Java driver for direct-to-database.
Type 5: highly-functional drivers with superior performance.

Q.20. What is socket. (RU BCA 2021)
Ans- In Java, a socket is one endpoint of a two-way communication link between two programs running on the network. It can be used to send and receive data. Sockets are bound to the port numbers and IP addresses, and they enable communication between the client and the server over the network.
Java provides the **java.net** package, which contains classes that provide the low-level communication details, allowing you to implement networking applications. The **java.net.Socket** class is used for creating a socket. It provides the necessary methods for connecting to a server, sending data, and receiving data.
Here's a basic overview of how sockets are used in Java:
Creating a socket:
Socket socket = new Socket(hostname, port);

Obtaining input and output streams for sending and receiving data:
InputStream input = socket.getInputStream();
OutputStream output = socket.getOutputStream();

Reading and writing data through the input and output streams.
Closing the socket when communication is complete:
socket.close();
Sockets are fundamental for implementing various network-related functionalities such as client-server communication, file transfer, and more.

Q.21 What is applet? (RU BCA 2021)
Ans: An applet is a small application designed to be executed within another application or a web browser. In the context of Java, an applet is a Java program that can be embedded into a web page. It runs in a restricted environment within the

Java Virtual Machine (JVM), which is installed on the client's computer. Applets were particularly popular in the early days of the internet for creating interactive web applications, games, and visualizations.
However, due to security concerns and the limitations of applets compared to other technologies, their usage has significantly declined in favour of more modern web technologies like JavaScript, HTML5, and other web application frameworks. As of my last knowledge update in September 2021, applets had largely been deprecated and were no longer supported in most modern web browsers.

Q.22. Describe socket based connectivity by providing suitable example. (RU BCA 2022)
Ans. Java Socket programming is used for communication between the applications running on different JRE Java Socket programming can be connection-oriented or connection-less. Socket and ServerSocket classes are used for connection-oriented socket programming and DatagramSocket and DatagramPacket classes are used for connection-less socket programming The client in socket programming must know two information:
1. IP Address of Server, and
2. Port number.
Here, we are going to make one-way client and server communication. In this application, client sends a message to the server, server reads the message and prints it. Here, two classes are being used: Socket and ServerSocket. The Socket class is used to communicate client and server. Through this class, we can read and write message. The ServerSocket class is used at server-side. The accept() method of ServerSocket class blocks the console until the client is connected. After the successful connection of client, it returns the instance of Socket at server-side.
Example of Java Socket Programming
Creating Server:
To create the server application, we need to create the instance of ServerSocket class. Here, we are using 6666 port number for the communication between the client and server. You may also choose any other port number. The accept() method waits for the client. If clients connects with the given port number, it returns an instance of Socket.

```
Server Socket ss= new Server Socket (6666);
Socket s=ss.accept()//establishes connection and waits for the client
```

Creating Client:
To create the client application, we need to create the instance of Socket class. Here, we need to pass the IP address or hostname of the Server and a port number. Here, we are using "localhost" because our server is running on same system.

```
Socket s=new Socket("localhost",6666);
import java.io.*;
import java.net.* public class MyServer {
public static void main(String[] args) {
try{
ServerSocket ss= new ServerSocket(6666);
Socket s=ss.accept()://establishes connection
Data Input Stream dis= new DataInput Stream (s. get
InputStream()).
String str(String)dis.readUTF();
System.out.println("message="+str);
ss.close();
}catch(Exception e) { System.out.println(e);}
}
}
```

File: MyClient.java

```
import java.io.*:
import java.net.*;
public class MyClient {
public static void main(String[] args) {
try{
Socket s= new Socket("localhost",6666);
Data Output Stream dout = new Data Output Stream (s.
get Output Stream());
dout writeUTF("Hello Server");
dout flush();

dout.close();
s.close();
}catch(Exception e)(System.out.println(e);}
```

```
}
}
```

Q.23. Why we need Syncronization? (RU BCA 2022)

Ans- If we do not use syncronization, and let two or more threads access a shared resource at the same time, it will lead to distorted results.

Consider an example, Suppose we have two different threads T1 and T2, T1 starts execution and save certain values in a file temporary.txt which will be used to calculate some result when T1 returns. Meanwhile, T2 starts and before TI returns, T2 change the values saved by T1 in the file temporary.txt (temporary.txt is the shared resource). Now obviously Tl will return wrong result.

To prevent such problems, synchronization was introduced. With synchronization in above case, once TI starts using temporary.txt file, this file will be locked(LOCK mode), and no other thread will be able to access or modify it until Tl returns Every Java object with a critical section of code gets a lock associated with the object. To enter critical section a thread need to obtain the corresponding object's lock.

Q.24. In what two way the threads can be created in java programming? which way is effective and why? explain. (RU BCA 2022)

Ans. Java provides built-in support for multithreading. Multithreading in Java contains two or more we can define a thread in the following two ways:

By extending Thread class

By implementing Runnable interface

In the first approach, Our class always extends Thread class. There is no chance of extending any other class. Hence we are missing Inheritance benefits. In the second approach, while implementing Runnable interface we can extends any other class. Hence we are able to use the benefits of Inheritance. Because of the above reasons, implementing Runnable interface approach is recommended than extending Thread class.

Runnable interface effective way for following reason: When we extend Thread class, we can't extend any other class even we require and When we implement Runnable, we can save a space for our class to extend any other class in future or now.

When we extend Thread class, each of our thread creates unique object and associate with it. When we implements Runnable, it shares the same object to multiple threads.

Implementing Runnable is the preferred way to do it. Here, you're not really specializing or modifying the thread's behavior. You're just giving the thread something to run. That means composition is the better way to go. Java only supports single inheritance, so you can only extend one class. Instantiating an interface gives a cleaner separation between your code and the implementation of threads. Implementing Runnable makes your class more flexible. If you extend Thread then the action you're doing is always going to be in a thread. However, if you implement Runnable it doesn't have to be. You can run it in a thread, or pass it to some kind of executor service, or just pass it around as a task within a single threaded application

```
class ThreadDemo extends Thread{
 public void run(){
System.out.println("thread is running...");
public static void main(String args[]){
ThreadDemo 11-new ThreadDemo():
t1.start():
}
}
```

Output: thread is running....

2)by Implementing Runnable Interface c.g

```
class RunnableDemo implements Runnable(
public void run(){
System.out.println("thread is running...");
}
public static void main(String args[]){
RunnableDemo rd-new RunnableDemo();
Thread 11 =new Thread(rd);
t1.start():
}
}
```

Output:thread is running...

implements Runnable" makes the code loosely-coupled and casier to read Because the code is split into two classes. Thread class for the thread specific code and your Runnable implementation class for your task that should be run by a thread code. "extends Thread" makes the code tightly coupled. Single class contains the thread code as well as the task that needs to be done by the thread.

Q.25.Discuss thread synchronization by explain its need implementation in a multithreading based program in Java. (RU BCA 2022)
Ans. Synchronization is a process of handling resource accessibility by multiple thread requests. The main purpose of synchronization is to avoid thread interference. At times when more than one thread try to access a shared resource, we need to ensure that resource will be used by only one thread at a time. The process by which this is achieved is called synchronization. The synchronization keyword in java creates a block of code referred to as critical section.
General Syntax:

```
synchronized (object)
{
//statement to be synchronized
}
```

Q.26. What is URL class in java? (RU BCA 2022)
Ans. The Java URL class represents an URL.URL is an acronym for Uniform Resource Locator. It points to a resource on the World Wide Web. A URL contains many information :
1. Protocol: In this case, http is the protocol.
2. Server name or IP Address: In this case www.javatpoint.com is the server name
3. Port Number: It is an optional http//www.parth.com:80/btech/, 80 is the number is not mentioned in the URL, it
4. File Name or directory name: In this case index.jsp is the file name.

Q.27 what is use of extends key word. (RU BCA 2022)
Ans. The extends keyword extends a class (indicates that a class is inherited from another class). In Java, it is possible to inherit attributes and methods from one class to another. We group the "inheritance concept into two categories:
subclass (child) - the class that inherits from another class
superclass (parent)- the class being inherited from to inherit from a class, use the extends keyword.

ONLINE RESOURCES

Practice Paper
Link: https://forms.gle/1QVMihthaP2QN7Kb7
QR Code:

Video Content
Link: https://www.youtube.com/playlist?list=PLzlh_31VWEFr99qHNKZpFZw-UtMpAwVPN
QR Code:

CHAPTER 7 - Java Streams and Lambda Expression

7.1 Enumerations and Enumerated Types

Enumerations, often referred to as enums, are a special data type in Java that allow you to define a set of named constants representing discrete values. Enumerations provide a way to group related constants and make your code more readable and maintainable. In this detailed overview, we'll explore enumerations and enumerated types in Java, covering their key concepts, syntax, usage, and best practices.

1. Key Concepts:

Enumeration: An enumeration is a set of named constant values. Enumerations are used to represent a fixed set of values, such as days of the week, months, or status codes.

Enum Type: An enum type is a data type that consists of a fixed set of enumeration constants. Enum types are defined using the enum keyword in Java.

Enum Constant: An enum constant is one of the named values of an enum type. Enum constants are implicitly public, static, and final.

2. Enum Syntax:

To define an enumeration in Java, you use the enum keyword followed by the name of the enum type and a list of constants enclosed in braces:

Example-

```
enum Day {
  SUNDAY, MONDAY, TUESDAY, WEDNESDAY, THURSDAY, FRIDAY, SATURDAY
}
```

3. Enum Usage:

Accessing Enum Constants: You can access enum constants using the dot notation:

Example-

```
Day today = Day.WEDNESDAY;
```

Switch Statements: Enums are commonly used with switch statements for improved readability and type safety:

Example-

```
switch (today) {
  case MONDAY:
    System.out.println("It's Monday.");
    break;
  case WEDNESDAY:
    System.out.println("It's Wednesday.");
    break;
  // Other cases...
}
```

Iterating Over Enum Constants: You can iterate over the constants of an enum using a for-each loop:

Example-

```
for (Day day : Day.values()) {
  System.out.println(day);
}
```

4. Best Practices:

Use enums when you have a fixed set of related constants that are logically grouped together. This improves code readability and reduces the risk of errors.

Name enums in singular form (e.g., Day instead of Days) to reflect that each constant represents a single value from the set.

Use uppercase letters for enum constants, as it is a common naming convention.

Consider providing additional information or behavior for each enum constant by adding fields, constructors, and methods.

5. Enum Constructors and Methods:

You can add constructors and methods to enums to enhance their functionality. Here's an example:

Example-

```
enum Color {
  RED(255, 0, 0),
  GREEN(0, 255, 0),
  BLUE(0, 0, 255);

  private int red;
```

```
    private int green;
    private int blue;

    Color(int red, int green, int blue) {
            this.red = red;
            this.green = green;
            this.blue = blue;
        }

        public int getRed() {
            return red;
        }

        public int getGreen() {
            return green;
        }

        public int getBlue() {
            return blue;
        }
    }
```

6. Use Cases:

Enums are used in various situations, including:

Representing days of the week, months, or other fixed sets of values.

Defining status codes, error codes, or result types in APIs.

Creating type-safe options for configuration or settings.

Modelling categories or types in domain-specific applications.

In summary, enumerations and enumerated types in Java are a powerful way to define named constants that represent a fixed set of values. They improve code readability, reduce errors, and can be enhanced with constructors and methods. By following best practices, developers can effectively use enums to represent related constants in their code

7.1.1 Usage of enumerated data type

An enumerated data type, often referred to as an "enum" in many programming languages, is a user-defined data type that consists of a set of named values, each of which represents a unique constant. Enumerations are used to create a set of symbolic names (enumerators) that represent a set of discrete values or options for a variable.

The primary usage of an enumerated data type is to improve code readability and maintainability by providing meaningful names for values instead of using raw, numeric constants. Enums make the code more self-explanatory and reduce the likelihood of errors when dealing with options or choices.

Here's an example in Java to illustrate the usage of an enumerated data type:

Example-

```
// Define an enum called "Day" representing days of the week
enum Day {
    SUNDAY, MONDAY, TUESDAY, WEDNESDAY, THURSDAY, FRIDAY, SATURDAY
}

public class EnumExample {
    public static void main(String[] args) {
        // Declare a variable of type "Day"
        Day today = Day.WEDNESDAY;

        // Use the enum value in a conditional statement
        if (today == Day.WEDNESDAY) {
            System.out.println("Today is Wednesday!");
        }

        // Enum values can be used in switch statements
        switch (today) {
            case MONDAY:
                System.out.println("It's a workday.");
                break;
```

```
        case SATURDAY:
        case SUNDAY:
          System.out.println("It's the weekend.");
          break;
        default:
          System.out.println("It's a regular weekday.");
      }
    }
}
```

In this example, we define an enum called Day, which represents the days of the week. We declare a variable today of type Day and initialize it with the value Day.WEDNESDAY. We then use this enum value in conditional statements and a switch statement to perform different actions based on the day of the week. This makes the code more readable and self-explanatory compared to using numeric constants or strings to represent days.

Enumerated data types are also used in other programming languages like C, C++, C#, and Python, and they serve a similar purpose of providing named constants for better code organization and readability.

7.2 Annotations and Custom Annotations

Annotations are a form of metadata that provide information about the code in your Java programs. Java annotations are introduced with the @ symbol and can be attached to classes, methods, fields, and other program elements. They serve various purposes, including adding documentation, specifying runtime behavior, and enabling code generation. Custom annotations, also known as user-defined annotations, allow developers to create their own custom metadata for their applications. In this, we'll explore annotations and custom annotations in Java, covering their key concepts, syntax, usage, and creation.

1. Key Concepts:

- **Annotations:** Annotations in Java are introduced with the @ symbol followed by an annotation type. They can be added to program elements to provide additional information or directives.
- **Annotation Types:** Java provides several built-in annotation types, including @Override, @Deprecated, and @SuppressWarnings, which serve various purposes.
- **Custom Annotations:** Developers can define their own custom annotations by creating annotation types using the @interface keyword. These custom annotations can be used to add application-specific metadata.

2. Annotation Syntax:

Example-

```
@AnnotationType(parameterName = value, ...)
```

@ symbol: Denotes the start of an annotation.

AnnotationType: The annotation type being applied.

parameterName = value: Parameters and their values can be included within parentheses.

Built-in Annotations:

@Override: Indicates that a method in a subclass is intended to override a method in the superclass.

@Deprecated: Marks a program element (e.g., method or class) as deprecated, signaling that it should not be used.

@SuppressWarnings: Suppresses compiler warnings for specific code sections.

4. Custom Annotations:

Custom annotations are user-defined and created using the @interface keyword. They can include attributes with default values and can be applied to program elements

Example-

```
import java.lang.annotation.*;

@Retention(RetentionPolicy.RUNTIME)
@Target(ElementType.METHOD)
public @interface MyAnnotation {
  String value() default "Default Value";
  int number();
}
```

5. Annotation Usage:

Annotations can be used for various purposes, including:

- **Documentation:** Annotations like @Override and Javadoc tags provide documentation for code.
- **Runtime Behavior:** Annotations can specify runtime behavior, such as transaction management in Spring Framework.
- **Code Generation:** Annotations are used to generate code (e.g., with Java Persistence API - JPA).

Custom Behavior: Custom annotations can add custom metadata to program elements, allowing developers to define their own semantics.

6. Custom Annotation Example:

Example-

```
@Retention(RetentionPolicy.RUNTIME)
@Target(ElementType.METHOD)
public @interface MyAnnotation {
  String value() default "Default Value";
  int number();
}
```

Example-

```
public class MyClass {
  @MyAnnotation(number = 42)
  public void myMethod() {
    // Method implementation
  }
}
```

7. Processing Annotations:

Java provides reflection APIs to inspect and process annotations at runtime. Libraries like Spring, Hibernate, and JUnit heavily rely on annotations for configuration and runtime behavior.

8. Best Practices:

Use built-in annotations for common purposes like documentation (@Override), deprecation (@Deprecated), and warnings suppression (@SuppressWarnings).

Create custom annotations when you need to add application-specific metadata or directives.

Follow naming conventions for custom annotation types, typically ending with "Annotation" (e.g., MyAnnotation).

9. Use Cases:

Custom annotations are commonly used in frameworks like Spring, Hibernate, and JUnit for configuration and behavior control.

Annotations can be used for RESTful web services, JSON processing, and custom logging.

In summary, annotations in Java are a powerful way to add metadata, documentation, and behavior to your code. Custom annotations provide flexibility to developers to define their own metadata and semantics for their applications. Understanding and effectively using annotations is essential for modern Java development.

7.3 Lambda Expressions and Functional Interfaces

Lambda expressions and functional interfaces are powerful features introduced in Java 8 that facilitate the adoption of functional programming paradigms within the language. They allow you to write more concise, expressive, and flexible code. In this, we'll explore lambda expressions, functional interfaces, their key concepts, syntax, usage, and best practices.

1. Key Concepts:

Lambda Expression: A lambda expression is an anonymous function (a function without a name) that can be used to implement a single abstract method from a functional interface.

Functional Interface: A functional interface is an interface that defines exactly one abstract method. Functional interfaces are used as the target types for lambda expressions and method references.

Syntax: A lambda expression consists of a parameter list, an arrow token (->), and a body.

2. Lambda Expression Syntax:

Example-

```
(parameter1, parameter2, ...) -> expression
```

Parameters: The input parameters for the lambda expression.

Arrow Token (->): Separates the parameters from the expression.

Expression: The code that represents the functionality of the lambda.

3. Functional Interfaces:

Java provides a set of built-in functional interfaces in the java.util.function package, including Predicate, Consumer, Function, and more. Developers can also define their custom functional interfaces.

4. Usage of Lambda Expressions:

Lambda expressions are widely used for various purposes:

Simplifying Code: They make code more concise, especially when implementing functional interfaces.

Collections: Lambda expressions are used with Java's stream API to perform operations on collections in a more declarative and functional style.

Concurrency: They are used in concurrent programming with Java's Executor framework and parallel streams.

5. Examples:

Example 1: Using Lambda with Functional Interface

```
// Using a lambda expression with Predicate (functional interface)
Predicate<Integer> isEven = (num) -> num % 2 == 0;
boolean result = isEven.test(4); // true
```

Example 2: Using Lambda with Streams

```
List<Integer> numbers = Arrays.asList(1, 2, 3, 4, 5);
int sum = numbers.stream()
            .filter(n -> n % 2 == 0)
            .mapToInt(Integer::intValue)
            .sum();
// sum is 6 (2 + 4)
```

6. Best Practices:

Use lambda expressions when they enhance code readability and maintainability.
Prefer built-in functional interfaces from java.util.function for common use cases.
Keep lambda expressions simple and avoid excessive complexity within them.

7. Functional Interfaces in Java:

Commonly used built-in functional interfaces include:

Predicate<T>: Represents a boolean-valued function of one argument.
Consumer<T>: Represents an operation that accepts a single input argument and returns no result.
Function<T, R>: Represents a function that takes one argument and produces a result.
Supplier<T>: Represents a supplier of results.
UnaryOperator<T> and BinaryOperator<T>: Represents operations on a single operand or two operands, respectively.

8. Benefits:

Improved code readability and conciseness.
Enhanced support for functional programming paradigms.
Facilitates parallel and concurrent programming.

In summary, lambda expressions and functional interfaces in Java provide a powerful way to work with functions as first-class citizens in the language. They enable more expressive and concise code and are extensively used in modern Java development, particularly in collections processing, parallelism, and functional programming. Understanding these concepts is essential for writing modern Java applications.

7.4 Java Streams and Stream API

Java Streams and the Stream API, introduced in Java 8, provide a powerful way to work with sequences of data in a functional and declarative manner. They enable you to perform operations on data such as filtering, mapping, and reducing without the need for explicit loops. In this detailed overview, we'll explore Java Streams, the Stream API, their key concepts, syntax, usage, and best practices.

1. Key Concepts:

Stream: A stream is a sequence of data elements that can be processed in a functional and parallel manner. It does not store data but operates on the source data structure (e.g., collections or arrays).

Stream Operations: Stream operations can be categorized into two types: intermediate operations and terminal operations. Intermediate operations transform a stream into another stream, while terminal operations produce a result or side effect.

2. Stream API Syntax:

The Stream API provides a set of methods that can be chained together to create a pipeline of operations. Here's the general syntax for using the Stream API:

Example-

```
streamSource
  .filter(predicate)
  .map(transformation)
  .reduce(identity, accumulator);
```

3. Usage of Java Streams:

Java Streams are used for various purposes, including:

Data Transformation: You can filter, map, and transform data elements to create a new stream with modified or refined data.

Data Reduction: You can perform aggregation operations like sum, average, or count on data elements.

Data Filtering: Filtering allows you to select elements based on specific conditions.

Parallel Processing: Streams can be processed in parallel to leverage multi-core processors for improved performance.

4. Examples:

Example 1: Filtering and Mapping

```
List<String> names = Arrays.asList("Alice", "Bob", "Charlie", "David");

List<String> filteredNames = names.stream()
   .filter(name -> name.length() > 4)
   .map(String::toUpperCase)
   .collect(Collectors.toList());

// filteredNames contains ["ALICE", "CHARLIE"]
```

Example 2: Sum of Integers

```
List<Integer> numbers = Arrays.asList(1, 2, 3, 4, 5);

int sum = numbers.stream()
   .reduce(0, (a, b) -> a + b);

// sum is 15
```

5. Best Practices:

Use Streams when working with collections or arrays to simplify and clarify code.
Avoid mutating data during Stream operations; prefer immutability.
Be cautious when using parallel streams; not all operations benefit from parallelism.

6. Stream API Methods:

Common Stream API methods include:

filter(Predicate<T> predicate): Filters elements based on the given predicate.
map(Function<T, R> mapper): Transforms elements using the provided mapping function.
reduce(T identity, BinaryOperator<T> accumulator): Aggregates elements into a single result.
collect(Collector<T, A, R> collector): Collects elements into a collection or other result.
forEach(Consumer<T> action): Applies an action to each element in the stream.
parallelStream(): Converts a sequential stream to a parallel stream for concurrent processing.

7. Benefits:

Simplifies data manipulation and transformation.
Encourages functional and declarative programming style.
Facilitates parallel processing and can improve performance.

In summary, Java Streams and the Stream API provide a powerful and expressive way to work with data sequences. They offer a functional and declarative approach to data manipulation, making your code more concise and readable. Understanding and using Java Streams is essential for modern Java development.

7.5 Optional Class and Null Handling

The Optional class in Java is introduced to address the problem of null references and to provide a more robust way of handling potentially absent values. It's a container that may or may not contain a non-null value. In this detailed overview, we'll explore the Optional class and its usage for null handling in Java.

1. The Problem with Null References:

Null references in Java can lead to NullPointerExceptions at runtime when trying to access or manipulate a null object. Handling these null references can be error-prone and reduce code reliability.

2. Introduction to the Optional Class:

The Optional class is part of the java.util package (introduced in Java 8) and provides a more structured and safer way to deal with the absence of values.

3. Key Concepts:

Creation: You can create an Optional instance using factory methods like of, ofNullable, or by using the empty method.

Presence Check: You can check if an Optional contains a value using methods like isPresent or ifPresent.

Value Extraction: To extract the value from an Optional, you can use methods like get, but it should be done cautiously to avoid NoSuchElementException. A safer approach is to use methods like orElse, orElseGet, or orElseThrow.

4. Usage of Optional for Null Handling:

Example 1: Using Optional to Avoid Null

```
public Optional<String> findNameById(int id) {
   // Simulated logic to find a name by ID
   if (id == 1) {
      return Optional.of("Alice");
   } else {
      return Optional.empty();
```

```
    }
}

Optional<String> nameOptional = findNameById(1);
String name = nameOptional.orElse("Unknown"); // "Alice"
```

Example 2: Using ifPresent to Avoid Null

```
public void printName(Optional<String> nameOptional) {
    nameOptional.ifPresent(name -> System.out.println("Name: " + name));
}

printName(findNameById(1)); // Prints "Name: Alice"
```

5. Benefits:

Improved Code Reliability: Optional encourages explicit handling of potentially null values, reducing the risk of NullPointerExceptions.

More Expressive: It makes your code more expressive by clearly indicating where values may be absent.

6. Drawbacks:

Overuse: Overusing Optional for non-nullable values can lead to unnecessarily verbose code.

Performance: Creating Optional instances can have a slight performance overhead compared to direct null checks.

7. Best Practices:

Use Optional when dealing with methods that may return null values.

Avoid using Optional for fields or method parameters that are guaranteed to be non-null.

8. Real-World Scenarios:

Optional is commonly used in situations where a method may return a potentially absent value, such as when querying databases or working with optional configuration parameters.

In conclusion, the Optional class in Java provides a safer and more expressive way to handle potentially null values, reducing the risk of NullPointerExceptions. While it's a valuable tool for certain scenarios, it should be used judiciously, primarily for methods that return optional or nullable values.

7.6 Reading and Writing Properties Files

Properties files are a common way to store configuration data in Java applications. They are simple text files that contain key-value pairs, making them easy to read and write. In this detailed overview, we'll explore how to read and write properties files in Java.

1. Reading Properties Files:

1.1. Using java.util.Properties:

Java provides the java.util.Properties class to read properties files. Here's how to read a properties file:

Example-

```
import java.io.FileInputStream;
import java.io.IOException;
import java.util.Properties;

public class ReadPropertiesFile {
    public static void main(String[] args) {
        try (FileInputStream input = new FileInputStream("config.properties")) {
            Properties properties = new Properties();
            properties.load(input);

            // Access properties by key
            String username = properties.getProperty("db.username");
            String password = properties.getProperty("db.password");

            System.out.println("Username: " + username);
            System.out.println("Password: " + password);
        } catch (IOException e) {
            e.printStackTrace();
        }
    }
}
```

1.2. Using java.nio.file (Java 7+):

You can use the java.nio.file package for reading properties files in a more modern way:

Example-

```
import java.io.IOException;
import java.nio.file.Files;
import java.nio.file.Path;
import java.nio.file.Paths;
import java.util.Properties;

public class ReadPropertiesFile {
  public static void main(String[] args) {
    Path path = Paths.get("config.properties");
    try {
      Properties properties = new Properties();
      properties.load(Files.newBufferedReader(path));

      // Access properties by key
      String username = properties.getProperty("db.username");
      String password = properties.getProperty("db.password");

      System.out.println("Username: " + username);
      System.out.println("Password: " + password);
    } catch (IOException e) {
      e.printStackTrace();
    }
  }
}
```

2. Writing Properties Files:

2.1. Using java.util.Properties:

To write properties to a file using java.util.Properties, you can use the store method:

Example-

```
import java.io.FileOutputStream;
import java.io.IOException;
import java.util.Properties;

public class WritePropertiesFile {
  public static void main(String[] args) {
    Properties properties = new Properties();
    properties.setProperty("db.username", "myuser");
    properties.setProperty("db.password", "mypassword");

    try (FileOutputStream output = new FileOutputStream("config.properties")) {
      properties.store(output, "Database Configuration");
    } catch (IOException e) {
      e.printStackTrace();
    }
  }
}
```

2.2. Using java.nio.file (Java 7+):

Here's how to write properties to a file using java.nio.file:

Example-

```
import java.io.IOException;
import java.nio.file.Files;
import java.nio.file.Path;
import java.nio.file.Paths;
import java.util.Properties;

public class WritePropertiesFile {
  public static void main(String[] args) {
    Path path = Paths.get("config.properties");
    Properties properties = new Properties();
```

```
        properties.setProperty("db.username", "myuser");
        properties.setProperty("db.password", "mypassword");

        try {
            Files.createDirectories(path.getParent()); // Create parent directories if needed
            properties.store(Files.newBufferedWriter(path), "Database Configuration");
        } catch (IOException e) {
            e.printStackTrace();
        }
    }
}
```

3. Best Practices:

Use properties files for configuration data that may change over time or for data that should be externalized from the code.

Handle exceptions and I/O operations properly when reading and writing properties files.

Consider using a more structured configuration management solution (e.g., Spring Boot configuration) for complex configurations.

In summary, reading and writing properties files in Java is straightforward and commonly used for storing configuration data. The java.util.Properties class and java.nio.file package provide convenient methods for working with properties files in both older and newer Java versions.

7.7 Working with Regular Expressions (Regex)

Regular expressions, often referred to as regex or regexp, provide a powerful and flexible way to search, match, and manipulate text patterns in Java. Java's java.util.regex package provides classes and methods for working with regular expressions. In this overview, we'll explore how to work with regular expressions in Java, covering key concepts, syntax, usage, and best practices.

1. Key Concepts:

Regular Expression: A regular expression is a pattern that defines a set of strings. It can be used to search for, match, and manipulate text based on that pattern.

Metacharacters: Metacharacters are special characters in regex that have a predefined meaning. For example, . matches any character, * matches zero or more occurrences, and + matches one or more occurrences.

Character Classes: Character classes allow you to specify a set of characters to match. For example, [a-zA-Z] matches any uppercase or lowercase letter.

Quantifiers: Quantifiers specify how many times a character or group of characters should be matched. For example, a{2,4} matches 2 to 4 consecutive 'a' characters.

2. Using Regex in Java:

Java provides the java.util.regex package for working with regular expressions. The primary classes are Pattern and Matcher.

Pattern Class: This class compiles a regex pattern into a Pattern object, which can then be used for matching.

Matcher Class: The Matcher class is used to apply a regex pattern to a given input string and perform various matching operations.

3. Syntax for Common Regex Patterns:

Matching Digits: \d matches any digit (0-9).

Matching Word Characters: \w matches any word character (alphanumeric and underscore).

Matching Spaces: \s matches any whitespace character (space, tab, newline).

Anchors: ^ matches the start of a line, $ matches the end of a line.

4. Examples:

Example 1: Basic Pattern Matching

```
import java.util.regex.*;

public class RegexExample {
    public static void main(String[] args) {
        String text = "The quick brown fox jumps over the lazy dog.";
        String pattern = "fox";

        Pattern regex = Pattern.compile(pattern);
        Matcher matcher = regex.matcher(text);

        if (matcher.find()) {
            System.out.println("Match found: " + matcher.group());
```

```
        } else {
            System.out.println("No match found.");
        }
    }
}
```

Example 2: Extracting Email Addresses

```
import java.util.regex.*;
import java.util.ArrayList;
import java.util.List;

public class EmailExtractor {
    public static void main(String[] args) {
        String text = "Email me at john@example.com or jane@example.org.";

        Pattern pattern = Pattern.compile("\\b[A-Za-z0-9._%+-]+@[A-Za-z0-9.-]+\\.[A-Z|a-z]{2,7}\\b");
        Matcher matcher = pattern.matcher(text);

        List<String> emails = new ArrayList<>();
        while (matcher.find()) {
            emails.add(matcher.group());
        }

        System.out.println("Email addresses found:");
        for (String email : emails) {
            System.out.println(email);
        }
    }
}
```

5. Best Practices:

Compile and reuse Pattern objects when you need to perform multiple matches with the same regex pattern.

Be mindful of performance when working with complex regex patterns, as they can be computationally expensive.

Test your regex patterns thoroughly to ensure they match the intended text.

6. Use Cases:

Regex is commonly used for tasks such as data validation, text parsing, and searching within text data. It is widely employed in tasks like email validation, data extraction from text, and search functionality in text editors.

In summary, working with regular expressions in Java provides a powerful tool for text manipulation and pattern matching. Understanding the syntax and using the java.util.regex package allows you to perform various text-related operations efficiently and effectively.

7.8 Working with XML using Java

XML (Extensible Markup Language) is a widely used format for structuring and exchanging data. Java provides several libraries and APIs for working with XML data, making it possible to parse, create, modify, and manipulate XML documents. In this detailed overview, we'll explore how to work with XML using Java, covering key concepts, libraries, and best practices.

1. Key Concepts:

XML Document: An XML document is a structured data file that contains a hierarchy of elements, attributes, and text content.

Element: An element is a fundamental unit in XML, composed of a start tag, content, and an end tag. For example, <book>Title</book>.

Attribute: An attribute is a property or characteristic of an element, defined within the start tag. For example, <book genre="fiction">Title</book>.

XML Parsing: Parsing is the process of reading an XML document and converting it into a usable data structure in memory.

XML Serialization: Serialization is the process of converting data structures in memory into an XML document.

2. Java Libraries for XML Handling:

Java provides several libraries and APIs for working with XML, including:

DOM (Document Object Model): Represents XML as a tree-like structure in memory, allowing for easy navigation and modification. Classes are in the javax.xml package.

SAX (Simple API for XML): Provides a streaming approach to XML parsing, allowing you to process XML documents sequentially. Classes are in the org.xml.sax package.

StAX (Streaming API for XML): Offers a pull-based approach for reading and writing XML data. Classes are in the javax.xml.stream package.

JAXB (Java Architecture for XML Binding): Allows you to bind XML data to Java objects and vice versa. Classes are in the javax.xml.bind package.

3. Parsing XML:

Using DOM:

Example-

```
import org.w3c.dom.*;
import javax.xml.parsers.*;
import java.io.*;

public class DOMParser {
  public static void main(String[] args) throws Exception {
    DocumentBuilderFactory factory = DocumentBuilderFactory.newInstance();
    DocumentBuilder builder = factory.newDocumentBuilder();
    Document document = builder.parse(new File("data.xml"));

    // Access and manipulate XML elements and attributes here
  }
}
```

Using SAX:

Example-

```
import org.xml.sax.*;
import org.xml.sax.helpers.*;
import java.io.*;

public class MyHandler extends DefaultHandler {
  public void startElement(String uri, String localName, String qName, Attributes attributes) throws SAXException {
    // Process XML start element
  }

  public void characters(char[] ch, int start, int length) throws SAXException {
    // Process XML text content
  }

  // Implement other SAX handler methods as needed
}
```

Using StAX:

Example-

```
import javax.xml.stream.*;
import java.io.*;

public class StAXParser {
  public static void main(String[] args) throws Exception {
    XMLInputFactory factory = XMLInputFactory.newInstance();
    XMLStreamReader reader = factory.createXMLStreamReader(new FileReader("data.xml"));

    while (reader.hasNext()) {
      int event = reader.next();
      if (event == XMLStreamConstants.START_ELEMENT) {
        // Process XML start element
      } else if (event == XMLStreamConstants.CHARACTERS) {
        // Process XML text content
      }
```

```
        }
    }
}
```

4. Creating and Modifying XML:

Using DOM:
Example-

```
DocumentBuilderFactory factory = DocumentBuilderFactory.newInstance();
DocumentBuilder builder = factory.newDocumentBuilder();
Document document = builder.newDocument();

Element rootElement = document.createElement("root");
document.appendChild(rootElement);

Element childElement = document.createElement("child");
childElement.setTextContent("Hello, XML!");
rootElement.appendChild(childElement);

// Serialize the document to a file or other output
```

Using JAXB (for Java Object Binding):
Example-

```
@XmlRootElement
public class MyObject {
    private String data;

    // Getter and setter for data

    public static void main(String[] args) throws Exception {
        MyObject obj = new MyObject();
        obj.setData("Hello, XML!");

        JAXBContext context = JAXBContext.newInstance(MyObject.class);
        Marshaller marshaller = context.createMarshaller();
        marshaller.marshal(obj, new File("data.xml"));
    }
}
```

5. Best Practices:

Use DOM when you need to navigate, modify, or construct an XML document in a tree-like structure.
Use SAX or StAX for streaming processing of large XML documents to conserve memory.
Consider using JAXB for easy conversion between Java objects and XML.

6. Use Cases:

XML is commonly used for data exchange between systems, configuration files, web services, and data storage.
Java's XML handling capabilities are valuable for processing XML data in various scenarios.

In summary, working with XML in Java involves parsing, creating, and manipulating XML documents using libraries like DOM, SAX, StAX, and JAXB. Understanding these libraries and their use cases is essential for handling XML data effectively in Java applications.

7.9 Introduction to JSON Processing

JSON (JavaScript Object Notation) is a lightweight data-interchange format widely used for data serialization and exchange between web services and applications. Java provides several libraries and APIs for processing JSON data, making it possible to parse, create, modify, and manipulate JSON objects. In this introduction, we'll explore the basics of JSON processing in Java, covering key concepts, libraries, and usage.

1. Key Concepts:

JSON Object: A JSON object is an unordered collection of key-value pairs, represented by curly braces {}. Each key is a string, and values can be strings, numbers, objects, arrays, booleans, or null.

JSON Array: A JSON array is an ordered list of values, represented by square brackets []. Values in an array can be of different types, including other arrays or objects.

Parsing: Parsing is the process of converting a JSON string into a structured data object in memory.

Serialization: Serialization is the process of converting data structures in memory into a JSON string.

2. Java Libraries for JSON Processing:

Java provides several libraries and APIs for working with JSON data, including:

Jackson: A popular high-performance library for JSON processing in Java. It provides both simple and advanced features for JSON parsing and generation.

Gson: Developed by Google, Gson is a library for parsing JSON in Java and converting Java objects to JSON and vice versa.

JSON-P (JSON Processing API): Part of the Java EE standard, JSON-P provides a standard API for parsing and generating JSON. It is available in the javax.json package.

3. Parsing JSON:

Using Jackson:

Example-

```
import com.fasterxml.jackson.databind.JsonNode;
import com.fasterxml.jackson.databind.ObjectMapper;

public class JsonParser {
   public static void main(String[] args) throws Exception {
      String jsonString = "{\"name\":\"Alice\",\"age\":30}";

      ObjectMapper objectMapper = new ObjectMapper();
      JsonNode jsonNode = objectMapper.readTree(jsonString);

      String name = jsonNode.get("name").asText();
      int age = jsonNode.get("age").asInt();

      System.out.println("Name: " + name);
      System.out.println("Age: " + age);
   }
}
```

Using Gson:

Example-

```
import com.google.gson.JsonObject;
import com.google.gson.JsonParser;

public class JsonParser {
   public static void main(String[] args) {
      String jsonString = "{\"name\":\"Alice\",\"age\":30}";

      JsonParser jsonParser = new JsonParser();
      JsonObject jsonObject = jsonParser.parse(jsonString).getAsJsonObject();

      String name = jsonObject.get("name").getAsString();
      int age = jsonObject.get("age").getAsInt();

      System.out.println("Name: " + name);
      System.out.println("Age: " + age);
   }
}
```

4. Creating and Modifying JSON:

Using Jackson:

Example-

```
import com.fasterxml.jackson.databind.ObjectMapper;
import com.fasterxml.jackson.databind.node.ObjectNode;

public class JsonCreator {
```

```
    public static void main(String[] args) throws Exception {
        ObjectMapper objectMapper = new ObjectMapper();
        ObjectNode jsonNode = objectMapper.createObjectNode();

        jsonNode.put("name", "Bob");
        jsonNode.put("age", 25);

        String jsonString = objectMapper.writeValueAsString(jsonNode);
        System.out.println(jsonString);
    }
}
```

Using Gson:
Example-

```
import com.google.gson.JsonObject;

public class JsonCreator {
    public static void main(String[] args) {
        JsonObject jsonObject = new JsonObject();

        jsonObject.addProperty("name", "Bob");
        jsonObject.addProperty("age", 25);

        String jsonString = jsonObject.toString();
        System.out.println(jsonString);
    }
}
```

5. Best Practices:

Choose a JSON library based on your project's requirements, performance, and ease of use.
Validate JSON data to ensure it conforms to the expected schema before processing.
Handle exceptions and errors when parsing and working with JSON data.

6. Use Cases:

JSON is commonly used for data interchange in web services, configuration files, and communication between front-end and back-end systems. Java's JSON processing libraries are essential for handling JSON data in various applications.

In summary, JSON processing in Java involves parsing JSON strings into structured data objects and creating JSON strings from data structures. Understanding JSON libraries like Jackson and Gson, along with their usage, is essential for working with JSON data effectively in Java applications.

Exercise

Exercise 1 – MCQ

Q 1. In Java, which of the following is a valid functional interface from the Java Standard Library?
a) Serializable
b) b) Runnable
c) c) Map
d) d) String

Q 2. What is the primary purpose of the Java Stream API?
a) To manage database connections.
b) To create graphical user interfaces.
c) To work with sequences of data in a functional and declarative style.
d) To handle asynchronous I/O operations.

Exercise 2 – True/ False

Q 1. In Java, enumerations (enums) are used to represent a fixed set of constants and cannot contain methods or fields.
Q 2. Internationalization (i18n) is the process of adapting a Java application to support multiple languages and cultures, while localization (L10n) refers to the process of translating the application's user interface into various languages.

Exercise 3 – Fill in the blanks

Q 1. Annotations in Java are used for adding _______ information to code elements, and custom annotations can be created using the @interface keyword.

Q 2. In Java, the Pattern class is used to compile regular expressions, while the Matcher class is used to _______ a regular expression against an input string.

Exercise 4 – Match case

Q 1. Match the Java concept with its description:

i. Regular Expressions (Regex) ()

ii. Optional Class ()

iii. Lambda Expressions ()

iv. Java Streams and Stream API ()

Descriptions:

a. A technique used for pattern matching and text searching in strings.

b. A class used to represent the absence of a value or a nullable result.

c. An anonymous function that can be passed as an argument to a method.

d. A feature for processing sequences of data in a functional and declarative style.

Exercise 5 – One word answer

Q 1. What is the purpose of the default keyword when used in an interface in Java?

Q 2. What is the keyword used in Java to create an instance of a class?

Exercise 6 – Small answer

Q 1. What is the purpose of the break statement in a Java switch statement?

Q 2. In Java, what is the primary role of the StringBuilder class?

Exercise 7 – Long answer

Q 1. Explain the concept of Java Streams and provide an example of how you can use them to filter a collection of data.

Q 2. Describe the concept of internationalization (i18n) and localization (L10n) in Java. Provide an example scenario where internationalization and localization are important in software development.

Answer:

Exercise 1. Q 1: b) Runnable

Q 2: c) To work with sequences of data in a functional and declarative style.

Exercise 2. Q 1: True Q 2: True

Exercise 3. Q 1: metadata Q 2: match

Exercise 4. Q 1: i. Regular Expressions (Regex) ()- a ii. Optional Class ()- b

iii. Lambda Expressions () -c iv. Java Streams and Stream API ()-d

Exercise 5. Q 1: Multiple Q 2: new

Previous Year Questions

Q 1. What is the usage of enumerated data type? Give examples. (SPPU – BCA - 2015)

ONLINE RESOURCES

Practice Paper

Link: https://forms.gle/qGCqvGVpWDgcTzXs7

QR Code:

Video Content

Link: https://www.youtube.com/playlist?list=PLzlh_31VWEFp0IUemjbkD4iDOYU4C6gKC

QR Code:

CHAPTER 8 - Concepts of DSA IN Java

8.1 Java LinkedList

A LinkedList in Java is a data structure that represents a collection of elements, where each element is stored as a separate object called a node. These nodes are connected through references to form a chain-like structure. In this detailed overview, we'll explore Java LinkedList, covering its key concepts, characteristics, usage, and best practices.

1. Key Concepts:

- **Node:** Each element in a LinkedList is encapsulated within a node object. A node typically contains two fields: the data (element) and a reference (or link) to the next node in the sequence.
- **Head:** The head is the first node in the LinkedList. It serves as the entry point and is used to access the elements in the list.
- **Tail:** The tail is the last node in the LinkedList. It does not have a reference to the next node and usually has a null reference.

2. Characteristics of LinkedList:

- **Dynamic Size:** LinkedLists can dynamically grow or shrink in size. Elements can be easily added or removed from any position within the list.
- **Insertions and Deletions:** Inserting or deleting elements in a LinkedList is more efficient than arrays because it requires changing references, not shifting elements.
- **Random Access:** LinkedLists do not support direct random access to elements. To access an element at a specific index, you must traverse the list from the head.
- **Memory Overhead:** LinkedLists have higher memory overhead than arrays because of the additional storage required for node references.

3. Java LinkedList Implementation:

In Java, you can use the java.util.LinkedList class, which implements the java.util.List interface. This class provides a standard implementation of a doubly-linked list.

Creating a LinkedList:

Example-

```
LinkedList<String> linkedList = new LinkedList<>();
```

1. Adding Elements:

Example-

```
linkedList.add("Apple");
linkedList.add("Banana");
linkedList.add("Cherry");
```

2. Accessing Elements:

Example-

```
String firstElement = linkedList.getFirst();
String lastElement = linkedList.getLast();
String elementAtIndex = linkedList.get(1);
```

3. Iterating Through Elements:

Example-

```
for (String fruit : linkedList) {
   System.out.println(fruit);
}
```

4. LinkedList vs. ArrayList:

LinkedList: Best suited for frequent insertions and deletions, especially in the middle of the list. It has a higher memory overhead due to node references.

ArrayList: Best suited for frequent random access to elements. It is more memory-efficient than LinkedList when you don't need frequent insertions and deletions.

5. Best Practices:

- Use LinkedList when you need efficient insertions and deletions in the middle of the list or when you don't require frequent random access.
- Be mindful of performance implications when working with large LinkedLists, as traversing them can be slower than ArrayLists.
- Consider using java.util.Deque (double-ended queue) when you need a LinkedList with both stack and queue operations.
- When iterating over a LinkedList, use an iterator (Iterator or enhanced for loop) for efficient traversal.

6. Common Operations:

LinkedLists support various common operations:

Adding Elements: Use add() or addFirst()/addLast() methods to insert elements at the beginning or end of the list.
Removing Elements: Use remove() or removeFirst()/removeLast() methods to remove elements. You can also use removeFirstOccurrence() or removeLastOccurrence().
Inserting at Specific Positions: Use add(index, element) to insert an element at a specific position.
Getting Elements: Use get(index) to retrieve an element at a specific index.
Size: Use size() to get the number of elements in the list.

7. Use Cases:

LinkedLists are suitable for scenarios where you need efficient insertions and deletions in the middle of the list or when the list size may change frequently. Some use cases include:
Implementing data structures like stacks and queues.
Implementing certain algorithms, such as graph algorithms, where dynamic updates are common.
Handling collections of items where elements may be frequently added or removed.

In summary, Java LinkedList is a dynamic data structure that provides efficient insertion and deletion operations at the cost of slower random access. It is a valuable tool when you need to manage a collection of elements with frequent changes in size or when you want to implement specific data structures or algorithms that benefit from its characteristics.

8.2 Java HashMap

A HashMap in Java is a widely used data structure that implements the Map interface, representing a collection of key-value pairs. It allows you to store and retrieve data efficiently using a hashing mechanism. In this detailed overview, we'll explore Java HashMap, covering its key concepts, characteristics, usage, and best practices.

1. Key Concepts:

Key-Value Pairs: A HashMap stores data as key-value pairs, where each key is unique, and each key maps to a single value.
Hashing: Hashing is the process of converting a key into an index (hash code) within an array. This index is used to store and retrieve the associated value.
Buckets: HashMap internally maintains an array of "buckets" or "slots" where key-value pairs are stored. Each bucket can hold multiple pairs.
Collision Handling: Collisions occur when two keys generate the same hash code. HashMap uses a mechanism called chaining to handle collisions, where multiple key-value pairs with the same hash code are stored as a linked list within the same bucket.

2. Characteristics of HashMap:

Fast Retrieval: HashMap provides fast retrieval of values based on keys. It has an average time complexity of O(1) for get() and put() operations.
Unordered: The order of key-value pairs in a HashMap is not guaranteed to be preserved. If you need ordering, consider using a LinkedHashMap.
No Duplicate Keys: HashMap does not allow duplicate keys. If you attempt to add a duplicate key with a different value, the new value will overwrite the existing one.
Null Values: HashMap allows one null key and multiple null values.

3. Java HashMap Implementation:

In Java, you can use the java.util.HashMap class to create and work with HashMaps.

Creating a HashMap:

Example-
```
HashMap<String, Integer> hashMap = new HashMap<>();
```
1. Adding Key-Value Pairs:

Example-
```
hashMap.put("Alice", 25);
hashMap.put("Bob", 30);
hashMap.put("Charlie", 22);
```
2. Accessing Values:

Example-
```
int age = hashMap.get("Alice");
```
3. Removing Entries:

Example-
```
hashMap.remove("Bob");
```
4. Iterating Through Entries:

Example-
```
for (Map.Entry<String, Integer> entry : hashMap.entrySet()) {
   String name = entry.getKey();
   int age = entry.getValue();
   System.out.println(name + ": " + age);
```

}

4. Best Practices:

Choose appropriate data types for keys and values based on your use case.

- Use descriptive and meaningful keys.
- Be cautious when using mutable objects as keys, as changes to the key's state can affect the HashMap's behavior.
- Use the containsKey() method to check if a key exists before performing operations.
- Be aware of the load factor (the ratio of elements to buckets). If the load factor exceeds a certain threshold, the HashMap is automatically resized, which can be a performance cost.
- When specifying an initial capacity, consider the expected number of elements to reduce resizing.

5. Common Operations:

HashMaps support various common operations:

- **Adding Key-Value Pairs:** Use put(key, value) to add key-value pairs.
- **Getting Values:** Use get(key) to retrieve the value associated with a key.
- **Removing Entries**: Use remove(key) to delete an entry based on the key.
- **Size:** Use size() to get the number of key-value pairs in the HashMap.
- **Checking for Existence:** Use containsKey(key) to check if a key exists.

6. Use Cases:

- HashMaps are suitable for various use cases, including:
- Storing and retrieving data with fast access times based on keys.
- Implementing caches and memorization for optimization.
- Managing configurations and settings.
- Counting occurrences of items in collections.

In conclusion, Java HashMap is a versatile and efficient data structure for storing and retrieving key-value pairs. It provides fast access times and is widely used in various programming scenarios. By following best practices and understanding its characteristics, developers can leverage HashMaps effectively in their applications for efficient data management.

8.3 Java HashSet

A HashSet in Java is an implementation of the Set interface, which represents an unordered collection of unique elements. It is part of the Java Collections Framework and is commonly used for storing and manipulating data where uniqueness and order are not important. In this detailed overview, we'll explore Java HashSet, covering its key concepts, characteristics, usage, and best practices.

1. Key Concepts:

- **Set:** A Set is a collection of elements that do not allow duplicates. In the case of a HashSet, it ensures that no duplicate elements are stored.
- **Unordered:** HashSet does not guarantee any specific order of elements. Elements are stored in an order determined by their hash codes.
- **Hashing**: HashSet uses a hashing mechanism to store and retrieve elements efficiently. It computes the hash code of each element to determine its position in an internal array.

2. Characteristics of HashSet:

- **Uniqueness:** HashSet enforces the uniqueness of elements, ensuring that duplicate values are not allowed. Adding a duplicate element has no effect.
- **Fast Operations:** HashSet provides fast operations for adding, removing, and checking for the presence of elements. It has an average time complexity of O(1) for these operations.
- **Null Values**: HashSet allows one null element. Adding multiple null elements has no effect because null is considered a single value.
- **Iteration**: Elements in a HashSet can be iterated through using an iterator or an enhanced for loop, but the order of iteration is not guaranteed.

3. Java HashSet Implementation:

In Java, you can use the java.util.HashSet class to create and work with HashSets.

Creating a HashSet:

Example-

```
HashSet<String> hashSet = new HashSet<>();
```

1. Adding Elements:

Example-

```
hashSet.add("Apple");
hashSet.add("Banana");
hashSet.add("Cherry");
```

2. Removing Elements:

Example-

```
hashSet.remove("Banana");
```

3. Checking for Existence:

Example-

```
boolean containsCherry = hashSet.contains("Cherry");
```

4. Iterating Through Elements:

Example-

```
for (String fruit : hashSet) {
   System.out.println(fruit);
}
```

4. Best Practices:

- Choose appropriate data types for elements based on your use case.
- Use HashSet when you need to ensure the uniqueness of elements and order is not important.
- Be cautious when using mutable objects as elements, as changes to the object's state can affect the HashSet's behavior.
- Use the contains() method to check if an element exists before performing operations.
- Consider specifying an initial capacity when creating a HashSet to reduce resizing if you know the expected number of elements.

5. Common Operations:

HashSet supports various common operations:

- **Adding Elements:** Use add(element) to add elements.
- **Removing Elements**: Use remove(element) to delete an element.
- **Checking for Existence:** Use contains(element) to check if an element exists.
- **Size:** Use size() to get the number of elements in the HashSet.
- **Clearing**: Use clear() to remove all elements from the HashSet.

6. Use Cases:

- HashSet is suitable for various use cases, including:
- Removing duplicates from a collection.
- Checking for the presence of elements in a dataset.
- Implementing efficient membership tests.
- Managing unique identifiers or keys in a data structure.

In summary, Java HashSet is a versatile and efficient data structure for maintaining a collection of unique elements. It provides fast operations for adding, removing, and checking for element existence. By following best practices and understanding its characteristics, developers can leverage HashSet effectively in their applications for managing unique data sets.

8.4 Java Iterator

In Java, an Iterator is an interface that provides a way to access elements in a collection sequentially without exposing the underlying data structure. Iterators are widely used in Java Collections Framework to traverse and manipulate collections such as ArrayLists, HashSets, and LinkedLists. In this detailed overview, we'll explore Java Iterator, covering its key concepts, methods, usage, and best practices.

1. Key Concepts:

- **Iterator Interface:** The java.util.Iterator interface defines the methods for iterating over a collection. It is part of the Java Collections Framework.
- **Sequential Access**: Iterators allow you to traverse elements in a collection sequentially, from the beginning to the end, without exposing the underlying data structure.
- **Methods:** The Iterator interface provides three primary methods: hasNext(), next(), and remove(). The remove() method is optional and is used to remove the last element returned by next().

2. Iterator Methods:

- **hasNext():** This method returns true if there are more elements to iterate, and false if the end of the collection has been reached.
- **next():** This method returns the next element in the collection and advances the iterator to the following element. If there are no more elements, it throws a NoSuchElementException.
- **remove():** This method is used to remove the last element returned by next(). It can only be called once per call to next(). If it is called without a preceding call to next(), it throws an IllegalStateException.

3. Java Iterator Implementation:

Here's an example of using an Iterator with an ArrayList:

Example-

```
import java.util.ArrayList;
import java.util.Iterator;

public class IteratorExample {
  public static void main(String[] args) {
```

```
        ArrayList<String> fruits = new ArrayList<>();
        fruits.add("Apple");
        fruits.add("Banana");
        fruits.add("Cherry");

        Iterator<String> iterator = fruits.iterator();
        while (iterator.hasNext()) {
            String fruit = iterator.next();
            System.out.println(fruit);
        }
    }
}
```

4. Best Practices:

Always use an Iterator to traverse collections when you need sequential access. Avoid using index-based loops like for loops.

Use the enhanced for-each loop (for iterating collections) whenever possible, as it simplifies the code and reduces the risk of off-by-one errors.

Be cautious when modifying a collection while iterating over it using an Iterator. Use the Iterator's remove() method for safe removal.

When using a remove() operation with an Iterator, make sure you call hasNext() before calling remove() to ensure that there are more elements to remove.

Be aware of concurrent modification exceptions when modifying a collection outside the Iterator while iterating over it.

5. Use Cases:

Iterators are suitable for various use cases, including:

Traversing and processing elements in collections, arrays, or custom data structures.

Implementing algorithms like searching, filtering, or transforming data.

Creating custom iterators for custom data structures.

Reading data from external sources sequentially, such as files or network streams.

In conclusion, Java Iterator is a fundamental interface that provides a standardized way to traverse and manipulate elements in collections. It promotes clean and efficient code for iterating over data structures, and following best practices helps avoid common pitfalls. Iterators are a crucial part of the Java Collections Framework and are widely used in Java programming.

8.5 Java Wrapper Classes

Wrapper classes in Java provide a way to represent primitive data types (e.g., int, char, boolean) as objects. These classes are part of the Java Standard Library and are used when you need to treat primitive data types as objects, such as when working with collections or using certain Java APIs that require objects. In this detailed overview, we'll explore Java Wrapper Classes, covering their key concepts, characteristics, usage, and best practices.

1. Key Concepts:

Primitive Data Types: Java has eight primitive data types: byte, short, int, long, float, double, char, and boolean. These data types are not objects and do not have methods or fields.

Wrapper Classes: Wrapper classes are a set of classes, one for each primitive data type, that allow you to create objects representing primitive values. They provide useful methods and behaviors not available in primitive data types.

2. Characteristics of Wrapper Classes:

Object Representation: Wrapper classes wrap primitive values in an object, allowing you to use them in object-oriented contexts.

Immutable: Wrapper objects are immutable, meaning their values cannot be changed once they are created. Any modification results in the creation of a new object.

Null Values: Wrapper classes can represent null values, which is not possible with primitive data types.

Utility Methods: Wrapper classes provide useful methods for converting, parsing, and comparing values, among other operations.

3. Java Wrapper Classes:

Here are the eight wrapper classes in Java:

Byte: Represents a byte value.

Short: Represents a short value.

Integer: Represents an int value.

Long: Represents a long value.

Float: Represents a float value.

Double: Represents a double value.

Character: Represents a char value.

Boolean: Represents a boolean value.

4. Java Wrapper Class Implementation:

Creating wrapper objects:

Example-

Integer intObj = Integer.valueOf(42); // Creating an Integer object with value 42
Boolean boolObj = Boolean.valueOf(true); // Creating a Boolean object with value true

1. Unboxing (converting wrapper objects to primitive values):

Example-

int intValue = intObj.intValue(); // Unboxing to int
boolean boolValue = boolObj.booleanValue(); // Unboxing to boolean

5. Autoboxing and Unboxing:

Java introduced autoboxing and unboxing to simplify the use of wrapper classes:

Autoboxing: Automatic conversion of primitive types to their corresponding wrapper objects. For example, Integer i = 42; is equivalent to Integer i = Integer.valueOf(42);.

Unboxing: Automatic conversion of wrapper objects to their primitive values. For example, int n = i; is equivalent to int n = i.intValue();.

6. Best Practices:

Use wrapper classes when working with collections (e.g., ArrayList, HashSet) because they require objects, not primitives.

Be mindful of potential null values when working with wrapper objects, as they can be null.

Be cautious when comparing wrapper objects using ==, as it compares references, not values. Use equals() for value comparisons.

When dealing with performance-critical code, consider the overhead of using wrapper classes compared to primitive types.

7. Use Cases:

Wrapper classes are used in various situations:

Storing primitive values in collections like ArrayList, where only objects are allowed.

Working with APIs that require objects, such as certain Java libraries or frameworks.

Handling null values in situations where primitive types cannot represent null.

Performing mathematical operations on values represented as objects.

In summary, Java Wrapper Classes provide a bridge between primitive data types and objects, allowing you to use primitive values in object-oriented contexts. They offer utility methods and enable the representation of null values. While autoboxing and unboxing simplify their usage, it's important to understand their characteristics and best practices for effective and error-free programming.

8.6 Java Regular Expressions

Regular expressions, often referred to as regex or regexp, are a powerful tool for pattern matching and text manipulation in Java. They provide a way to search, match, and manipulate strings based on patterns defined using a special syntax. In this detailed overview, we'll explore Java Regular Expressions, covering their key concepts, syntax, usage, and best practices.

1. Key Concepts:

Pattern Matching: Regular expressions are patterns used to match and search for strings within a larger text or document.

Metacharacters: Special characters (e.g., *, +, ?, ., [,]) have predefined meanings in regular expressions.

Quantifiers: Quantifiers specify how many times a character or group of characters should be repeated (e.g., * for zero or more times, + for one or more times, ? for zero or one time).

Character Classes: Character classes (e.g., [a-zA-Z], [0-9], [^abc]) allow you to match a set of characters at a specific position in the string.

Groups and Capturing: Parentheses ( ) are used to create groups, and you can capture and extract matched portions of the string.

2. Java Regular Expression Classes:

Java provides the java.util.regex package for working with regular expressions. Key classes and interfaces include:

Pattern: Represents a compiled regular expression pattern.

Matcher: Represents the result of applying a pattern to a string and provides methods for text manipulation.

PatternSyntaxException: Represents an exception thrown when there's a syntax error in a regular expression.

3. Java Regular Expression Syntax:

Here are some common regular expression constructs:

a. Basic Matching:

.: Matches any character except a newline.

a: Matches the character 'a'.

b. Character Classes:

[abc]: Matches any of the characters 'a', 'b', or 'c'.

[^abc]: Matches any character except 'a', 'b', or 'c'.

[a-z]: Matches any lowercase letter from 'a' to 'z'.

c. Predefined Character Classes:

\d: Matches any digit (equivalent to [0-9]).

\w: Matches any word character (equivalent to [a-zA-Z0-9_]).

\s: Matches any whitespace character (e.g., space, tab, newline).

d. Quantifiers:

*: Matches zero or more of the preceding element.

+: Matches one or more of the preceding element.

?: Matches zero or one of the preceding element.

{n}: Matches exactly 'n' occurrences.

{n,}: Matches 'n' or more occurrences.

{n,m}: Matches between 'n' and 'm' occurrences.

e. Anchors:

^: Matches the start of a line.

$: Matches the end of a line.

f. Groups and Capturing:

(abc): Creates a capturing group that matches 'abc'.

g. Alternation:

a|b: Matches either 'a' or 'b'.

4. Java Regular Expression Example:

Here's an example of using regular expressions in Java to match email addresses:

Example-

```
import java.util.regex.*;

public class RegexExample {
    public static void main(String[] args) {
        String text = "Contact us at info@example.com or support@company.com for assistance.";

        Pattern pattern = Pattern.compile("\\b\\w+@\\w+\\.\\w+\\b");
        Matcher matcher = pattern.matcher(text);

        while (matcher.find()) {
            System.out.println("Email found: " + matcher.group());
        }
    }
}
```

5. Best Practices:

Compile regular expressions using Pattern.compile() when you need to match the same pattern multiple times for efficiency.

Use \ to escape metacharacters if you want to match them as literal characters (e.g., * to match an asterisk).

Be mindful of greedy quantifiers (*, +) that match as much as possible. Use non-greedy quantifiers (*?, +?) when you want to match as little as possible.

Use character classes and predefined character classes (\d, \w, \s) to simplify pattern creation.

Consider using tools like online regex testers to test and debug your regular expressions.

6. Use Cases:

Regular expressions are used in various situations, including:

Validating input (e.g., email addresses, phone numbers, dates).

Extracting data (e.g., parsing log files, extracting URLs).

Replacing or cleaning text (e.g., removing HTML tags, formatting text).

Search and replace operations within text editors and IDEs.

In conclusion, Java Regular Expressions provide a powerful and flexible way to work with text and patterns. By understanding the key concepts, syntax, and best practices, developers can effectively use

8.7 Java Threads

Threads are a fundamental part of Java, allowing concurrent execution of code. Threads are used for multitasking and parallelism, enabling programs to perform multiple tasks concurrently. In this detailed overview, we'll explore Java Threads, covering their key concepts, creation, management, synchronization, and best practices.

1. Key Concepts:

Thread: A thread is the smallest unit of execution in a Java program. Multiple threads can run concurrently within a single Java process.

Multithreading: Multithreading is the concurrent execution of multiple threads to perform tasks in parallel.
Thread State: Threads can be in various states, including new, runnable, blocked, waiting, timed waiting, and terminated.
Concurrency: Concurrency is the ability of a program to handle multiple tasks and make progress on all of them.
Synchronization: Synchronization is a mechanism used to ensure that only one thread can access a shared resource at a time, preventing data corruption.

2. Creating Threads:

There are two main ways to create threads in Java:

Extending the Thread Class: You can create a custom class that extends the Thread class and overrides the run() method.

Example-

```
class MyThread extends Thread {
    public void run() {
        // Thread logic here
    }
}

MyThread thread = new MyThread();
thread.start();
```

Implementing the Runnable Interface: You can create a class that implements the Runnable interface and provides a run() method. Then, you can pass an instance of this class to a Thread constructor.

Example-

```
class MyRunnable implements Runnable {
    public void run() {
        // Thread logic here
    }
}

Thread thread = new Thread(new MyRunnable());
thread.start();
```

3. Thread Management:

Starting Threads: Use the start() method to begin the execution of a thread. Starting a thread multiple times will result in an IllegalThreadStateException.
Joining Threads: You can use the join() method to make one thread wait for the completion of another thread.
Interrupting Threads: The interrupt() method is used to interrupt a thread's execution. You can check if a thread is interrupted using isInterrupted().
Thread Priority: Threads can have priority levels ranging from Thread.MIN_PRIORITY to Thread.MAX_PRIORITY. Higher-priority threads are given preference in execution.

4. Synchronization:

Synchronization is used to prevent race conditions and ensure that only one thread accesses a shared resource at a time.
You can use the synchronized keyword on methods or blocks to create synchronized sections.

Example-

```
public synchronized void synchronizedMethod() {
    // Synchronized method logic
}

public void someMethod() {
    synchronized (lockObject) {
        // Synchronized block logic
    }
}
```

The wait(), notify(), and notifyAll() methods are used for inter-thread communication and coordination.

5. Best Practices:

Use higher-level concurrency utilities from the java.util.concurrent package (e.g., ExecutorService, ThreadPoolExecutor) for better thread management.
Prefer implementing the Runnable interface over extending the Thread class, as it separates the task from the thread.
Avoid using stop(), suspend(), and resume() methods, as they are deprecated and can lead to thread instability.
Properly handle exceptions within threads to avoid silent thread termination.

Use thread pools for managing and reusing threads to reduce overhead.

6. Use Cases:

Threads are used in various scenarios, including:
GUI applications to keep the UI responsive while performing background tasks.
Web servers to handle multiple client requests simultaneously.
Parallel processing to improve performance in tasks like data processing and rendering.
Real-time systems for tasks requiring precise timing.
In summary, Java threads enable concurrent execution of code, allowing programs to perform multiple tasks simultaneously. Understanding thread creation, management, synchronization, and best practices is essential for developing efficient and robust multithreaded applications.

8.8 Life cycle of a thread.

The life cycle of a thread in a multi-threaded program typically goes through several stages, from its creation to its termination. The thread life cycle in Java can be described using the following states:
New: In this initial state, a thread is created but has not yet started its execution. The thread is not yet eligible to run.
Runnable: Once a thread is started using the start() method, it enters the "Runnable" state. In this state, the thread is eligible to run but may not necessarily be executing at a given moment. The thread scheduler of the operating system or Java's runtime environment determines when it will run.
Running: When the thread is executing its code, it is in the "Running" state. Only one thread can be in this state at any given time on a single CPU core. If there are multiple CPU cores, multiple threads can be in this state concurrently.
Blocked/Waiting: A thread can transition to the "Blocked" or "Waiting" state under various conditions:
Blocked: When a thread is waiting for a resource (e.g., I/O operation, synchronized block) or waiting for a condition to be met, it enters the "Blocked" state. It cannot continue execution until the resource or condition becomes available.
Waiting: Threads can explicitly enter the "Waiting" state by calling methods like Object.wait() or Thread.sleep(). They remain in this state until another thread wakes them up or the specified time period elapses.
Timed Waiting: Threads can enter the "Timed Waiting" state when they call methods like Thread.sleep() with a specific time duration or Object.wait() with a timeout. They wait for the specified duration before transitioning back to the "Runnable" state.
Terminated/Dead: A thread can enter the "Terminated" or "Dead" state in one of several ways:
When the run() method of the thread completes its execution, the thread naturally terminates and enters the "Terminated" state.
If an unhandled exception occurs within the thread, it terminates abnormally, also entering the "Terminated" state.
The Thread.stop() method (deprecated) can forcefully terminate a thread, but it is not recommended due to potential data corruption and synchronization issues.
Here's a visual representation of the thread life cycle:
Example-

```
 +-------------------+
 |                   |
 v                   |
New -> Runnable -> Running
 |       |     |
 |       |     |
 v       |     v
Blocked  |  Timed Waiting
 |       |     |
 |       |     |
 v       |     v
Blocked  |  Terminated
 |       |
 |       |
 v       v
Waiting Terminated
```

In summary, a thread's life cycle involves transitioning between different states, such as New, Runnable, Running, Blocked, Waiting, Timed Waiting, and Terminated, based on its activities and external factors. Proper thread management, synchronization, and error handling are crucial for managing thread life cycles effectively and ensuring the correct behavior of multi-threaded applications.

8.9 Assigning Priorities to Threads:

In Java, you can assign priorities to threads using the setPriority() method, which is a member of the Thread class. The setPriority() method takes an integer argument that represents the priority level of the thread. Thread priorities are indicated by integer values ranging from 1 (lowest priority) to 10 (highest priority), and there are three static constants in the Thread class to represent these priority levels:

Thread.MIN_PRIORITY with a value of 1.
Thread.NORM_PRIORITY with a value of 5 (default priority).
Thread.MAX_PRIORITY with a value of 10.
Here's an example of how to assign priorities to threads in Java:

Example-

```
class MyThread extends Thread {
   public MyThread(String name) {
      super(name);
   }

   public void run() {
      System.out.println(getName() + " is running with priority " + getPriority());
   }
}

public class ThreadPriorityExample {
   public static void main(String[] args) {
      MyThread thread1 = new MyThread("Thread 1");
      MyThread thread2 = new MyThread("Thread 2");
      MyThread thread3 = new MyThread("Thread 3");

      // Assign priorities to threads
      thread1.setPriority(Thread.MIN_PRIORITY);
      thread2.setPriority(Thread.NORM_PRIORITY);
      thread3.setPriority(Thread.MAX_PRIORITY);

      // Start the threads
      thread1.start();
      thread2.start();
      thread3.start();
   }
}
```

In this example, we create three threads (thread1, thread2, and thread3) and assign different priorities to them using the setPriority() method. We then start the threads, and each thread prints its name and priority level.

8.10 Thread Priority Usage

Thread priorities are used to influence the scheduling of threads by the Java Virtual Machine's (JVM) thread scheduler. Threads with higher priorities are given preference over threads with lower priorities when it comes to CPU time. However, thread priority is only a hint to the scheduler, and the actual behavior may vary depending on the JVM and the operating system.

Here are some considerations when using thread priorities:

Default Priority: When you create a thread, it inherits the priority of its parent thread. By default, threads have a normal priority (Thread.NORM_PRIORITY), which is typically 5.

Higher Priority Tasks: Threads with higher priority are scheduled more frequently by the JVM, making them suitable for tasks that require immediate attention or high processing speed.

Lower Priority Tasks: Threads with lower priority are scheduled less frequently, making them suitable for background or less critical tasks that can yield CPU time to higher-priority threads.

Avoid Excessive Reliance: Relying heavily on thread priorities for task coordination can lead to unpredictable behavior and should be used judiciously. It's often better to use other synchronization mechanisms like locks, semaphores, or condition variables for better control over thread execution.

In summary, you can assign priorities to threads in Java using the setPriority() method, but it's essential to use them carefully, considering their limitations and the specific requirements of your multithreaded application. Prioritizing threads can help you achieve better control over task scheduling and resource allocation.

8.11 Thread and a Process

Aspect	Thread	Process
Definition	A thread is the smallest unit of execution within a process. Multiple threads can exist within a single process.	A process is an independent program that runs in its own memory space.
Creation	Threads are created within a process and share the same memory space.	Processes are independent and have their memory space, and they may create child processes.
Communication	Threads within the same process can easily communicate and share data.	Inter-process communication (IPC) mechanisms are required for communication between processes.
Resource Overhead	Threads within the same process share resources, leading to lower resource overhead.	Processes have higher resource overhead as each has its memory space and resources.
Synchronisation	Threads can synchronise and coordinate with other threads within the same process using synchronization mechanisms.	Processes require more complex synchronization mechanisms and IPC for coordination.

8.12 Java Lambda Expressions

Lambda expressions were introduced in Java 8 and have since become a powerful feature of the language. They allow you to write concise and expressive code by representing a block of code as a function that can be passed around and executed. In this detailed overview, we'll explore Java Lambda Expressions, covering their key concepts, syntax, usage, functional interfaces, and best practices.

1. Key Concepts:

Lambda Expression: A lambda expression is a concise representation of an anonymous function (a function without a name) that can be passed as an argument to methods, stored in variables, or returned from methods.

Functional Interface: A functional interface is an interface that defines exactly one abstract method (also known as a functional method). Lambda expressions can be used wherever functional interfaces are expected.

Syntax: A lambda expression consists of parameters, an arrow (->), and a body. The body can be a single expression or a block of code.

2. Lambda Expression Syntax:

The basic syntax of a lambda expression is as follows:

Example-

(parameters) -> expression or statement

(parameters): Represents the input parameters (if any) to the lambda expression.

->: The arrow operator separates the parameters from the body of the lambda.

expression or statement: Represents the code to be executed when the lambda is invoked.

3. Functional Interfaces:

Functional interfaces are the cornerstone of lambda expressions in Java. They are interfaces with a single abstract method and are annotated with the @FunctionalInterface annotation.

Here are some commonly used functional interfaces:

- **Runnable:** Represents a task that can be executed concurrently.
- **Callable**: Represents a task that can be executed and returns a result.
- **Consumer<T>:** Accepts a single argument and performs an operation on it.
- **Supplier<T>:** Provides a value.
- **Function<T, R>:** Accepts an argument of type T and returns a result of type R.
- **Predicate<T>:** Evaluates a condition on an argument of type T.
- **Comparator<T>:** Compares two values of type T.

4. Lambda Expression Examples:

Here are some examples of lambda expressions:

Lambda that takes no arguments:

Example-

```
() -> System.out.println("Hello, Lambda!");
```

Lambda with a single argument:

Example-

```
(name) -> System.out.println("Hello, " + name);
```

Lambda with multiple arguments:

Example-

```
(x, y) -> {
  int sum = x + y;
  System.out.println("Sum: " + sum);
}
```

5. Usage of Lambda Expressions:

Lambda expressions are commonly used in various scenarios, including:

Collections: Lambda expressions simplify iteration and processing of collections using methods like forEach, map, filter, and reduce.

Multithreading: They are used with the Runnable and Callable interfaces to create threads and execute tasks concurrently.

GUI Applications: Lambda expressions simplify event handling in graphical user interfaces.

Functional Programming: They enable functional programming constructs like map, reduce, and filter.

6. Best Practices:

Use lambda expressions for code that is concise and enhances readability.

Prefer existing functional interfaces (e.g., Consumer, Function) over creating custom functional interfaces.

Be aware of variable scoping rules and effectively final variables when using lambda expressions.

Keep lambda expressions simple and avoid complex logic within them.

7. Example:

Using lambda expressions with the ArrayList class:

Example-

```
List<String> names = new ArrayList<>();
names.add("Alice");
names.add("Bob");
names.add("Charlie");

// Using a lambda expression to iterate and print names
names.forEach(name -> System.out.println("Hello, " + name));
```

In summary, Java Lambda Expressions provide a concise and expressive way to represent anonymous functions. They are a key feature of Java 8 and later versions, enabling functional programming constructs and simplifying code in various scenarios. Understanding the syntax, functional interfaces, and best practices for using lambda expressions is essential for writing clean and efficient Java code.

8.13 Concurrent Collections

Concurrent collections are a set of data structures in Java designed for use in multi-threaded or concurrent programming scenarios. They provide thread-safe operations for accessing and modifying data, ensuring that multiple threads can work together without causing data corruption or synchronization issues. In this overview, we'll explore the concept of concurrent collections, some commonly used concurrent collection classes, and their usage in Java.

1. Why Use Concurrent Collections:

In multi-threaded applications, when multiple threads access and manipulate shared data structures concurrently, synchronization is necessary to avoid race conditions and maintain data consistency. Traditional collections (e.g., ArrayList or HashMap) are not thread-safe by default, and improper synchronization can lead to issues like data corruption or performance bottlenecks.

1. Concurrent collections offer several advantages:

Thread Safety: They provide built-in thread-safety, eliminating the need for explicit synchronization.

Improved Performance: They use fine-grained locking techniques to improve concurrent access performance.

Scalability: They are designed to handle a high level of concurrency without performance degradation.

2. Common Concurrent Collection Classes:

Java provides a variety of concurrent collection classes, including:

ConcurrentHashMap: A concurrent version of HashMap that allows multiple threads to read and write without blocking.

ConcurrentLinkedQueue and ConcurrentLinkedDeque: Thread-safe implementations of a singly-linked and doubly-linked queue, respectively.

CopyOnWriteArrayList and CopyOnWriteArraySet: These collections create a new copy of the underlying data structure whenever it's modified, ensuring thread safety during iterations.

BlockingQueue and its implementations like LinkedBlockingQueue and ArrayBlockingQueue: These provide thread-safe blocking operations for producer-consumer scenarios.

3. Example Usage:

Using ConcurrentHashMap:

Example-

```
import java.util.concurrent.ConcurrentHashMap;

public class ConcurrentMapExample {
    public static void main(String[] args) {
        ConcurrentHashMap<String, Integer> map = new ConcurrentHashMap<>();

        map.put("one", 1);
        map.put("two", 2);

        int value = map.get("two"); // Thread-safe read

        map.put("three", 3); // Thread-safe write
    }
}
```

Using BlockingQueue (Producer-Consumer Pattern):

Example-

```
import java.util.concurrent.*;

public class ProducerConsumerExample {
    public static void main(String[] args) {
        BlockingQueue<Integer> queue = new LinkedBlockingQueue<>();

        // Producer thread
        Thread producer = new Thread(() -> {
            try {
                queue.put(1); // Add an item to the queue
            } catch (InterruptedException e) {
                Thread.currentThread().interrupt();
            }
        });

        // Consumer thread
        Thread consumer = new Thread(() -> {
            try {
                int item = queue.take(); // Remove an item from the queue (waits if empty)
                // Process the item
            } catch (InterruptedException e) {
                Thread.currentThread().interrupt();
            }
        });

        producer.start();
        consumer.start();
    }
}
```

4. Best Practices:

Choose the appropriate concurrent collection class based on the specific concurrency requirements of your application.
Be cautious with blocking operations in concurrent collections, as they can lead to deadlocks if not used correctly.
Use these collections in multi-threaded scenarios, but be aware that they may introduce additional overhead compared to non-concurrent collections.

5. Use Cases:

Concurrent collections are commonly used in scenarios where multiple threads need to access and manipulate shared data structures, such as caching, thread pools, and producer-consumer patterns.

In summary, concurrent collections in Java provide thread-safe alternatives to traditional collections, enabling safe and efficient multi-threaded programming. Understanding the available concurrent collection classes and their usage is essential for building concurrent and scalable applications in Java.

8.14 Custom Data Structures and Implementations

Custom data structures are user-defined data structures tailored to specific application needs. Java allows developers to create custom data structures by implementing classes and interfaces. In this overview, we'll explore the concept of custom data structures, their design considerations, and provide examples of custom data structure implementations in Java.

1. Design Considerations for Custom Data Structures:

When designing custom data structures in Java, consider the following factors:

Data Representation: Determine how the data will be stored and organized within the structure. Choose appropriate data types and structures based on the use case.

Access Patterns: Understand how the data structure will be accessed, whether it's more frequently read or modified, and design for optimal performance in common use cases.

Thread Safety: Decide if the data structure needs to be thread-safe. If so, implement proper synchronization mechanisms or use concurrent data structures.

API Design: Define a clear and consistent API (methods and operations) for interacting with the data structure, following Java conventions.

2. Custom Data Structure Examples:

Here are examples of custom data structures implemented in Java:

Example 1: Custom LinkedList

```
public class CustomLinkedList<T> {
    private Node<T> head;

    private static class Node<T> {
        T data;
        Node<T> next;

        Node(T data) {
            this.data = data;
        }
    }

    public void add(T data) {
        Node<T> newNode = new Node<>(data);
        if (head == null) {
            head = newNode;
        } else {
            Node<T> current = head;
            while (current.next != null) {
                current = current.next;
            }
            current.next = newNode;
        }
    }

    // Implement other methods like remove, contains, size, etc.
}
```

Example 2: Custom Stack

```
public class CustomStack<T> {
    private LinkedList<T> stack = new LinkedList<>();

    public void push(T item) {
        stack.addFirst(item);
    }

    public T pop() {
        if (isEmpty()) {
            throw new EmptyStackException();
        }
```

```
        return stack.removeFirst();
    }

    public T peek() {
        if (isEmpty()) {
            throw new EmptyStackException();
        }
        return stack.getFirst();
    }

    public boolean isEmpty() {
        return stack.isEmpty();
    }

    // Implement other methods like size, clear, etc.
}
```

Example 3: Custom Binary Search Tree (BST)

```
public class CustomBST<T extends Comparable<T>> {
    private Node<T> root;

    private static class Node<T> {
        T data;
        Node<T> left;
        Node<T> right;

        Node(T data) {
            this.data = data;
        }
    }

    public void insert(T data) {
        root = insertRec(root, data);
    }

    private Node<T> insertRec(Node<T> root, T data) {
        if (root == null) {
            return new Node<>(data);
        }

        if (data.compareTo(root.data) < 0) {
            root.left = insertRec(root.left, data);
        } else if (data.compareTo(root.data) > 0) {
            root.right = insertRec(root.right, data);
        }
        return root;
    }

    // Implement other methods like search, delete, traversal, etc.
}
```

3. Best Practices:

Follow Java naming conventions and provide clear and consistent method names and documentation.

Consider performance implications when designing custom data structures. Optimize for common use cases.

Test your custom data structures thoroughly to ensure correctness and reliability.

4. Use Cases:

Custom data structures are suitable for various use cases, such as optimizing data access patterns, implementing specific algorithms, or modelling domain-specific concepts.

In summary, custom data structures in Java allow developers to create specialized data structures tailored to their application's needs. When designing and implementing custom data structures, careful consideration of design, API, and performance is essential to create efficient and reliable solutions.

8.15 Understanding Big O Notation and Algorithm Efficiency

Big O notation is a mathematical notation used in computer science to analyze and describe the performance and efficiency of algorithms and data structures. It provides a way to characterize how the runtime or space requirements of an algorithm grow relative to the size of the input data. Understanding Big O notation is crucial for optimizing code and selecting the right algorithms and data structures. In this overview, we'll explore the concept of Big O notation, its importance, and how it applies to Java programming.

1. Importance of Algorithm Efficiency:

Efficiency is a critical factor in software development for the following reasons:

Scalability: As data sizes increase, the performance of algorithms and data structures becomes a critical concern.

Resource Utilization: Efficient algorithms and data structures use fewer system resources (CPU, memory, etc.), reducing operational costs.

User Experience: Faster algorithms result in a better user experience, particularly in real-time applications.

2. Big O Notation Basics:

Big O notation describes the upper bound or worst-case performance of an algorithm concerning the input size. It characterizes how an algorithm's runtime or space requirements grow relative to the size of the input data.

Common Big O notations include:

O(1): Constant time. The algorithm's runtime or space usage remains constant, regardless of input size. (e.g., array indexing)

O(log n): Logarithmic time. The algorithm's performance grows logarithmically with the input size. (e.g., binary search)

O(n): Linear time. The algorithm's runtime or space usage grows linearly with the input size. (e.g., iterating through an array)

O(n log n): Linearithmic time. Common in efficient sorting algorithms like merge sort and quicksort.

O(n^2): Quadratic time. The algorithm's performance grows quadratically with the input size. (e.g., nested loops)

O(2^n): Exponential time. The algorithm's runtime or space usage doubles with each input size increase. (e.g., naive recursive algorithms)

3. Applying Big O Notation in Java:

Understanding Big O notation in Java involves analyzing algorithms and data structures to assess their efficiency. Here's an example using Java code:

```
public class BigONotationExample {
  // O(1) - Constant time
  public static void printFirstElement(int[] array) {
    System.out.println(array[0]);
  }

  // O(n) - Linear time
  public static void printAllElements(int[] array) {
    for (int element : array) {
      System.out.println(element);
    }
  }

  // O(n^2) - Quadratic time
  public static void printPairs(int[] array) {
    for (int i = 0; i < array.length; i++) {
      for (int j = 0; j < array.length; j++) {
        System.out.println(array[i] + ", " + array[j]);
      }
    }
  }

  public static void main(String[] args) {
    int[] array = {1, 2, 3, 4, 5};

    printFirstElement(array); // O(1)
    printAllElements(array);  // O(n)
```

```
        printPairs(array);        // O(n^2)
    }
}
```

4. Best Practices:

Consider algorithm efficiency from the beginning of your software design.

Profile and benchmark code to identify performance bottlenecks.

Choose appropriate data structures and algorithms based on the problem's characteristics and expected input size.

Utilize libraries and built-in functions optimized for common tasks whenever possible.

5. Use Cases:

Big O notation is used in optimizing search algorithms (e.g., binary search), sorting algorithms (e.g., merge sort), and data structures (e.g., hash tables).

It plays a crucial role in designing efficient database queries and optimizing resource usage in distributed systems.

In summary, Big O notation is a fundamental concept in computer science and software development. It helps analyze and compare algorithmic efficiency, enabling developers to make informed decisions about algorithm selection and optimization strategies in Java and other programming languages.

8.16 Sorting Algorithms (e.g., Merge Sort, Quick Sort)

Sorting algorithms are essential in computer science for organizing data efficiently. Java provides several built-in sorting algorithms in the java.util package. Here, we'll explain two common sorting algorithms, Merge Sort and Quick Sort, using minimal code.

1. Merge Sort:

Merge Sort is a divide-and-conquer algorithm that divides the input array into smaller halves, sorts them, and then merges them back together.

Example-

```
import java.util.Arrays;

public class MergeSortExample {
    public static void main(String[] args) {
        int[] arr = {12, 11, 13, 5, 6, 7};

        mergeSort(arr, 0, arr.length - 1);

        System.out.println("Sorted array: " + Arrays.toString(arr));
    }

    private static void mergeSort(int[] arr, int left, int right) {
        if (left < right) {
            int mid = (left + right) / 2;

            mergeSort(arr, left, mid);
            mergeSort(arr, mid + 1, right);

            merge(arr, left, mid, right);
        }
    }

    private static void merge(int[] arr, int left, int mid, int right) {
        int n1 = mid - left + 1;
        int n2 = right - mid;

        int[] leftArr = new int[n1];
        int[] rightArr = new int[n2];

        for (int i = 0; i < n1; i++) {
            leftArr[i] = arr[left + i];
        }
        for (int j = 0; j < n2; j++) {
            rightArr[j] = arr[mid + 1 + j];
```

```
        }

        int i = 0, j = 0, k = left;
        while (i < n1 && j < n2) {
            if (leftArr[i] <= rightArr[j]) {
                arr[k++] = leftArr[i++];
            } else {
                arr[k++] = rightArr[j++];
            }
        }

        while (i < n1) {
            arr[k++] = leftArr[i++];
        }

        while (j < n2) {
            arr[k++] = rightArr[j++];
        }
    }
}
```

2. Quick Sort:

Quick Sort is another divide-and-conquer algorithm that partitions the array into smaller subarrays, with elements less than a chosen pivot on one side and elements greater on the other side.

Example-

```
import java.util.Arrays;

public class QuickSortExample {
    public static void main(String[] args) {
        int[] arr = {10, 7, 8, 9, 1, 5};

        quickSort(arr, 0, arr.length - 1);

        System.out.println("Sorted array: " + Arrays.toString(arr));
    }

    private static void quickSort(int[] arr, int low, int high) {
        if (low < high) {
            int pi = partition(arr, low, high);

            quickSort(arr, low, pi - 1);
            quickSort(arr, pi + 1, high);
        }
    }

    private static int partition(int[] arr, int low, int high) {
        int pivot = arr[high];
        int i = low - 1;

        for (int j = low; j < high; j++) {
            if (arr[j] < pivot) {
                i++;

                int temp = arr[i];
                arr[i] = arr[j];
                arr[j] = temp;
            }
```

```
        }

        int temp = arr[i + 1];
        arr[i + 1] = arr[high];
        arr[high] = temp;

        return i + 1;
    }
}
```

These are simplified examples of Merge Sort and Quick Sort algorithms in Java. In practice, you'd need to handle edge cases, additional optimizations, and various data types, but these code snippets provide a basic understanding of how these sorting algorithms work.

8.17ArrayList and Vector

Aspect	Array List	Vector
Synchronisation	Not synchronised by default.	Synchronised by default, ensuring thread safety.
Performance	Generally faster than Vector because of lack of synchronisation.	Slower than ArrayList due to synchronisation overhead.
Thread Safety	Not thread-safe. Multiple threads can access ArrayList concurrently, leading to potential issues in multi-threaded environments.	Thread-safe by design. Operations are synchronised, making it safe for concurrent access by multiple threads.
Legacy	Introduced in Java 2 (JDK 1.2).	Introduced in Java 1.0 and considered a legacy class.
Iterator	The iterator returned by ArrayList is not synchronised.	The iterator returned by Vector is synchronised.
Performance Impact	In a single-threaded environment, ArrayList typically offers better performance due to the lack of synchronization.	In a multi-threaded environment, the Vector's synchronisation ensures data consistency but may impact performance.
Use Cases	Suitable for non-concurrent, single-threaded scenarios where synchronisation is not required.	Suitable for scenarios where thread safety is a concern, such as multi-threaded applications or legacy code that requires synchronization.

8.18 Interthread Communication in Java

Interthread communication is a fundamental concept in Java and other multi-threaded programming environments. It allows threads to synchronize their activities and exchange data, enabling collaboration and coordination among threads within a program. Java provides mechanisms for interthread communication using methods like wait(), notify(), and notifyAll() that are associated with objects that use synchronized blocks or methods.

Here are some key points about interthread communication in Java:

Object-Level Locks: Java's interthread communication mechanisms are built on top of the object-level locks provided by the synchronized keyword. Threads can synchronize on a shared object and use this synchronization to coordinate their activities.

Wait and Notify: The wait() method is called by a thread within a synchronized block to voluntarily release the lock on the object and wait for another thread to notify it. The notify() method is used to wake up one waiting thread, and notifyAll() is used to wake up all waiting threads associated with the same object.

Usage Pattern:

A producer thread can use wait() to wait until a certain condition is met (e.g., a buffer is not full).

A consumer thread can use notify() or notifyAll() to signal the producer when it has consumed an item, allowing the producer to resume producing.

Threads should be inside a synchronized block when they call wait(), notify(), or notifyAll() on the same object.

Race Conditions and Deadlocks: Incorrect usage of interthread communication can lead to race conditions (e.g., missed signals) or deadlocks (e.g., two threads waiting for each other). Careful synchronization and coordination are necessary to avoid these issues.

Blocking and Wake-Up: Threads calling wait() are blocked and do not consume CPU resources, which is efficient. When they are notified and wake up, they become runnable and compete for CPU time.

Use Cases: Interthread communication is commonly used in scenarios where threads need to collaborate, such as producer-consumer problems, thread pooling, and handling shared resources like buffers or queues.

Thread Safety: Proper use of interthread communication can ensure thread safety in multi-threaded applications, where multiple threads access shared resources concurrently. It helps in avoiding data corruption and race conditions.

Here's a simple example of producer-consumer using wait() and notify():

Example-

```
class SharedResource {
  private int data;
  private boolean available = false;

  synchronized void produce(int value) {
    while (available) {
      try {
        wait(); // Wait if data is available
      } catch (InterruptedException e) {
        Thread.currentThread().interrupt();
      }
    }
    data = value;
    available = true;
    System.out.println("Produced: " + data);
    notify(); // Notify waiting consumer
  }

  synchronized int consume() {
    while (!available) {
      try {
        wait(); // Wait if data is not available
      } catch (InterruptedException e) {
        Thread.currentThread().interrupt();
      }
    }
    available = false;
    System.out.println("Consumed: " + data);
    notify(); // Notify waiting producer
    return data;
  }
}
```

Interthread communication is a powerful mechanism for managing the synchronization and cooperation of threads in Java, allowing them to work together efficiently while avoiding conflicts and ensuring thread safety.

8.19 Multithreaded Programming in Java

Multithreaded programming in Java refers to the practice of writing programs that execute multiple threads concurrently within the same process. A thread is the smallest unit of execution within a program, and multithreading allows multiple threads to execute independently and share resources like memory space, but with their own execution contexts.

In Java, multithreaded programming is made easier and more accessible through the java.lang.Thread class and the java.util.concurrent package. You can create and manage threads to perform tasks concurrently, taking advantage of the capabilities of modern multi-core processors.

Benefits of Multithreaded Programming in Java:

Improved Performance: Multithreading allows programs to make better use of multi-core processors. By dividing tasks into multiple threads, each core can work on a different thread simultaneously, increasing the program's overall performance and efficiency.

Responsive User Interfaces: Multithreading is crucial for building responsive graphical user interfaces (GUIs). The user interface can run in one thread while time-consuming operations like data processing or networking occur in separate threads. This prevents the UI from becoming unresponsive.
Concurrency: Multithreading enables concurrent execution of tasks. This is valuable for applications like web servers, where multiple clients can be served simultaneously without waiting for one request to complete before processing the next one.
Resource Sharing: Threads within the same process can share resources, such as variables and objects, which can lead to more efficient memory usage and communication between components of the program.
Task Parallelism: Multithreading is beneficial for tasks that can be executed in parallel. For example, image processing, video encoding, and scientific simulations can be divided into smaller tasks and executed concurrently, reducing processing time.
Simplified Code: Multithreading can simplify code in certain scenarios. For instance, you can encapsulate complex tasks in separate threads, making the code easier to manage and maintain.
Efficient Task Scheduling: Java provides built-in mechanisms for managing thread scheduling and synchronization, making it easier to handle complex concurrency scenarios.
Real-Time Systems: Multithreading is essential for building real-time systems, such as video games or embedded systems, where tasks need to be executed within strict time constraints.
Parallel Data Processing: In data-intensive applications, such as data analytics or database management systems, multithreading can be used to process data in parallel, significantly reducing processing times.
Scalability: Multithreaded programs are often more scalable because they can take advantage of additional CPU cores as hardware evolves, without requiring extensive code changes.

Exercise

Exercise 1 – MCQ

Q 1. In Java, which data structure allows for constant time (O(1)) average-case access to elements by their keys?
a) Linked List
b) ArrayList
c) HashMap
d) Stack

Q 2. Which sorting algorithm has an average time complexity of O(n log n) and is known for its efficiency and stability?
a) Bubble Sort
b) Quick Sort
c) Selection Sort
d) Merge Sort.

Exercise 2 – True/ False

Q 1. Big O notation provides an exact measure of the running time of an algorithm in seconds.
Q 2. In Java, you can create custom data structures by extending existing Java classes, such as ArrayList or LinkedList, to suit specific application needs.

Exercise 3 – Fill in the blanks

Q 1. In Java, concurrent collections provided by the java.util.concurrent package are designed to handle _______ access by multiple threads without the need for explicit synchronization.
Q 2. The time complexity of the Bubble Sort algorithm in the worst-case scenario is _______.

Exercise 4 – One word answer

Q 1. What data structure represents a collection of elements with no duplicates in Java?
Q 2. What is the process of converting a data type into a sequence of bytes called?

Exercise 5 – Small answer

Q 1. In the context of data structures, what does "collision" refer to?
Q 2. What is the primary advantage of using a HashMap over other data structures when it comes to key-value storage?

Exercise 6 – Long answer

Q 1. Describe the key differences between an ArrayList and a LinkedList in Java. Provide scenarios in which one data structure may be more advantageous than the other.
Q 2. Explain the concept of Big O notation in the context of algorithm analysis. Provide an example of an algorithm and its corresponding Big O notation.

Answer:

Exercise 1. Q 1: C) HashMap Q 2: d) Merge Sort
Exercise 2. Q 1: False Q 2: False
Exercise 3. Q 1: concurrent Q 2: O(n^2)
Exercise 4. Q 1: i. Regular Expressions (Regex) ()- a ii. Optional Class ()- b

iii. Lambda Expressions () -c iv. Java Streams and Stream API ()-d
Exercise 5. Q 1: Set Q 2: Serialization

Previous Year Questions

Q 1. Describe how to create a thread with an example. (JNTU -B.Tech.- 2018)
Q 2. How to assign priorities to threads? (JNTU -B.Tech. -2017)
Q 3. Write a program to explain thread priorities usage. (JNTU -B.Tech.- 2018
Q 4. What is a vector? How does it differ from array, list? (JNTU -B.Tech. -2017)
Q 5. How to achieve synchronization among threads? Write suitable code. (JNTU -B.Tech. -2017)
Q 6. What is the difference between a thread and a process? (JNTU -B.Tech. -2017)
Q 7. Differentiate between ArrayList and Vector. (JNTU -B.Tech.- 2016)
Q 8. Describe the need of thread synchronization. How is it achieved in Java programming? Explain with a suitable program. (JNTU -B.Tech.- 2016)
Q 9. List the thread states. (JNTU -B.Tech.- 2016)
Q 10. Differentiate between thread and process. (SPPU – BCA - 2015)
Q 11. What is the difference between array and vector? (SPPU – BCA - 2015)
Q 12. What is an Array? How it differs from Vector? (SPPU – BCA - 2015)
Q 13. Does Java support thread priorities? Justify your answer with suitable discussion. (SPPU – BCA - 2015)
Q 14. What is vector? How is it different from an array? (Aryabhatta University BCA 2014)
Q 15. Describe the compete life cycle of a thread. (Aryabhatta University BCA 2014)
Q 16. What is multithreaded programming? What are its benefits? What are the various ways of creating a Thread in java? Explain each one of them step by step with suitable code. (Punjab Technical University MCA -2015
Q 19. Write short notes on Interthread communication (IGNOU MCA 2011)
Q 21. Event Handling in Java (IGNOU MCA 2011)
Q 22. What is meant by thread priority? (IGNOU MCA 2013)
Q 23. What is multithreading? Explain the steps for creating thread in Java. (IGNOU MCA 2013)
Q 24. How does Java support inter thread communication? (JNTU -B.Tech.- 2018)

Previous Year Solved Papers

Q. 1. Write short notes on: a Hash Table (RU BCA 2018)
Ans- A hash table is a data structure that implements an associative array abstract data type, a structure that can map keys to values. It is also known as a hash map in some programming languages. Hash tables use a technique called hashing, which involves converting a key into a hash code and then using this code to locate the data associated with the key. The hash code is used as an index to locate the desired data in the table, enabling fast retrieval and storage of data.
Key points about hash tables include:
Key-Value Mapping: Hash tables store data in key-value pairs, allowing efficient retrieval of data based on the associated key.
Hashing Function: A hashing function is used to generate the hash code from the key, which is then used to index the data in the table.
Collisions Handling: Collisions occur when two different keys hash to the same index. Hash tables use various collision resolution techniques, such as separate chaining and open addressing, to manage collisions and store multiple values associated with the same hash code.
Complexity: Hash tables provide fast access and insertion of data, with an average time complexity of O(1) for basic operations, assuming a good hash function and minimal collisions.
Usage: Hash tables are widely used in various applications, such as database indexing, caching mechanisms, symbol tables in compilers, and implementing associative arrays in programming languages.
Load Factor: Hash tables have a load factor that determines the threshold for resizing the table to maintain efficient performance. Resizing helps manage the number of collisions and ensures that the hash table maintains its performance characteristics even as the number of entries increases.
Hash tables are a fundamental data structure used to implement various data storage and retrieval mechanisms efficiently. Their speed and versatility make them a key component in the development of many high-performance applications and algorithms.

ONLINE RESOURCES

Practice Paper

Link: https://forms.gle/SbFHDSwDXt8DRuCZ8

QR Code:

Video Content
Link: https://www.youtube.com/playlist?list=PLzlh_31VWEFoGGSn-_dSQRG5zgAOuHqA3

QR Code:

YouTube Videos Playlists for all Chapters

Chapter 1
Link: https://www.youtube.com/playlist?list=PLzlh_31VWEFqq_6dtNq3PMGwN99a0zTGH

QR Code:

Chapter 2
Link: https://www.youtube.com/playlist?list=PLzlh_31VWEFpzLNIlz8zQoR64L6DdxMVa

QR Code:

Chapter 3
Link: https://www.youtube.com/playlist?list=PLzlh_31VWEFoaNYQU5ofj-8LS23gOwTYt

QR Code:

Chapter 4
Link: https://www.youtube.com/playlist?list=PLzlh_31VWEFqhMzp2tHykbBba3OwuUUjL

QR Code:

Chapter 5
Link: https://www.youtube.com/playlist?list=PLzlh_31VWEFoUtTRRmg89RrahGM58tcGA

QR Code:

Chapter 6
Link: https://www.youtube.com/playlist?list=PLzlh_31VWEFr99qHNKZpFZw-UtMpAwVPN

QR Code:

Chapter 7
Link: https://www.youtube.com/playlist?list=PLzlh_31VWEFp0IUemjbkD4iDOYU4C6gKC

QR Code:

Chapter 8
Link: https://www.youtube.com/playlist?list=PLzlh_31VWEFoGGSn-_dSQRG5zgAOuHqA3

QR Code:

Core Java Textbook Playlist
Link: https://www.youtube.com/playlist?list=PLzlh_31VWEFofK7phOZSB9OO9rP1bkaxB

QR Code:

Advanced Java Playlist:
Link : https://www.youtube.com/playlist?list=PLzlh_31VWEFoZXs-3KLPda_DVlN9lPJyg

QR Code :

Java Interview Playlist:
Link: https://www.youtube.com/playlist?list=PLzlh_31VWEFryjvGNIVtyBVYvddpxKexP

QR Code:

Java EE 7 Application Developer (Paper Code - 1Z0-900) Playlist.
Link: https://www.youtube.com/playlist?list=PLzlh_31VWEFodNsy-MeBm7RdKGWAO4TzF

QR Code:

Oracle Certified Professional Java Programmer OCPJP (Paper Code - 1Z0-809) Playlist.
Link: https://www.youtube.com/playlist?list=PLzlh_31VWEFqzXoVrZjKV6cZQKi7iG2D9

QR Code:

Oracle Certified Master Java Enterprise Architect (OCMJEA)(Paper Code - 1Z0-807) Playlist.
Link: https://www.youtube.com/playlist?list=PLzlh_31VWEFqdceCx1Pivwi5ypdvfVaEs

QR Code:

Oracle Certified Master Java Enterprise Architect (OCMJEA)(Paper Code - 1Z0-807) Playlist.
Link: https://www.youtube.com/playlist?list=PLzlh_31VWEFr90bIgv56c3xabjV50iFLV

QR Code:

Core Java Textbook Playlist.
Link: https://www.youtube.com/playlist?list=PLzlh_31VWEFofK7phOZSB9OO9rP1bkaxB

QR Code: